Exam Ref AZ-900
Microsoft Azure
Fundamentals

Jim Cheshire

Exam Ref AZ-900 Microsoft Azure Fundamentals

Published with the authorization of Microsoft Corporation by:
Pearson Education, Inc.
Hoboken, NJ

ISBN-13: 978-0-13-687718-9
ISBN-10: 0-13-687718-4

Library of Congress Control Number: 2020940854

3 2020

TRADEMARKS

WARNING AND DISCLAIMER

SPECIAL SALES

For information about buying this title in bulk quantities, or for special sales opportunities (which may include electronic versions; custom cover designs; and content particular to your business, training goals, marketing focus, or branding interests), please contact our corporate sales department at corpsales@pearsoned.com or (800) 382-3419.

For government sales inquiries, please contact governmentsales@pearsoned.com.

For questions about sales outside the U.S., please contact intlcs@pearson.com.

CREDITS

EDITOR-IN-CHIEF
Brett Bartow

EXECUTIVE EDITOR
Loretta Yates

ASSISTANT SPONSORING EDITOR
Charvi Arora

DEVELOPMENT EDITOR
Rick Kughen

MANAGING EDITOR
Sandra Schroeder

SENIOR EDITOR
Tracey Croom

COPY EDITOR
Rick Kughen

INDEXER
Cheryl Ann Lenser

PROOFREADER
Abigail Manheim

TECHNICAL EDITOR
Tim Warner

EDITORIAL ASSISTANT
Cindy Teeters

INTERIOR COMPOSITOR
codeMantra

COVER DESIGNER
Twist Creative Seattle

I dedicate this book to my wife, Becky, my daughter, Hope, and my son, James.

—JIM CHESHIRE

Contents at a glance

Contents

Acknowledgments

I'd like to express my deep gratitude to the following people, without whom this book would not have been possible.

Thank you to Loretta for bringing me into this project. After two decades of working together on numerous projects, you still seem to find a way to bring freshness and excitement to each one. Thank you, Rick, for painstakingly editing every corner of this book to make it a better reading experience. Thanks to Tim for all the times you made me take a second look at my approach and for adding real value with your ideas. Thanks to Charvi for taking care of all the details that keep everything on track. Finally, thank you to all the people at Microsoft Press who worked so hard to create this book from the digital manuscript.

About the author

Jim Cheshire is a technology enthusiast with more than 25 years of experience in various roles within IT. Jim has authored more than 15 books on technology, and he's held numerous training sessions on Microsoft Azure, both in private enterprises and through Safari's Live Training program. Jim is heavily involved in Azure and is in his 22nd year at Microsoft. He's currently working on the design and implementation of the training ecosystem used to train Microsoft support engineers. You can follow Jim and interact with him on Twitter at @az900examref.

Introduction

Both businesses and individuals are adopting cloud technologies at a breakneck pace, and Microsoft Azure is often the choice for cloud-based applications and services. The purpose of the AZ-900 exam is to test your understanding of the fundamentals of Azure. The exam includes high-level concepts that apply across all of Azure to important concepts that are specific to a particular Azure service. Like the exam, this book is geared toward giving you a broad understanding of Azure itself as well as many common services and components in Azure.

While we've made every effort possible to make the information in this book accurate, Azure is rapidly evolving, and there's a chance that some of the screens in the Azure portal are slightly different now than they were when this book was written. It's also possible that other minor changes have taken place, such as minor name changes in features and so on.

In this edition of the book, we've meticulously reviewed the content in the first edition and updated everything to reflect the current state of Azure. We've also reorganized the book and added new content to reflect the current state of the AZ-900 exam. Microsoft has recently added new concepts, services, and Azure features to the AZ-900 exam, and we've added those to this edition. We've also corrected a few things and made quite a few changes based on reader feedback from the first edition.

This book covers every major topic area found on the exam, but it does not cover every exam question. Only the Microsoft exam team has access to the exam questions, and Microsoft regularly adds new questions to the exam, making it impossible to cover specific questions. You should consider this book a supplement to your relevant real-world experience and other study materials. In many cases, we've provided links in the "More Info" sections of the book, and these links are a great source for additional study.

Organization of this book

This book is organized by the "Skills measured" list published for the exam. The "Skills measured" list is available for each exam on the Microsoft Learning website: *http://aka.ms/examlist*. Each chapter in this book corresponds to a major topic area in the list, and the technical tasks in each topic area determine a chapter's organization. Because the AZ-900 exam covers six major topic areas, this book contains six chapters.

Preparing for the exam

Microsoft certification exams are a great way to build your resume and let the world know about your level of expertise. Certification exams validate your on-the-job experience and product knowledge. Although there is no substitute for on-the-job experience, preparation through study and hands-on practice can help you prepare for the exam. We recommend that you augment your exam preparation plan by using a combination of available study materials and courses. For example, you might use the Exam Ref and another study guide for your "at home" preparation and take a Microsoft Official Curriculum course for the classroom experience. Choose the combination that you think works best for you.

Note that this Exam Ref is based on publicly available information about the exam and the author's experience. To safeguard the integrity of the exam, authors do not have access to the live exam.

Microsoft certifications

Microsoft certifications distinguish you by proving your command of a broad set of skills and experience with current Microsoft products and technologies. The exams and corresponding certifications are developed to validate your mastery of critical competencies as you design and develop, or implement and support, solutions with Microsoft products and technologies both on-premises and in the cloud. Certification brings a variety of benefits to the individual and to employers and organizations.

> **MORE INFO**   **ALL MICROSOFT CERTIFICATIONS**
>
> For information about Microsoft certifications, including a full list of available certifications, go to *http://www.microsoft.com/learn*.

Quick access to online references

Throughout this book are addresses to webpages that the author has recommended you visit for more information. Some of these links can be very long and painstaking to type, so we've shortened them for you to make them easier to visit. We've also compiled them into a single list that readers of the print edition can refer to while they read.

Download the list at *https://MicrosoftPressStore.com/ ExamRefAZ900SecondEdition/ downloads*

The URLs are organized by chapter and heading. Every time you come across a URL in the book, find the hyperlink in the list to go directly to the webpage.

Errata, updates, & book support

We've made every effort to ensure the accuracy of this book and its companion content. You can access updates to this book—in the form of a list of submitted errata and their related corrections—at:

> *https://MicrosoftPressStore.com/ ExamRefAZ900SecondEdition/errata*

> If you discover an error that is not already listed, please submit it to us at the same page.

> For additional book support and information, please visit

> *https://MicrosoftPressStore.com/Support.*

> Please note that product support for Microsoft software and hardware is not offered through the previous addresses. For help with Microsoft software or hardware, go to *https://support.microsoft.com.*

Stay in touch

Let's keep the conversation going! We're on Twitter:

> *http://twitter.com/MicrosoftPress.*

> You can also follow the author of this book, Jim Cheshire, on Twitter at @az900examref.

CHAPTER 1

Describe cloud concepts

Cloud computing has been part of information technology (IT) for more than 20 years. During that time, it has evolved into a complex collection of cloud services and cloud models. Before you begin the process of moving to the cloud, it's important that you understand key concepts and services related to the cloud.

There are many reasons for moving to the cloud, but one of the primary benefits is removing some of the IT burden from your company. The cloud allows you to take advantage of a cloud provider's infrastructure and investments, and it makes it easier to maintain consistent access to your applications and data. You'll also gain the benefit of turnkey solutions for backing up data and ensuring your applications can survive disasters and other availability problems. Hosting your data and applications in the cloud is often more cost-effective than investing in infrastructure and on-premises IT resources.

Once you decide to take advantage of the cloud, you need to understand the different cloud offerings available to you. Some cloud services provide an almost hands-off experience, while others require you to manage some of the systems yourself. Finding the right balance for your needs requires that you fully understand each type of service.

This chapter covers the benefits of using the cloud, the different cloud services that are available, and cloud models that enable a variety of cloud configurations.

Skills covered in this chapter:

- Identify the benefits and considerations of using cloud services
- Describe the differences between categories of cloud services
- Describe the differences between types of cloud computing

Skill 1.1: Identify the benefits and considerations of using cloud services

Today's companies rely heavily on software solutions and access to data. In fact, in many cases, a company's most valuable assets are directly tied to data and applications. Because of that, investment in IT has grown tremendously over the past couple of decades. Reliance in on-premises IT departments worked well in the early days of IT, but access to data and applications has become such a critical part of day-to-day operations that localized IT systems have become inefficient on many levels.

When making decisions about what to move to the cloud, evaluate your decisions against the benefits that cloud computing can provide.

> **This section covers:**
> - High availability
> - Scalability, elasticity, and agility
> - Fault tolerance and disaster recovery
> - Capital and operational expenditures
> - The consumption-based model

High availability

The availability of data and applications is a core requirement for any application, whether it is on-premises or in the cloud. If your data or application isn't available to you, nothing else matters. There are many reasons why you might lose availability, but the most common issues are:

- A network outage
- An application failure
- A system outage (such as a virtual machine outage)
- A power outage
- A problem with a reliant system, such as an external database

In a perfect world, you experience 100 percent availability, but if any of the above problems occur, that percentage will begin to decrease. Therefore, it's critical that your infrastructure minimize the risk of problems that affect the availability of your application.

Cloud providers offer a *service-level agreement* (SLA) that guarantees a certain level of availability as a percentage. An SLA will usually guarantee an uptime of close to 100 percent, but it only covers systems that are controlled by the cloud provider.

An application hosted in the cloud might be one that is developed by your company, but it can also be one provided to you by the cloud provider.

Network outage

All applications require some level of network connectivity. Users of an application require network connectivity to the computers that run the application. The application requires network connectivity to required back-end systems such as database servers. Applications might also call into other applications using a network. If any of these network connections fail, they can cause a lack of availability.

Cloud providers invest a lot of money in network infrastructure, and by moving to the cloud you gain the benefit of that infrastructure and the additional reliability that comes with it. If something within that infrastructure fails, the cloud provider diagnoses and fixes it, often before you even realize there's a problem.

Application failure

An application failure is often the result of a software bug, but it can also be caused by application design.

In some cloud scenarios, you are still responsible for application failures, but your cloud provider likely provides you with tools that you can use to diagnose these failures more easily. For example, Azure offers a service called Application Insights that integrates with your application to give you detailed information about the performance and reliability of your application. Application developers can often use this information to get right to the code where a problem is happening, dramatically reducing the time needed for troubleshooting.

Cloud providers offer other features that can reduce availability problems caused by application failure. You can often test new versions of an application in a protected environment without affecting real users. When you're ready to move actual users to a new version, you can often move a small number of users first to ensure things are working correctly. If you discover problems, the cloud often makes it easy to roll things back to the prior version.

System outage

A system outage occurs when the computer running a particular system becomes unavailable. In the on-premises world, that computer might be a server running a database or another part of the application. In the cloud, these systems run inside of *virtual machines*, or VMs.

VMs are software-based computers that run on a physical computer. A single computer can run multiple VMs, and each VM has its own isolated operating system and applications. All VMs running on a computer share the CPU, memory, and storage of the host computer they run on.

Depending on the cloud service you choose, you might or might not be responsible for maintaining VMs. However, whether you or your cloud provider maintains them, the cloud provider will constantly monitor the health of VMs and will have systems in place to recover an unhealthy VM.

Power outage

Reliable electricity is critical to availability. Even a quick power flicker can cause computers to reboot and systems to restart. When that happens, your application is unavailable until all systems are restored.

Cloud providers invest heavily in battery-operated power backups and other redundant systems in order to prevent availability problems caused by power outages. In a situation where a large geographic area is affected by a power outage, cloud providers offer you the ability to run your application from another region that isn't affected.

Problems with a reliant system

Your application might use systems that aren't in the cloud or that are hosted by a different cloud provider. If those systems fail, you might lose availability. By hosting your application in the cloud, you gain the benefit of troubleshooting, alerting, and diagnostics tools that the cloud provider offers.

Now that you have an understanding of some of the things that can affect availability and you understand some general advantages of the cloud that help alleviate those problems, let's review some of the specific ways the cloud can help you ensure high availability.

Scalability, elasticity, and agility

Computing resources aren't free. Even if you're using virtual machines, the underlying resources such as disk space, CPU, and memory cost money. The best way to minimize cost is to use only the resources necessary for your purposes. The challenge is that resource needs can change often and quickly.

Consider a situation where you are hosting an application in the cloud that tracks sales data for your company. If your sales staff regularly enters information on daily sales calls at the end of the day, you might need additional computing resources to handle that load. Those same resources aren't needed during the day when the sales staff is making sales calls and not using the application.

You might also host a web application in the cloud that is used by external customers. Depending on the usage pattern, you might want to add additional computing resources on certain days or during certain times. You might also need to quickly adapt to more users if your company receives unexpected publicity from the media or some other means.

Scaling and *elasticity* allow you to easily deal with these kinds of scenarios. Scaling is the process of adding additional resources or additional power for your application. There are two variations of scaling: horizontal scaling (often referred to as *scaling out*) and vertical scaling (often referred to as *scaling up*).

When you scale out, you add additional VMs for your application. Each VM you add is identical to other VMs servicing your application. Scaling out provides additional resources to handle additional load.

When you scale up, you move to a new VM with additional resources. For example, you might determine that you need a more powerful CPU and more memory for your application. In that case, scaling up will allow you to move your application to a more powerful VM.

NOTE   SCALING UP OFTEN ADDS FEATURES

When you scale up, you often not only add more CPU power and memory, but you also often gain additional features because of the added power. For example, scaling up might give you solid-state disk drives or other features not available at lower tiers.

Figure 1-1 shows an example of scaling up a web application hosted in Azure.

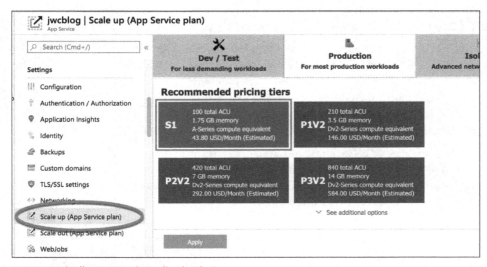

FIGURE 1-1 Scaling up a web application in Azure

REAL WORLD   SCALING GOES BOTH WAYS

In addition to scaling out and scaling up, you can also *scale in* and *scale down* to decrease resource usage. In a real-world situation, you would want to increase computing resources when needed and reduce them when demand goes down.

Cloud providers make it easy to scale your application, and they offer the ability to scale automatically based on the usage pattern for your application. You can scale automatically based on things like CPU usage and memory usage, and you can also scale based on other metrics that are specific to the type of application. The concept of automatically scaling is referred to as *elasticity*.

EXAM TIP

In Azure, you can scale automatically by configuring Auto-Scale. Auto-Scale is an Azure service that can automatically scale applications running in many Azure services based on usage patterns, resource utilization, time of day, and much more.

One major benefit of the cloud is that it allows you to quickly scale. For example, if you are running a web application in Azure and you determine that you need two more VMs for your application, you can scale out to three VMs in seconds. Azure takes care of allocating the resources for you. All you have to do is tell Azure how many VMs you want and you're up and running. This kind of speed and flexibility in the cloud is often called cloud *agility*.

> **MORE INFO** **MORE INFORMATION ON SCALING BEST PRACTICES**
>
> For more information on scaling in Azure, see the documentation at *https://docs.microsoft.com/azure/architecture/best-practices/auto-scaling*.

Fault tolerance and disaster recovery

In a complex cloud environment, things are bound to go wrong from time to time. In order to maintain a high level of availability, cloud providers implement systems that monitor the health of cloud resources and take action when a resource is determined to be unhealthy, thereby ensuring that the cloud is *fault tolerant*.

EXAM TIP

Don't confuse fault tolerance with scaling. Scaling allows you to react to additional load or resource needs, but it's always assumed that all the VMs you are using are healthy. Fault tolerance happens without any interaction from you, and it's designed to automatically move you from an unhealthy system to a healthy system if things go wrong.

In addition to monitoring the health of VMs and other resources, cloud providers design their infrastructure in such a way as to ensure fault tolerance. For example, if you have an application running on two VMs in Azure, Microsoft ensures that those two VMs are allocated within the infrastructure so that they are unlikely to be affected by system failures.

> **MORE INFO** **FAULT TOLERANCE IN AZURE**
>
> You don't have to understand the technical details of how Azure implements fault tolerance for the AZ-900 exam, but if you're interested in learning more, check out *https://msdn.microsoft.com/magazine/mt422582.aspx*.

Fault tolerance is designed to deal with failure at a small scale; for example, fault tolerance can move you from an unhealthy VM to a healthy VM. However, there are times when much larger failures can occur. For example, natural disasters in a region can affect all resources in that particular region. Not only can something like that impact availability, but without a plan in place, disasters can also mean the loss of valuable data.

REAL WORLD **DISASTER RECOVERY AND GOVERNMENTS**

Depending on what kind of data you store, you might be required to have a disaster recovery plan in place. Cloud providers typically comply with standards imposed by laws such as the Health Insurance Portability and Accountability Act (HIPAA), and they often provide compliance tools you can use to ensure compliance. You'll learn more about compliance and Azure in Chapter 5, "Describe identity, governance, privacy, and compliance features."

Disaster recovery not only means having reliable backups of important data, but it also means that the cloud infrastructure can replicate your application's resources in an unaffected region so that your data is safe and your application availability isn't affected. Disaster recovery plans are commonly referred to as *Business Continuity and Disaster Recovery* (BCDR) plans, and most cloud providers have services that can help you develop and implement a plan that works for your particular needs.

Capital and operational expenditures

So far, we've talked only about the availability benefit of moving to the cloud, but there are also economic benefits that affect the way expenditures are allocated in your company. Let's consider both the on-premises model and the cloud model.

On-premises model

In the on-premises model, a business purchases physical computer hardware to be used for its IT needs. Because these computers are physical assets that are intended to be used for more than one year, they are usually purchased as *capital expenses*.

There are several drawbacks to this model. When a business purchases computer hardware, it will typically keep that hardware in service until the return on that investment is realized. In the fast-evolving environment of computers, this can mean that hardware is outdated long before it makes financial sense to replace it. Another major drawback to this method is that it is not an agile approach. It might take months to requisition and configure new hardware, and in the era of modern IT, that approach often makes no sense.

MORE INFO **TYING UP MONEY**

Businesses need money for day-to-day operations, and when you have large amounts of money tied up in capital expenses, it can dramatically reduce the amount of money you can put toward your daily operations.

Cloud model

When you move to the cloud, you no longer rely on your on-premises computing hardware. Instead, you essentially rent hardware from the cloud provider. Because you aren't purchasing physical assets, you move your IT costs from capital expenses to *operating expenses* or day-to-day expenses for your business. Unlike capital expenses, operating expenses are tracked on a month-by-month basis, so it's much easier to adjust them based on need.

Another major benefit of the cloud model is reduced costs. When you use cloud resources, you are using resources made available from a large pool of resources owned by the cloud provider. The cloud provider pays for these resources up-front, but because of the large scale of resources they purchase, the cost to the cloud provider is greatly reduced. The reduction in cost that is realized when purchasing large numbers of a resource is referred to as the *principle of economies of scale*, and those savings are passed on to consumers of the cloud.

The consumption-based model

Cloud providers take savings a step further by offering the ability to use only those computing resources you require at any particular time. This is typically referred to as a *consumption-based model*, and it's often applied at many levels in cloud computing.

As we've already discussed, you can scale your application to use only the number of VMs you need, and you can choose how powerful those VMs are. You can adjust their number and power as your needs require. However, many cloud providers also offer services that allow you to pay only for time that you consume computer resources. For example, you can have application code hosted in a cloud provider and pay only for time that the code is actually executing on a VM. When no one is using the application, you don't pay for any resources.

> *MORE INFO* **CONSUMPTION-BASED COMPUTING**
>
> For an example of a consumption-based model, see "Serverless computing" in Chapter 3, "Describe core solutions and management tools on Azure."

As you can see, the cloud model offers many economic benefits over the on-premises model, and that's just one reason why businesses are rapidly moving to the cloud.

Skill 1.2: Describe the differences between categories of cloud services

As you've learned, one of the benefits of moving to the cloud is that you offload some of the responsibility of your infrastructure to the cloud provider. Moving to the cloud, however, is not an all-or-nothing kind of thing. When you're evaluating your use of the cloud, you need to balance your need for controlling resources against the convenience of allowing the cloud provider to handle things for you.

In this skill section, we're going to discuss the shared responsibility model the cloud offers through three primary categories of cloud services: *Infrastructure-as-a-Service (IaaS)*, *Platform-as-a-Service (PaaS)*, and *Software-as-a-Service (SaaS)*.

Shared responsibility model

Each type of service comes with a different level of responsibility on your part, and this concept is often referred to as the *shared responsibility model*. An easy way to visualize this model is by using the cloud pyramid shown in Figure 1-2. The bottom of the cloud pyramid represents the greatest amount of control over your resources, but it also represents the greatest amount of responsibility on your part. The top of the pyramid represents the least amount of control, but it also represents the least amount of responsibility on your part.

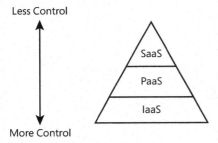

FIGURE 1-2 The cloud pyramid

Deciding on the right combination of control and responsibility requires that you understand each type of service and the pros and cons associated with them.

Infrastructure-as-a-Service (IaaS)

Infrastructure refers to the hardware that your application uses, and IaaS refers to the virtualized infrastructure offered by a cloud provider. When you create an IaaS resource, the cloud provider allocates a VM for your use. In some cases, the cloud provider might do the basic operating system install for you. In other situations, you might need to install the operating system yourself. In either case, you are responsible for installing other necessary services and your application.

Because you control the operating system install and installation of other services, IaaS gives you plenty of control over your cloud resources. However, it also means that you are responsible for making sure your operating system is patched with security updates, and if something goes wrong in the operating system, you're responsible for troubleshooting it.

The cloud provider is only responsible for providing the VM. You do, however, benefit from the underlying infrastructure in the area of fault tolerance and disaster recovery that we discussed earlier.

> **MORE INFO   REMOTE ACCESS TO IaaS VMs**
>
> You will have remote access to your IaaS VMs so that you can interact with them just as if you were using them in your on-premises environment. When you move to PaaS and SaaS services, you typically lose that capability because the infrastructure is managed by the cloud provider.

In Figure 1-3, you see an IaaS VM in the Azure portal. The Ubuntu Server, a Linux operating system, has been chosen for the VM. Once the VM is up and running, it will be using Ubuntu Server 18.04. Unless an update is installed, it will always be running that version, and Microsoft will never install patches or version updates.

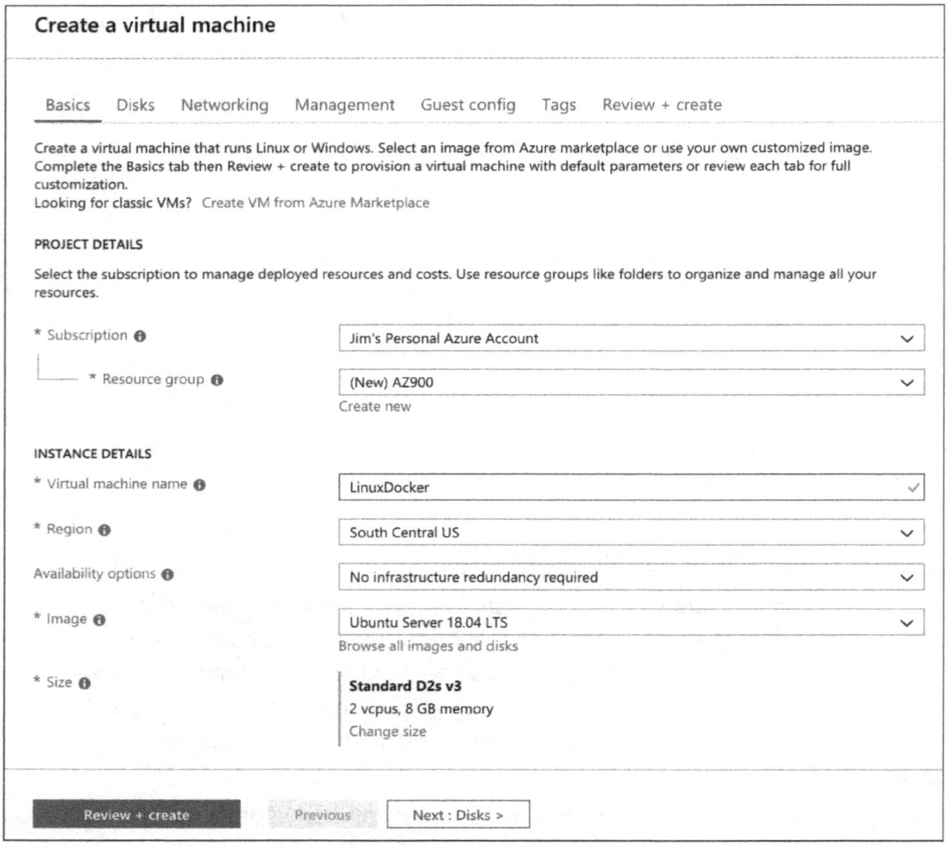

FIGURE 1-3 Creating an IaaS VM in Azure

Once you have an IaaS VM running in the cloud, you gain access to many services the cloud provider offers. For example, Microsoft offers Azure Security Center to ensure the security of your IaaS VMs, Azure Backup to make backing up data easy, Azure Log Analytics to help with troubleshooting any problems you might have, and much more.

> **MORE INFO**   **MORE INFORMATION ON IaaS AND AZURE**
>
> For more information on IaaS and Azure, see the documentation at *https://bit.ly/az900-whatisiaas.*

IaaS services allow you to control costs effectively because you only pay for them when you are using them. If you stop your IaaS VM, your billing stops for the resource. This makes IaaS an ideal choice if you need developers to have a platform for testing an application during release. Developers can start an IaaS VM, test the application as a team, and then stop the IaaS VM when testing is complete.

Another popular use of IaaS is when you need one or more powerful VMs for a temporary period. For example, you might need to analyze a large amount of data for a project. By utilizing IaaS VMs for your project, you can keep costs to a minimum, create resources quickly as you need them, and gain all the processing power you need.

IaaS services benefit from scaling and elasticity that we discussed earlier. If you need more VMs, you can scale out to accommodate that and then scale in when those resources are no longer needed. If you need more CPU power, more memory, or more disk space, you can quickly scale up to gain those benefits and then scale down when they're no longer needed.

In a nutshell, IaaS services are a great choice if you want to let someone else manage the hardware infrastructure (which can include both the computers and the network) related to your application, but you want to maintain control of what's installed in the operating system. In an IaaS environment, the cloud provider isn't going to install something on the operating system for you, so the current state of what's installed on your VMs is always known to you. If this is important for your particular needs, IaaS might be the right choice for you. Also, IaaS is a great choice if you occasionally need high-end VMs for specific needs.

IaaS is also a great choice if you want your application and configuration in the cloud, but you want the option of not paying for it when you aren't using it. By stopping your VM, you can avoid the costs associated with it, and when you need to use your application again, you can simply start your VM and pick up right where you left off.

Platform-as-a-Service (PaaS)

In a PaaS environment, a cloud provider still provides the infrastructure for you, but they also provide the operating system, software installed in the operating system to help you connect to databases and network systems (often referred to as *middleware*), and many features that enable you to build and manage complex cloud applications.

PaaS sits right in the middle of the cloud pyramid. PaaS services offer you the flexibility of controlling the application, but they offload management and control of the underlying systems to the cloud provider. If you are deploying your own application to the cloud and you want to minimize your management investment, a PaaS service is often the best choice.

> **NOTE PaaS AND VMs**
>
> A PaaS service also uses VMs provided by the cloud provider. However, a user typically has no visibility into those VMs. In most cases, they're entirely managed by the cloud provider.

Suppose you need to run a web application that uses the PHP framework to connect to a back-end database system. If you were to choose IaaS for your application, you'd need to ensure that you install and configure PHP on your VM. You'd then need to install and configure the software necessary to connect to your back-end database. In a PaaS scenario, you simply deploy your web application to the cloud provider, and everything else is taken care of for you.

In Figure 1-4, we have a web application in Azure App Service, one of the PaaS offerings in Azure. It has been created on a VM that's maintained by Microsoft. Notice the option to choose either Linux or Windows, but the operating system is still managed by Microsoft. We also have the option to enable Application Insights, a service in Azure that provides deep insight into how an application is performing, making it easier to troubleshoot problems if they occur.

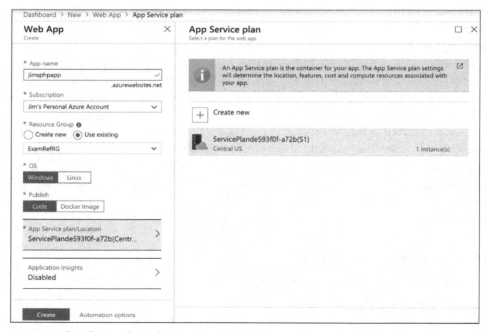

FIGURE 1-4 Creating a web app in Azure App Service

One more interesting thing in Figure 1-4 is the option to publish either your code or a Docker image. Docker is a technology that makes it easy to package your application and the components that it requires into an image that you can then deploy and run on another computer in another environment, as long as that computer has Docker installed on it. In Azure App Service, you don't have to worry about Docker installation or configuration. It's automatically included on all App Service VMs as part of Microsoft's PaaS offering, and it's completely managed and maintained by Microsoft.

Some of the other PaaS services are

- Azure CDN
- Azure Cosmos DB
- Azure SQL Database
- Azure Database for MySQL
- Azure Storage
- Azure Synapse Analytics

In a PaaS offering, cloud providers offer numerous application frameworks such as PHP, Node.js, ASP.NET, .NET Core, Java, Python, and more. The cloud provider usually provides multiple versions of each framework, so you can choose a version that you know is compatible with your application. The cloud provider will also ensure that common components necessary for data connectivity from your application to other systems are installed and configured. That usually means that your application code works without you having to do any kind of complex configuration. In fact, this is one of the main benefits of using a PaaS service; you can often move your application from on-premises to a cloud environment by simply deploying it to the cloud. This concept is often referred to as *lift-and-shift*.

Because the cloud provider controls the operating system and what's installed on the VM, they can provide additional capabilities to you by adding their own features. For example, suppose you want to add a log-in feature to your web application, and you want to allow users to log in with a Microsoft, Facebook, or Google account. If you want to add this capability on-premises or in an IaaS environment, you need some developers to build it for you, a task that isn't easy and one that requires specialized knowledge. You must either have developers in your company who already have those skills, or you'll have to hire them. However, cloud providers often offer features like this in their PaaS services, and enabling them is as easy as flipping a switch and doing some minor configuration specific to your app.

A PaaS service also benefits from all of the other enhancements offered by the cloud; you get fault tolerance, elasticity, easy and quick scaling, backup and disaster recovery features, and more. In fact, features such as backing up and restoring data are oftentimes more user-friendly and feature-rich in a PaaS environment because the cloud provider installs customized software on the PaaS VMs to add functionality.

As you can see, there are real benefits to allowing the cloud provider to control what's installed on the VMs running your application, but there can also be drawbacks. For example, the cloud provider controls when patches and updates are applied to both the operating system and to other components installed on the VMs. You'll usually be given advance notice of major changes so that you can test your application on-premises first and avoid any downtime, but you do lose the flexibility and control of deciding when to update the VM.

> **MORE INFO   MORE INFORMATION ON PaaS AND AZURE**
>
> For more information on PaaS offerings in Azure, see *https://bit.ly/az900-whatispaas.*

Software-as-a-Service (SaaS)

As you've learned, IaaS requires you to control both the operating system and middleware components along with your application. When you move to PaaS, you offload the control of the operating system and middleware components to the cloud provider, and you're responsible only for your application code. As you move to the top of the cloud pyramid and into the SaaS realm, the cloud provider controls everything. In other words, a SaaS service is software provided by a cloud provider that's installed on infrastructure completely controlled by the hosting provider.

SaaS services offer you the flexibility of a pay-as-you-go model. Essentially, you rent your software from a service provider. Users of the software usually access the software from a web browser, but they might also install applications that will only work as long as you are paying for the SaaS service. One huge benefit of web-based software is that it works from just about any device, including smart phones. Because of that, SaaS services enable connectivity and productivity for field staff using devices they already own.

When using a SaaS service, not only do you benefit from using software written and maintained by someone else, but you can also benefit from allowing the cloud provider to maintain and configure the application. For example, if your company offers corporate email, you can choose to use the Microsoft 365 SaaS service. By using the Exchange Online service in Microsoft 365, you can take advantage of enterprise-ready email solutions without having to hire IT staff and building infrastructure to support it. Instead, Microsoft maintains the system for you. Not only do you benefit from the flexibility and reliability of the cloud, but you can also rest easy knowing that Microsoft is ensuring your Exchange services are always available to your users.

SaaS services aren't just for the enterprise. In fact, most people use SaaS services all the time without even realizing it. If you use Hotmail or Gmail or another online email service, you're using a SaaS service. The cloud provider hosts the email software in the cloud, and you log in and use that software using your web browser. You don't have to know anything about the software. The cloud provider can offer new features with software updates, and those new features are available to you automatically without any action on your part. If the cloud provider finds a problem with the software, they can resolve it with a patch without you even realizing anything happened.

Some of the SaaS services Microsoft makes available are

- Microsoft 365
- Xbox Live

- OneDrive
- Power Automate (previously Microsoft Flow)

MORE INFO **MORE INFORMATION ON SₐₐS AND AZURE**

For more information on SaaS services and Azure, see *https://bit.ly/az900-whatissaas*.

Comparing service types

We've already discussed some of the advantages and disadvantages of each type of cloud service, and the cloud pyramid provides a visual representation of how types of cloud services differ related to your responsibility and what you can control. In order to solidify these concepts, let's look at a comparison of each service type.

As you've learned, IaaS provides you with the greatest flexibility. You can install your own software and your own components, and you control when the software and operating system are updated. An additional benefit is that you pay for your resources only when they're being used, so IaaS has the ability to reduce your operational expenses. Even though you can save costs by turning off VMs you aren't using, the higher costs associated with installing and maintaining your VMs might offset that benefit.

PaaS services offer you some of the same flexibility of IaaS services without the need to manage the infrastructure. In a PaaS service, you are responsible only for the application that's installed in the cloud. This can be your own application, or an application developed by someone else (for example, a WordPress system or an e-commerce solution), but in either case, you are responsible for the application. PaaS services are popular for developer teams who are looking to move on-premises applications to the cloud easily and quickly, and they typically offer many different deployment options to make that as easy as possible. PaaS services also offer more features than IaaS services because the cloud provider installs their own software and features on the platform. Any application running in a PaaS service, however, can be affected by updates and version changes in the underlying software, and that can mean increased costs associated with testing an application before the cloud provider rolls out changes.

SaaS services are quite a bit different than IaaS or PaaS services because they are completely managed and maintained by the cloud provider. You don't have the option of installing any of your own software with a SaaS service, so the deciding factor is related entirely to whether the provided software meets your needs. The benefit of a SaaS service is that it largely removes the IT burden from your company, and it enables everyone in your company to access the software on multiple devices from just about anywhere Internet access is available. You also benefit from data backup that the cloud provider includes in their infrastructure. If you have a need to customize the application or have any control over its configuration, however, SaaS might not be a good choice for you.

Skill 1.3: Describe the differences between types of cloud computing

In the simplest sense, the cloud usually represents infrastructure and applications that are accessible over the Internet. The examples covered so far are the more traditional cloud experience where anyone on the Internet can access your application. While you might have some means of authenticating people using your application so that the wrong people don't get access, your application is still running on VMs that are connected to the Internet and are accessible over public networks.

The traditional cloud model is referred to as the *public cloud*. In addition to a public cloud model, businesses can also use a *private cloud* where the infrastructure is dedicated to them. Finally, a *hybrid cloud* model represents a mixture of public and private cloud models.

This section covers:

- Cloud computing
- The public cloud
- The private cloud
- The hybrid cloud

Cloud computing

When I started this chapter, I said that the cloud *usually* represents infrastructure and applications that are available over the Internet. When most people think of the cloud, they think of it in this context, but cloud resources aren't always connected to the public Internet.

A better way of thinking of cloud computing is to think of it as many computing resources all connected by a network, but even that definition doesn't fully describe the cloud. Cloud computing also means systems that are scalable, agile, and so forth. If you combine those concepts along with distributed computing resources accessible on a network, you have the makings of cloud computing.

As you can see, it's a bit tough to clearly define cloud computing, but a discussion of the different cloud models should help you to better understand what cloud computing is.

The public cloud

The most common cloud model is the public cloud. In a public cloud model, you use shared infrastructure that is accessible on a public network. The network, storage, and VMs that your application uses are provided by a cloud provider and shared between all consumers of the public cloud. Microsoft Azure, Amazon Web Services (AWS), and Google Cloud Platform are examples of public clouds.

> **NOTE CLOUDS AND THE INTERNET**
>
> Many cloud services might provide access from the Internet, but that doesn't necessarily mean they are available to anyone on the Internet. In most cases, access requires authentication.
>
> You'll learn more about securing cloud resources in Chapter 4, "Describe general security and network security features."

The public cloud model is beneficial in that it makes it easy and fast to move to the cloud. Because the cloud provider already has the infrastructure in place and configured for you, all you have to do is decide on the type of cloud service you want and you're off and running. You also benefit from the ability to scale quickly and efficiently because the cloud provider has resources already provisioned and ready for your use when needed.

As we discussed earlier, another advantage to the public cloud model is that you can control costs more efficiently because you only pay for the resources you are using. If you need to scale out to more VMs, the cloud provider has them available and waiting for you. You don't have to maintain a pool of resources yourself. Instead, you take advantage of the resources the cloud provider has invested in.

> **IMPORTANT MULTITENANT ENVIRONMENT**
>
> Because you are sharing resources in a public cloud with other people who are using that public cloud, you'll often see public clouds referred to as a multitenant environment.

While the flexibility and convenience of the public cloud is attractive, it comes with some disadvantages. First of all, you do give up some control of the infrastructure when using the public cloud. How much control depends on where you land on the cloud pyramid, but no matter what, the cloud provider is going to control some portion of your infrastructure.

There might also be security concerns with operating in the public cloud. The network involved in the public cloud is the public Internet, and it's available to anyone with an Internet connection. That means you will need to have security measures in place to avoid unauthorized access to your application and data. Cloud providers realize this, and they provide security measures to help protect you, but those measures might not meet your security requirements.

Another disadvantage of the public cloud is that it locks you into the specific configuration defined by the cloud provider. For example, suppose you have an application that needs a large amount of disk storage, but you only need a single-CPU system to run it. In order to meet your disk space requirements, the cloud provider might require you to scale up to a high-powered, multi-CPU VM, thereby increasing your costs unnecessarily.

> **MORE INFO** **MORE INFORMATION ON PUBLIC CLOUDS**
>
> For more information on public clouds and Azure, see *https://bit.ly/az900-publiccloud*.

The private cloud

The private cloud model provides many of the attractive benefits of the cloud (things like easy scaling and elasticity) in a private environment that is dedicated to a single company. A private cloud can be hosted in an on-premises environment, but it can also be hosted on a third-party hosting provider.

> **IMPORTANT** **SINGLE-TENANT ENVIRONMENT**
>
> Because the resources in a private cloud are dedicated to a single organization, you will often see the private cloud referred to as a *single-tenant environment*.

Two of the main reasons why companies choose a private cloud are privacy and regulatory concerns. Unlike the public cloud, private clouds operate on a private network that is only accessible by a single organization. Businesses like banks and medical providers might have regulations in place that require certain data be inaccessible from the Internet, and in those situations, a private cloud might be a good choice. Another common consumer of private clouds is the cruise ship industry. Cruise ships operate in remote areas where Internet access isn't available, but they still want to take advantage of the benefits of the cloud for day-to-day operations of complex ship systems.

EXAM TIP

You'll often hear that a private cloud consists of infrastructure that is owned by an individual company, but that's not actually always true. If a company runs a private cloud on-premises, they will usually own the hardware and infrastructure used for the private cloud, but it's also possible to host a private cloud in a third-party data center. In that situation, the infrastructure is owned by the hosting provider, but it's still completely dedicated to the single company paying for the private cloud. The bottom line is that the difference between a public and a private cloud is the privacy of infrastructure and data. It doesn't really matter who owns the infrastructure.

There are some disadvantages to a private cloud. If you are hosting your private cloud on-premises, you will likely spend as much on IT as you would in a non-cloud environment. You will have to pay for hardware and virtualized systems for your cloud, and you'll need IT staff who are capable of managing the software and infrastructure for your cloud.

Avoiding IT costs is one of the primary reasons that companies choose to use a third-party hosting provider for private clouds, but that choice also has some drawbacks. For example, once you offload management of your private cloud to a third party, you lose control of important considerations such as the security of your data. It's often impossible to achieve full transparency when dealing with third-party providers, and you can't always guarantee that data on your private cloud network will remain secured in a way that you require.

> **MORE INFO**   **MORE INFORMATION ON PRIVATE CLOUDS**
>
> For more information on private clouds, see *https://bit.ly/az900-privatecloud*.

The hybrid cloud

As you might expect, hybrid clouds are a mixture of public and private clouds. In a hybrid cloud environment, you might have an application that is running within the public cloud, yet it accesses data that is securely stored on-premises. You might also have a scenario where your application and most of its resources are located on a private cloud, but you want to use services or infrastructure that are located in a public cloud. Indeed, the various scenarios that are suitable for a hybrid model are almost endless.

Hybrid cloud models are often a company's first foray into the cloud. Many companies have legacy on-premises systems that are expensive to move to the cloud, yet they might want to take advantage of some of the benefits of the cloud. In such a scenario, a company might move only part of a particular system to the cloud, leaving the legacy system on-premises until a later time.

Not all companies adopting a hybrid cloud model are doing so because of legacy systems. In some situations, a company might want to maintain complete control over part of their infrastructure or data. They might decide to build out on-premises infrastructure in tandem with building their public cloud presence.

> **IMPORTANT**   **HYBRID DOESN'T ALWAYS INCLUDE ON-PREMISES**
>
> Remember, a private cloud is a cloud dedicated to a single organization. It doesn't have to be located on-premises. It can also be hosted at a third-party data center, so a hybrid cloud model might be the combination of a third-party data center and a public cloud.

When companies adopt a hybrid model, they often require the capability of connecting the private, on-premises network with the public cloud network. Cloud providers offer many technologies to make that possible. In Microsoft Azure, Virtual Networks, Hybrid Connections, and Service Bus are just some examples of such technologies.

> **MORE INFO   MORE INFORMATION ON AZURE NETWORKING**
>
> We'll cover more features of Azure networking in Chapter 2, Skill 2.2 and in Chapter 4, Skill 4.2.

While it might not be immediately obvious, a hybrid cloud model comes with several challenges. First of all, application development teams will need to ensure that data shared between the public and private cloud is compatible. This might require some specialized development skills and complex troubleshooting. The networking complexities in a hybrid environment can also be quite challenging, especially because network infrastructure at third-party providers might introduce problems that are difficult to troubleshoot. Finally, spreading application resources between a public and a private cloud might cause application slowdowns due to the geographical distance between systems running the application and the data the application uses. All these situations have to be carefully evaluated when deciding to use a hybrid cloud model.

In order to make hybrid cloud easier for its customers, Microsoft provides Azure Stack. Azure Stack is sold as a package, including software and validated hardware to run it. Azure Stack allows you to run Azure services on-premises, making it easy to then transfer applications to the cloud with a minimal amount of work. Because the hardware is part of Azure Stack and has been validated by Microsoft, you don't have the burden of attempting to determine hardware needs in order to deploy Azure Stack, but you do have to manage the on-premises hardware.

Thought experiment

Let's apply what you've learned in this chapter. You can find the answers in the section that follows.

You work for Contoso Medical Group (CMG), and your manager is frustrated with one of your commonly used applications. The CMG IT department is resource-constrained, and they are having difficulty ensuring the application is always available.

The development team has been updating the application frequently, but due to a lack of knowledge in deployment methods, they only have the option of directly copying files, and this is causing problems with tracking changes that are being made. At the same time, the development team has no data to show whether the application is running correctly.

The problem became critical two days ago when a deadline was approaching for updating medical records. The application experienced way more usage than normal, and the system was quickly overloaded and became unresponsive. The IT team determined the problem was the server running low on resources, but it took them two hours to build a second server to handle the load.

Your manager has come to you asking for a solution that addresses all of these issues. Whatever solution you offer must take into account that the medical data in this application is covered under HIPAA, and your manager wants CMG to retain all control of the data. Your manager also wants to carefully control costs.

You've decided that CMG should move the application to the cloud, but you need to sell the idea to your manager.

Answer the following questions:

1. What type of cloud service would you recommend?
2. How would you justify your choice related to the problems being encountered by the IT team?
3. How would you justify your choice related to the problems being encountered by the development team?
4. What other benefits will please your manager if your advice is followed?
5. How can you meet the requirements related to the medical records and the need to control them?

Thought experiment answers

In this section, we'll discuss the answers from the previous section.

1. A PaaS service makes the most sense in this situation. An IaaS environment would require your IT department to manage the VMs, and that would not meet your requirements. A SaaS service provides the software to you, and in this case, you need to run your company's custom application in the cloud.
2. The IT department is short on resources and is challenged in keeping the application available. In a PaaS service, the management of the VMs running the application is offloaded to the cloud provider. The cloud provider also offers an SLA so that your application is always available. The IT team will also benefit from easy scaling offered in a cloud environment, and instead of two hours, they can add more servers almost instantly.
3. In a PaaS service, the cloud provider offers flexible deployment options that make it easy to deploy an application using the method you prefer. They also provide logging so that the development team can track changes made to the application. Diagnostic features in a PaaS service (such as Azure's Application Insights) provide detailed data on how an application is performing and can alert you to code problems in an application.
4. Your manager wants to lower costs and moving to the cloud should meet that need. Your IT department has already built a second server, so that when additional need is required, you can meet it. However, the increased usage was temporary. Even so, it was related to a deadline for filing records, and the next time that deadline occurs, you'll

need that second server. By moving to the cloud, you benefit from easy scaling and elasticity so that you can scale out when you need the second server to handle load, and then you can easily scale back in to reduce your costs.

5. By adopting a hybrid cloud model, you can keep your sensitive medical data on-premises, while benefiting from the application itself running in the cloud.

Chapter summary

In this chapter, you learned some of the general concepts related to the cloud. You learned about the advantages of moving to the cloud, you learned about the different cloud service types, and you learned about the different cloud models available to you. Here are the key concepts from this chapter.

- Cloud providers offer service-level agreements (SLAs) that guarantee a certain level of availability, but only for those systems that are controlled by them.
- Moving to the cloud can help avoid downtime caused by network outages, system outages, and power outages. It can also help you if you need to diagnose problems with an application or problems with an external system that your application uses.
- You can scale up (or vertically) when you want to add additional CPUs or more memory using a more powerful VM.
- You can scale out (or horizontally) if you want to add more VMs to handle additional load.
- Cloud providers give you ways to automatically scale based on usage patterns, resource utilization, and times of day. This is referred to as *elasticity*.
- Cloud providers monitor the health of the infrastructure. When a VM becomes unhealthy, the cloud provider can automatically move you to a healthy VM without you having to do anything. This is called *fault tolerance*.
- Cloud providers also operate across multiple data centers that are in different regions of the world. If a natural disaster (or any other disaster) happens in one region, you can switch over to another region, assuming you have replicated your environment in multiple regions. This kind of planning is called Business Continuity and Disaster Recovery planning, and cloud providers often have features in place to make implementing a plan easy. This is often referred to as disaster recovery.
- Because you are using infrastructure owned by the cloud provider, moving to the cloud reduces your *capital expenses*, the major expenses that are incurred for infrastructure and other major purchases. Cloud providers take advantage of the *principle of economies of scale* by purchasing large amounts of infrastructure to be used by cloud consumers.
- Day-to-day expenses (*operational expenses*) can also be reduced in the cloud because you pay only for those resources you are using at any particular time. This *consumption-based model* is a key benefit of the cloud.

- The cloud pyramid outlines the idea that increased control over your resources means a larger responsibility on your part. Decreased control results in more responsibility on the cloud provider's part. This concept is called the *shared responsibility model.*

- Infrastructure-as-a-Service (IaaS) offers infrastructure running in the cloud, but you have to maintain the operating system and what's installed on that infrastructure. IaaS services offer you the most control in the cloud, but they also carry the largest management burden.

- Platform-as-a-Service (PaaS) offloads the management of the infrastructure, and it also offloads the operating system and components installed on the VMs to the cloud provider. You are responsible for your application. PaaS services also offer many additional features that make it easy to add functionality to an application without having to write complex code. Development teams also have a wide variety of deployment methods available, and the cloud provider often automates much of that process.

- Software-as-a-Service (SaaS) provides a hosted application in the cloud that is most commonly accessed using a web browser. In a SaaS service, the cloud provider manages everything for you. You are essentially renting the use of the software from the cloud provider. A big benefit of SaaS is that it makes applications easily accessible by employees in the field on any device.

- The public cloud model is sometimes referred to as a multitenant environment. Multiple companies and users share the same infrastructure. VMs and other infrastructure are allocated to users as they need them, and when they no longer need them, they are returned to the pool to be used by other users. The network is available publicly over the Internet, but you do have the ability to put security methods in place to control access to your resources.

- The private cloud model is sometimes referred to as a single-tenant environment. All infrastructure is private to an individual or a company, and the network is only available within the private cloud itself. It is not exposed to the Internet. In many cases, the infrastructure used in a private cloud is owned by the company, but not always. It's possible to host a private cloud in a third-party data center.

- A hybrid cloud model is a mixture of the public and private cloud models. Hybrid clouds are often used when a company needs to use on-premises resources in a cloud application.

CHAPTER 2

Describe core Azure services

In Chapter 1, "Describe cloud concepts," you learned about the cloud and how you can benefit from using cloud services. Microsoft Azure was mentioned, but not in much detail.

In this chapter, we dive into the many services and solutions that Azure offers. You'll gain an understanding of the key concepts in Azure's architecture, which apply to all Azure services. We cover Azure datacenters and ways that Microsoft implements fault tolerance and disaster recovery by spreading Azure infrastructure across the globe. You'll also learn about availability zones, which are Microsoft's solution for ensuring your services aren't affected when a particular Azure datacenter experiences a problem.

You'll also discover how to manage and track your Azure resources, and how you can work with resources as a group using Azure resource groups. You'll learn how to use resource groups to plan and manage Azure resources, and you'll learn how resource groups can help you categorize your operational expenses in Azure.

In order to really understand resource groups and how Azure works under the hood, it's important to understand Azure Resource Manager (ARM), the underlying system that Azure uses to manage your resources. You'll learn about the benefits that ARM provides, and you'll see how ARM opens up some powerful possibilities for quickly and easily deploying real-world solutions to Azure.

Once you have the foundational understanding of Azure, you'll dig into some of the core workload products that Microsoft provides, such as Azure virtual machines, Azure App Service, services that make it easy to work with containers and networking, and storage and database services. You'll also learn about the Azure Marketplace and how it enables the creation and deployment of complex solutions with minimal work on your part, and because of the "under the hood" knowledge you'll have from earlier in the chapter, the Azure Marketplace won't seem like black magic.

If you think that's a lot to cover, you're right! It's important for you to have an understanding of all these topics in order to pass the AZ-900 exam. With the foundational knowledge of the cloud from Chapter 1, "Describe cloud concepts," you'll find that understanding Azure-specific concepts will be easier than you think.

Skills covered in this chapter:

- Describe the core Azure architectural components
- Describe core resources available in Azure

Skill 2.1: Describe the core Azure architectural components

If you were to ask any CEO to list the five most important assets of their company, it is likely that the company's data would be near the top of the list. The world we live in revolves around data. Just look at companies like Facebook and Google. These companies offer services to us that we like. Everyone likes looking at pictures from friends and family on Facebook (mixed in with things we don't like so much), and many people use Google to look for things on the Internet. Facebook and Google don't offer those services because they want to be nice to us. They offer those services because it's a way for them to collect a large amount of data on their customers, and that data is their most valuable asset.

Facebook and Google aren't alone. Most companies have vast amounts of data that is key to their business and keeping that data safe is at the cornerstone of business decisions. That's why some companies are hesitant to move to the cloud. They're afraid of losing control of their data. Not only are they afraid that someone else might gain access to sensitive data, but they're also concerned about losing data that would be difficult (or even impossible) to re-create.

Microsoft is keenly aware of those fears, and Azure has been designed from the ground up to instill confidence in this area. Let's look at some core architectural components that help Microsoft deliver on the cloud promise.

> **This section covers:**
> - Azure regions and regional pairs
> - Availability zones
> - Resource groups
> - Azure subscriptions
> - Management groups
> - Azure Resource Manager (ARM)

Azure regions and regional pairs

The term "cloud" tends to make people think of Azure as a nebulous entity that you can't clearly see, but that would be a mistake. While there certainly are logical constructs to Azure, there are also physical components to it. After all, at the end of the day, we're talking about computers!

In order to provide Azure services to people around the world, Microsoft has created boundaries called *geographies*. A geography boundary is oftentimes the border of a country, and there's good reason for that. There are often regulations for data handling that apply to an entire country, and having a geography defined for a country allows Microsoft to ensure that data-handling regulations are in place. Many companies (especially ones that deal with sensitive data) are also much more comfortable if their data is contained within the confines of the country in which they operate.

There are numerous geographies in Azure. For example, there's a United States geography, a Canada geography, a UK geography, and so on. Each geography is broken out into two or more regions, each of which is typically hundreds of miles apart. As an example, within the United States geography, there are many regions, including the Central US region in Iowa, the East US region in Virginia, the West US region in California, and the South Central US region in Texas. Microsoft also operates isolated regions that are completely dedicated to government data because of the additional regulations that governmental data requires.

Within each geography, Microsoft has created another logical boundary called a *regional pair*. Each regional pair contains two regions within the geography. When Microsoft has to perform updates to the Azure platform, they perform those updates on one region in the regional pair. Once those updates are complete, they move to the next region in the regional pair. This ensures that your services operating within a regional pair aren't impacted by updates.

> **MORE INFO** **REGIONAL PAIRS**
>
> To benefit from regional pairs, you should make sure to deploy resources redundantly to each regional within the pair. You can find a list of all regional pairs by browsing to *https://bit.ly/ az900-regionpairs*.

> **EXAM TIP**
>
> The fact that each geography contains at least two regions separated by a large physical distance is important. That's how Azure maintains disaster recovery, and it's likely this concept will be included on the exam. We'll cover more about this later in this chapter.

At each region, Microsoft has built datacenters (physical buildings) that contain the physical hardware that Azure uses. These datacenters contain climate-controlled buildings that house the server racks containing physical computer hardware. Each region also operates on its own network infrastructure, and Microsoft has designed the networks for low latency. Therefore, any Azure services you have in a particular region will have reliable and fast network connectivity with each other.

> **MORE INFO** **CUSTOMERS ONLY SEE REGIONS**
>
> When a customer is creating Azure resources, only the region is visible. The concept of geographies is an internal implementation of Azure that customers don't really have visibility of when using Azure. Customers also don't have visibility into the concept of regional pairs, but they can see each region within a regional pair.

Each datacenter has an isolated power supply and power generators in case of a power outage. All the network traffic entering and exiting the datacenter goes over Microsoft's own fiber-optic network on fiber owned or leased by Microsoft. Even data that flows between regions across oceans travels over Microsoft's fiber-optic cables that traverse the oceans.

> **MORE INFO   DATACENTER POWER**
>
> As of 2018, all Microsoft's datacenters were using at least 50 percent natural power consisting of solar power, wind power, and so on. In 2020, the goal is 60 percent, and Microsoft has a goal of being carbon-neutral by the year 2030.
>
> In order to remove reliance on third-party power providers, Microsoft is also investing in the development of natural gas-powered, fully integrated fuel cells for power. Not only do fuel cells provide clean power, but they also remove the power fluctuations and other disadvantages of relying on the power grid. In late July 2020, Microsoft announced that it had developed a hydrogen-fueled cell that could run an Azure datacenter for 48 consecutive hours.

To ensure that data in Azure is safe from disasters and failures caused by possible problems in a particular region, customers are encouraged to replicate data in multiple regions. For example, if the South Central US region is hit by a devastating tornado (not out of the question in Texas), data that is also replicated to the North Central US region in Illinois is still safe and available. In order to ensure that applications are still performing as quickly as possible, Microsoft guarantees round-trip network performance of 2 milliseconds or less between regions.

Availability zones

The fact that regions are physically separated by hundreds of miles protects Azure users from data loss and application outages caused by disasters at a particular region. However, it's also important that data and applications maintain availability when a problem occurs at a particular datacenter within a region. For that reason, Microsoft developed availability zones.

> **NOTE   AVAILABILITY ZONE AVAILABILITY**
>
> Availability zones aren't available in all Azure regions, nor are they available for all Azure services in regions that support them. For the most up-to-date list of availability zone-enabled regions and services, see *https://bit.ly/az900-azones*.

There are at least three availability zones within each enabled region, and because each availability zone exists within its own datacenter in that region, each has a water supply, cooling system, network, and power supply that is isolated from other zones. By deploying an Azure service in two or more availability zones, you can achieve high availability in a situation where there is a problem in one zone.

EXAM TIP

Availability zones provide high-availability and fault tolerance, but they might not help you with disaster recovery. If there is a localized disaster, such as a fire in a datacenter housing one zone, you will benefit from availability zones. Because availability zones are located in the same Azure region, if there is a large-scale natural disaster such as a tornado, you might not be protected. In other words, availability zones are just one facet to an overall disaster recovery and fault-tolerant design.

Because Availability zones are designed to offer enhanced availability for infrastructure, not all services support availability zones. For example, Azure has a service called App Service Certificates that allows you to purchase and manage an SSL certificate through Azure. It wouldn't make any sense to host a certificate in App Service Certificates within an availability zone because it's not an infrastructure component.

Currently, availability zones are supported with the following Azure services.

- Windows virtual machines
- Linux virtual machines
- Virtual Machine Scale Sets
- Azure Kubernetes Service
- Managed disks
- Zone-redundant storage
- Standard Load Balancer
- Standard IP address
- VPN Gateway
- ExpressRoute Gateway
- Application Gateway V2
- Azure Firewall
- Azure Data Explorer
- Azure SQL Database
- Azure Cache for Redis
- Azure Cosmos DB
- Event Hubs
- Service Bus (Premium tier)
- Event Grid
- Azure AD Domain Services
- App Service Environments ILB

NOTE **KEEP UP WITH CHANGES IN AZURE**

You can keep up with all the news related to Azure updates by watching the Azure blog at *https://azure.com/blog.*

By deploying your service to two or more availability zones, you ensure the maximum availability for that resource. In fact, Microsoft guarantees an SLA of 99.99 percent uptime for Azure virtual machines only if two or more VMs are deployed into two or more zones. Figure 2-1 illustrates the benefit of running in multiple zones. As you can see, even though availability zone 3 has gone offline for some reason, zones 1 and 2 are still operational.

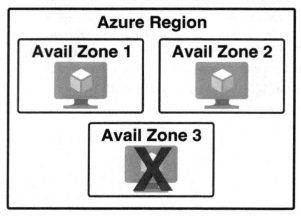

FIGURE 2-1 Azure virtual machine inside of three availability zones

NOTE **THE STATUS OF AZURE**

Microsoft operates a website that shows the status of all Azure services. If you notice a problem with your resources, you can check the Azure Status page at *https://status.azure.com*.

EXAM TIP

Don't confuse availability zones with availability sets. Availability sets allow you to create two or more virtual machines in different physical server racks in an Azure datacenter. Microsoft guarantees a 99.95 percent SLA with an availability set.

An availability zone allows you to deploy two or more Azure services into two distinct datacenters within a region. Microsoft guarantees a 99.99 percent SLA with availability zones.

There are two categories of services that support availability zones: *zonal* services and *zone redundant* services. Zonal services are services such as virtual machines, managed disks used in a virtual machine, and public IP addresses used in virtual machines. In order to achieve high availability, you must explicitly deploy zonal services into two or more zones.

NOTE **MANAGED DISKS AND PUBLIC IP ADDRESSES**

When you create a virtual machine in Azure and you deploy it to an availability zone, Azure will automatically deploy the managed disk(s) and public IP address (if one is configured) to the same availability zone.

Zone redundant services are services such as zone redundant storage and SQL Databases. To use availability zones with these services, you specify the option to make them zone redundant when you create them. (For storage, the feature is called ZRS or zone redundant storage. For SQL Database, there is an option to make the database zone redundant.) Azure takes care of the rest for you by replicating data automatically to multiple availability zones.

Resource groups

You should now be realizing that moving to the cloud might not be as simple as it first seemed. Creating a single resource in Azure is pretty simple, but when you're dealing with enterprise-level applications, you're usually dealing with a complex array of services. Not only that, but you might be dealing with multiple applications that use multiple services, and they might be spread across multiple Azure regions. Things can certainly get chaotic quickly.

Fortunately, Azure provides a feature that helps you deal with this kind of problem: the resource group. A resource group is a logical container for Azure services. By creating all Azure services associated with a particular application in a single resource group, you can then deploy and manage all of those services as a single entity.

Organizing Azure resources in a resource group has many advantages. You can easily set up deployments using a feature known as an ARM template. *ARM template* deployments are typically for a single resource group. You can deploy to multiple resource groups but doing so requires you to set up a complicated chain of ARM templates.

MORE INFO   **MORE ON ARM TEMPLATES**

You'll learn more about ARM templates in Skill 3.2, "Describe core solutions and management tools on Azure," in Chapter 3.

Another advantage to resource groups is that you can name a resource group with an easily recognizable name so that you can see all Azure resources used in a particular application at a glance. This might not seem so important until you actually start deploying Azure resources and realize that you have many more resources than you first thought. For example, when you create an Azure virtual machine, Azure creates not only a virtual machine, but it also creates a disk resource, network interface, public IP resource, and network security group. If you're looking at all your Azure resources, it can be hard to differentiate which resources go with which app. Resource groups solve that problem.

In Figure 2-2, you can see a lot of Azure services. Some of these were automatically created by Azure in order to support other services, and in many cases, Azure gives the resource an unrecognizable name.

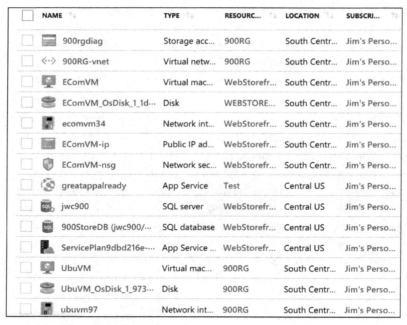

	NAME ↑↓	TYPE ↑↓	RESOURC... ↑↓	LOCATION ↑↓	SUBSCRI... ↑↓
☐	900rgdiag	Storage acc...	900RG	South Centr...	Jim's Perso...
☐	900RG-vnet	Virtual netw...	900RG	South Centr...	Jim's Perso...
☐	EComVM	Virtual mac...	WebStorefr...	South Centr...	Jim's Perso...
☐	EComVM_OsDisk_1_1d···	Disk	WEBSTORE...	South Centr...	Jim's Perso...
☐	ecomvm34	Network int...	WebStorefr...	South Centr...	Jim's Perso...
☐	EComVM-ip	Public IP ad...	WebStorefr...	South Centr...	Jim's Perso...
☐	EComVM-nsg	Network sec...	WebStorefr...	South Centr...	Jim's Perso...
☐	greatappalready	App Service	Test	Central US	Jim's Perso...
☐	jwc900	SQL server	WebStorefr...	Central US	Jim's Perso...
☐	900StoreDB (jwc900/...	SQL database	WebStorefr...	Central US	Jim's Perso...
☐	ServicePlan9dbd216e-···	App Service ...	WebStorefr...	Central US	Jim's Perso...
☐	UbuVM	Virtual mac...	900RG	South Centr...	Jim's Perso...
☐	UbuVM_OsDisk_1_973···	Disk	900RG	South Centr...	Jim's Perso...
☐	ubuvm97	Network int...	900RG	South Centr...	Jim's Perso...

FIGURE 2-2 All my Azure resources

In Figure 2-3, you can see resources that are in the *WebStorefront* resource group. These are the Azure resources used in the e-commerce storefront.

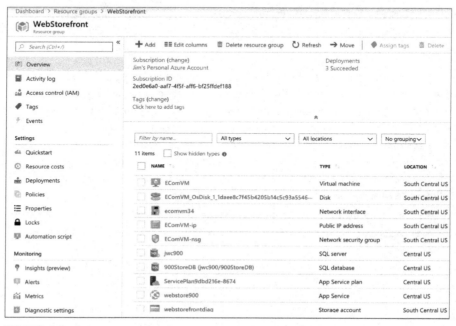

FIGURE 2-3 An Azure resource group

It's convenient to see all the resources associated with a particular app, but you aren't locked into that paradigm. This is a useful example, because it's a common use of resource groups; however, you can organize your resource groups any way you choose. Notice in Figure 2-3 that you see resources in several different Azure regions (Regions are in the Location column). If you have access to multiple Azure subscriptions, you can also have resources from multiple subscriptions in a single resource group.

If you look at the left side of Figure 2-3, you'll see a menu of operations that you can perform on your resource group. We won't go into all of these because it's out of scope for the AZ-900 exam, but there are a few that clarify the benefit of resource groups.

If you click **Resource Costs**, you can see the cost of all the resources in this resource group. Having that information at your fingertips is especially helpful in situations where you want to make sure certain departments in your company are charged correctly for their used resources. In fact, some companies will create resource groups for each department rather than creating resource groups scoped to applications. Having a Sales and Marketing resource group or an IT Support resource group, for instance, can help you immensely when reporting and controlling costs.

EXAM TIP

An Azure resource can only exist in one resource group. In other words, you can't have a virtual machine in a resource group called *WebStorefront* and also in a resource group called *SalesMarketing*, because it must be in one group or the other. You can move Azure resources from one resource group to another.

MORE INFO **MOVING AZURE RESOURCES**

Moving Azure resources between resource groups or subscriptions isn't without risk. Microsoft has documented some things you can do to avoid problems when moving resources. You can read that guidance by browsing to *https://bit.ly/az900-movingresources*.

You can also click **Automation Script** and Azure will generate an ARM template that you can use to deploy all these Azure resources. This is useful in a situation where you want to deploy these resources later or when you want to deploy them to another Azure subscription.

When you delete a resource group, all the resources in that resource group are automatically deleted. This makes it easy to delete multiple Azure resources in one easy step. Suppose you are testing a scenario and you need to create a couple of virtual machines, a database, a web app, and more. By placing all these resources in one resource group, you can easily delete that resource group after your testing and Azure will automatically delete all the resources in it for you. This is a great way to avoid unexpected costs associated with resources you are no longer using.

Azure subscriptions

You get an Azure subscription automatically when you sign up for Azure and all the resources you create are created inside that subscription. You can, however, create additional subscriptions that are tied to your Azure account. Additional subscriptions are useful in cases where you want to have some logical groupings for Azure resources or if you want to be able to report on resources used by specific groups of people.

Each Azure subscription has limits (sometimes called quotas) assigned to it. For example, you can have up to 250 Azure Storage accounts per region in a subscription, up to 25,000 virtual machines per region, and up to 980 resource groups per subscription across all regions.

MORE INFO **SUBSCRIPTION LIMITS**

You can find details on all limits for subscriptions at *https://bit.ly/az900-sublimits*.

EXAM TIP

Microsoft support can increase limits in some scenarios if you have a good business justification. Some limits, however, cannot be increased.

Figure 2-4 shows an Azure subscription in the Azure portal.

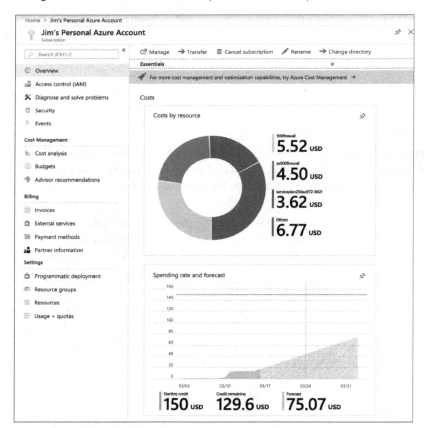

FIGURE 2-4 Azure subscription in the Azure portal

On the **Overview** blade, you can see a cost breakdown for each of the resources. You can also see the spending rate for the subscription, along with a forecasted cost by the end of the current month. If you click the **Costs By Resource** tile, you can see a further breakdown of the Azure expenses, as shown in Figure 2-5. In this view, you see costs by **Service Name**, **Location (Azure region)**, and **Resource Group**, along with a graph of the costs for the month.

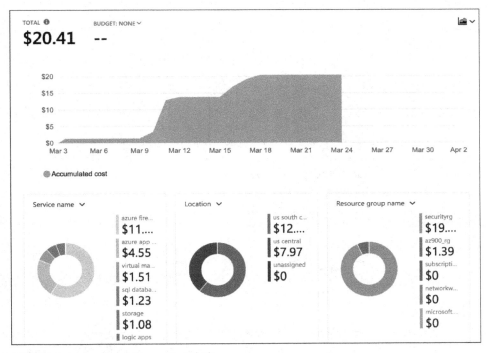

FIGURE 2-5 Azure subscription cost analysis

MORE INFO **CREATING BUDGETS**

You can manage your costs in Azure by creating budgets. You'll learn more about that in Chapter 6, "Describe Azure pricing, SLAs, and lifecycles."

Azure invoices are also available for the subscription from within the Azure portal. You can see all the past invoices by clicking Invoices in the menu for the subscription, as shown in Figure 2-6.

FIGURE 2-6 Azure invoices

You can create additional Azure subscriptions in your Azure account. This is useful in cases where you want to separate costs or if you are approaching a subscription limit on a resource. To create a new Azure subscription, type **subscription** in the search box and click **Subscriptions** as shown in Figure 2-7.

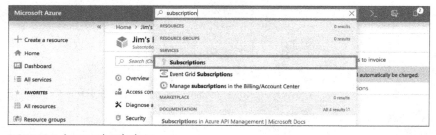

FIGURE 2-7 Azure subscriptions

To create a new subscription, click **Add** in the **Subscriptions** blade, as shown in Figure 2-8.

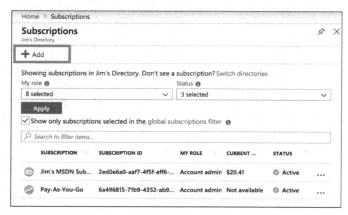

FIGURE 2-8 Creating a new subscription

After you click **Add**, you need to choose which type of subscription you want to create. There are several types of Azure subscriptions.

- **Free Trial**   Provides free access to Azure resources for a limited time. Only one free trial subscription is available per account, and you cannot create a new free trial if a previous one has expired.
- **Pay-As-You-Go**   You pay only for those resources you use in Azure. There's no up-front cost, and you can cancel the subscription at any time.
- **Pay-As-You-Go Dev/Test**   A special subscription for subscribers to Visual Studio that can be used for development and testing. This subscription offers discounted rates on VMs, but you cannot use this for production applications.

> **NOTE   AZURE SUBSCRIPTION TYPES**
>
> Depending on the type of Azure account you have, you might have additional subscription options.

> **EXAM TIP**
>
> Each subscription is associated with a unique identifier called a *subscription ID*. You can give each subscription a descriptive name to help you identify it, but Azure will always use the subscription ID to identify your subscription. When you talk to Microsoft about your Azure account, they'll also often ask for your subscription ID.

You now have an understanding of Azure subscriptions and how you can create additional subscriptions if needed. Once you've created additional subscriptions and resources in those subscriptions, you might find that managing all your resources becomes more cumbersome. To help with that, Microsoft has developed a feature called management groups.

Management groups

Management groups are a convenient way to apply policies and access control to your Azure resources. Much like a resource group, a management group is a container for organizing your resources. However, management groups can contain only Azure subscriptions or other management groups.

> **NOTE   AZURE IDENTITY AND GOVERNANCE**
>
> At this point, you aren't expected to understand concepts such as policies and access control. These concepts are introduced in Chapter 5, "Describe identity, governance, privacy, and compliance features."

In Figure 2-9, three management groups have been created for a company. The Sales Dept. management group contains subscriptions for the sales department. The IT Dept. management group contains a subscription and another management group, and two additional subscriptions are within that management group. The Training Dept. management group contains two subscriptions for the training department.

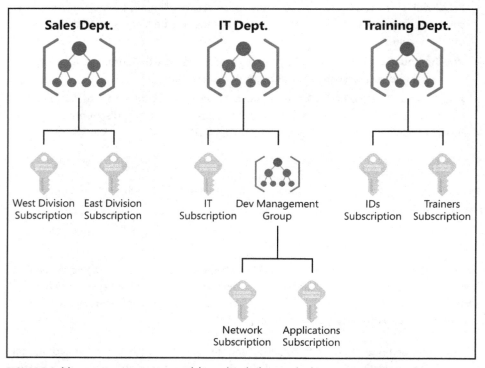

FIGURE 2-9 Management groups organizing subscriptions and other management groups

By organizing the subscriptions using management groups, you can have more precise control over who has access to which resources. You can also control the configuration of resources created within those subscriptions.

After you create a management group, you can move any of your subscriptions into that management group. You can also move a management group into another management group. There are, however, a few limitations:

- You're limited to a total of 10,000 management groups.
- A management group hierarchy can only support up to six levels.
- You cannot have multiple parents for a single management group or subscription.

Azure Resource Manager (ARM)

Almost all systems that are moved to the cloud consist of more than one Azure service. For example, you might have an Azure virtual machine for one part of your app; your data might be in an Azure SQL Database; you might have some sensitive data stored in Azure Key Vault; and you might have a web-based portion of your app hosted in Azure App Service.

If you must manage all these different Azure services separately, it can be quite a headache, and if you have multiple applications in the cloud, it can be even worse. Not only would it be confusing to keep track of which services are related to which applications, but when you add in the complexity of deploying updates to your application, things can really become disorganized.

In order to make it easier to deploy and manage Azure services, Microsoft developed Azure Resource Manager, or ARM. ARM is a service that runs in Azure, and it's responsible for all interaction with Azure services. When you create a new Azure service, ARM authenticates you to make sure you have the right access to create that resource, and then it talks to a *resource provider* for the service you're creating. For example, if you're creating a new web app in Azure App Service, ARM will pass your request on to the *Microsoft.Web* resource provider because it knows all about web apps and how to create them.

EXAM TIP

There are resource providers for every Azure service, but the names might not always make sense. For example, the *Microsoft.Compute* resource provider is responsible for creating virtual machine resources.

You don't have to know details on resource providers for the AZ-900 exam, but you should understand the general concept because you are expected to know about Azure Resource Manager.

In Chapter 3, you'll learn about using the Azure portal to create and manage Azure services. You'll also learn about how you can use command-line tools to do the same thing. Both the portal and the command-line tools work by using ARM, and they interact with ARM using the ARM application programming interface, or API. The ARM API is the same whether you're using the portal or command-line tools, and that means you get a consistent result. It also means that you can create an Azure resource with the portal and then make changes to it using command-line tools, allowing you the flexibility that cloud consumers need.

MORE INFO **VISUAL STUDIO AND ARM**

Visual Studio, Microsoft's development environment for writing applications, also can create Azure resources and deploy code to them. It does this using the same ARM API we've mentioned previously. In fact, you can think of the ARM API as your interface into the world of Azure. You really can't create or manage any Azure services without going through the ARM API.

The flow of a typical ARM request to create or manage a resource is straightforward. Tools such as the Azure portal, command-line tools, or Visual Studio make a request to the ARM API. The API passes that request to ARM where the user is authenticated and authorized to perform the action. ARM then passes the request to a resource provider, and the resource provider creates the new resource or modifies an existing resource. Figure 2-10 illustrates this flow and features a small sampling of the many Azure services that are available.

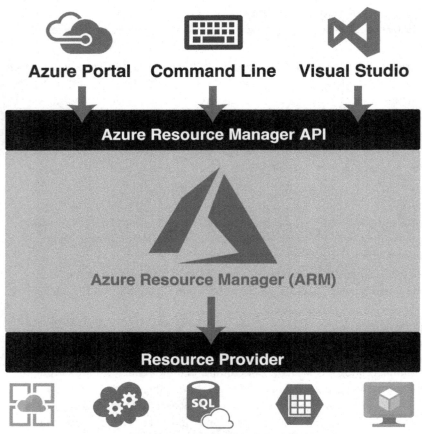

FIGURE 2-10 Azure Resource Manager

The request that is made to ARM isn't a complicated, code-based request. Instead, ARM uses *declarative syntax*. That means that, as a consumer of Azure, you tell ARM what you want to do, and ARM does it for you. You don't have to tell ARM *how* to do what you want. You simply have to tell it what you want. To do that, ARM uses files that are encoded in JavaScript Object Notation (or JSON) called *ARM templates*.

MORE INFO **ARM TEMPLATES**

You'll find out more about ARM templates in Skill 3.2 in Chapter 3, "Describe core solutions and management tools on Azure."

As you can see, ARM has many benefits, and you should be aware of these for your exam:

- ARM allows you to easily deploy multiple Azure resources at once.
- ARM makes it possible to reproduce any deployment with consistent results at any point in the future.
- ARM allows you to create declarative templates for deployment instead of requiring you to write and maintain complex deployment scripts.
- ARM makes it possible to set up dependencies so that your resources are deployed in the right order every time.

Throughout this skill section, you've learned about some of the benefits of using Azure. Because Azure regions are spread out across the world in different geographies, you can be assured that your data and apps are hosted where you need them to be and that any regulations or data requirements are complied with. You learned that there are multiple datacenters in each region, and by deploying your applications in availability zones, you can avoid effects from a failure in a particular datacenter.

You also learned about using resource groups to organize your Azure resources and how to use Azure subscriptions. Finally, you learned about management groups and Azure Resource Manager, or ARM. In the next skill section, you'll learn details about some of the core resources in Azure.

Skill 2.2: Describe core resources available in Azure

As we went over the core Azure architectural components, you noticed some references to some of the products available in Azure. In this skill section, we'll talk about some of the core workload products available in Azure.

This section covers:

- Azure virtual machines
- Azure App Service
- Azure Container Instances (ACI)
- Azure Kubernetes Service (AKS)
- Windows Virtual Desktop
- Virtual networks
- Azure VPN Gateway
- Virtual network peering
- ExpressRoute
- Container (Blob) Storage
- Disk Storage
- Azure Files
- Storage tiers
- Cosmos DB
- Azure SQL Database
- Azure Database for MySQL
- Azure Database for PostgreSQL
- The Azure Marketplace and its usage scenarios

Azure virtual machines

A virtual machine (VM) is a software-based computer that runs on a physical computer. The physical computer is considered the *host*, and it provides the underlying physical components such as disk space, memory, CPU power, and so on. The host computer runs software called a hypervisor that can create and manage one or more VMs, and those VMs are commonly referred to as *guests*.

The operating system on a guest doesn't have to be the same operating system that the host is running. If your host is running Windows 10, you can run a guest that uses Windows Server 2016, Linux, or many other operating systems. This flexibility makes VMs extremely popular. However, because the VMs running on a host use the physical systems on that host, if you have a need for a powerful VM, you'll need a powerful physical computer to host it.

By using Azure virtual machines, you can take advantage of powerful host computers that Microsoft makes available when you need computing power, and when you no longer need that power, you no longer have to pay for it.

To create an Azure virtual machine, log in to the Azure portal using your Azure account and then follow these steps, as shown in Figures 2-11 through 2-13.

1. Click **Create A Resource**.
2. Click **Compute**.
3. Click the **See All link**.
4. Click **Ubuntu Server**.

FIGURE 2-11 Creating a virtual machine

5. Click the **Create** button.
6. Next to **Resource Group**, click **Create New** to create a new resource group.
7. Enter **TestRG** as the resource group name and click **OK**.
8. Enter **TestVM** as your VM name.

FIGURE 2-12 Virtual machine settings

9. Scroll down and select **Password** for the authentication type.

10. Enter a username for your administrator account.

11. Enter a password you'd like to use for your administrator account.

12. Confirm the password.

13. Leave all the other settings as they are and click the **Next** button three times to move to the **Management** screen.

14. In the **Monitoring** section, set **Boot Diagnostics** to **Off**.

15. Click **Review + Create** to create your VM.

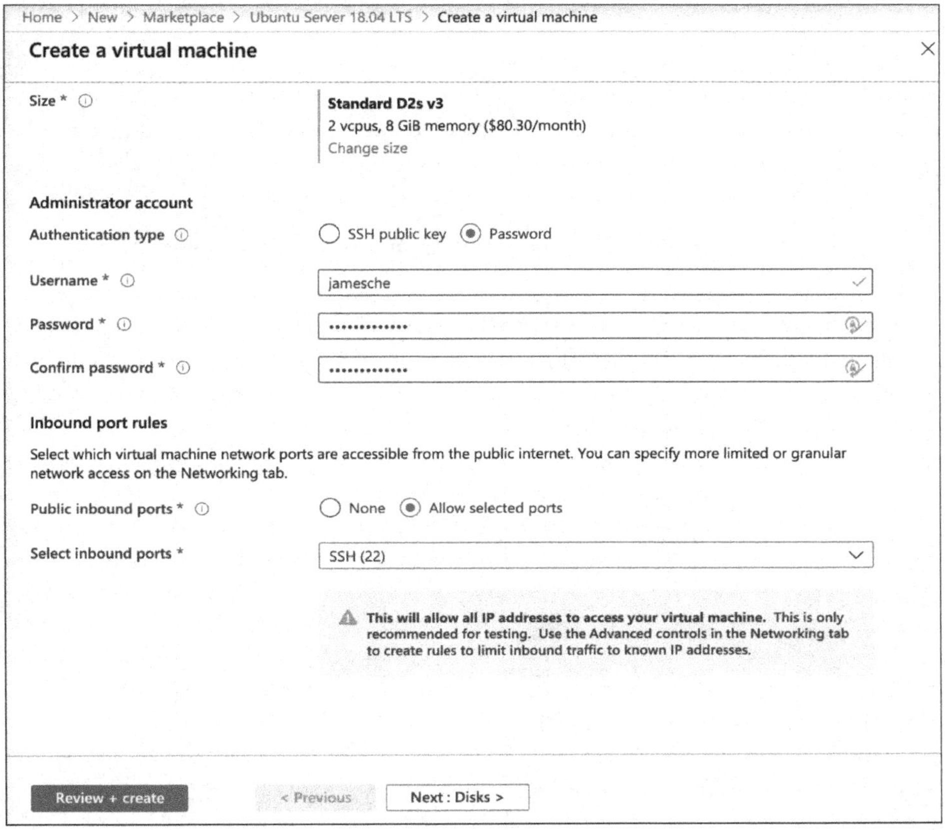

FIGURE 2-13 Virtual machine settings

After you click **Review + Create**, Azure will validate your settings to make sure you haven't left anything out. Once your validation has passed, you will see a **Create** button. Click the **Create** button to start the deployment of your new VM.

> **MORE INFO**   **HOW AZURE DEPLOYS YOUR VM**
>
> When you click **Create** to create your VM, the Azure portal is actually using an ARM template to deploy your VM. That ARM template contains parameters that are replaced with the information you entered for your VM. Every VM that is created in Azure is created using an ARM template. This ensures that the deployments are consistent.

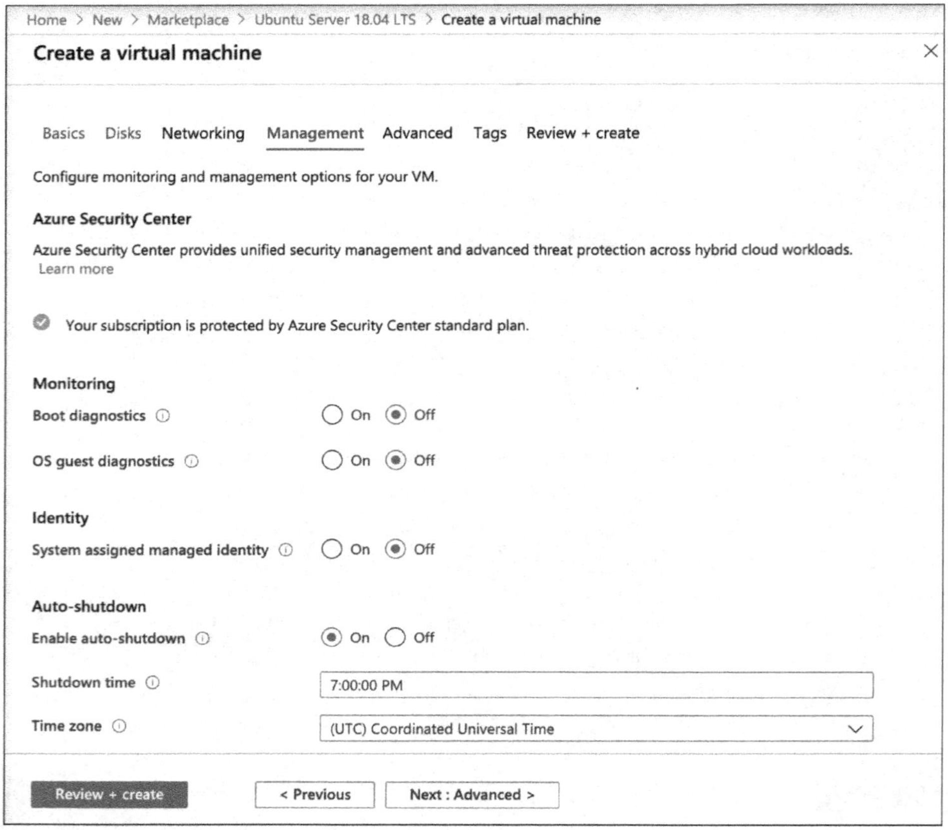

FIGURE 2-14 Virtual machine management settings

As your VM is being deployed, you'll see the status displayed in the Azure portal, as shown in Figure 2-15. You can see the Azure resources that are created to support your VM. You can see the resource name, the resource type (which starts with the resource provider), and the status of each resource.

Once all the resources required for your VM are created, your VM will be considered fully deployed. You'll then be able to click the **Go To Resource** button to see the management interface for your VM in the Azure portal, as shown in Figure 2-16.

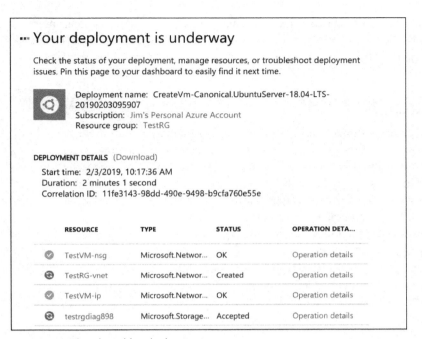

FIGURE 2-15 Virtual machine deployment

FIGURE 2-16 Viewing a virtual machine

Our new VM is a guest on a physical computer in an Azure datacenter. In that datacenter is a physical rack of computer servers, and our VM is hosted on one of those servers. The host computer is managed by Microsoft, but the VM is managed by you because this is an IaaS offering in Azure.

> **NOTE   VMs AND BILLING**
>
> You are charged for Azure VMs as long as they are running, and using the default settings as we have here led to a few expensive options. To stop billing for this VM, click the Stop button at the top of the screen shown in Figure 2-15. Azure will save the current state of the VM and billing will stop. You won't be able to use the VM while it's in a stopped state, but you will also avoid the billing of that VM. Keep in mind that unless you have configured a static IP address for your VM, your IP address will likely change the next time you start it.
>
> You can also stop a VM from within the guest operating system on the VM, but when you do that, you will still be charged for the resources the VM uses because it's still allocated to you. That means you'll still incur charges for managed disks and other resources. Once you finish this chapter, deleting the *TestRG* resource group will ensure you aren't charged for the VM.

As of right now, this VM is susceptible to downtime due to three types of events: *planned maintenance, unplanned maintenance*, and *unexpected downtime*.

Planned maintenance refers to planned updates that Microsoft makes to the host computer. This includes things like operating system updates, driver updates, and so on. In many cases, updates won't affect your VM, but if Microsoft installs an update that requires a reboot of the host computer, your VM will be down during that reboot.

Azure has underlying systems that constantly monitor the health of computer components. If one of these underlying systems detects that a component within the host computer might fail soon, Azure will flag the computer for unplanned maintenance. In an unplanned maintenance event, Azure will attempt to move your VM to a healthy host computer. When it does this, it preserves the state of the VM, including what's in memory and any files that are open. It only takes Azure a short time to move the VM, during which time it's in a paused state. In a case where the move operation fails, the VM will experience unexpected downtime.

In order to ensure reliability when a failure occurs in a rack within the Azure datacenter, you can (and you should) take advantage of a feature called availability sets. *Availability sets* protect you from maintenance events and downtime caused by hardware failures. To do that, Azure creates some underlying entities in an availability set called *update domains* and *fault domains*. (In order to protect yourself in the event of maintenance events or downtime, you must deploy at least two VMs into your availability set.)

Fault domains are a logical representation of the physical rack in which a host computer is installed. By default, Azure assigns two fault domains to an availability set. If a problem occurs in one fault domain (one computer rack), the VMs in that fault domain will be affected, but VMs in the second fault domain will not. This protects you from unplanned maintenance events and unexpected downtime.

Update domains are designed to protect you from a situation where the host computer is being rebooted. When you create an availability set, Azure creates five update domains by default. These update domains are spread across the fault domains in the availability set. If a reboot is required on computers in the availability set (whether host computers or VMs within the availability set), Azure will only reboot computers in one update domain at a time and it will wait 30 minutes for computers to recover from the reboot before it moves on to the next update domain. Update domains protect you from planned maintenance events.

Figure 2-17 shows the diagram that Microsoft uses to represent an availability set. In this diagram, the fault domains FD0, FD1, and FD2 encompass three physical racks of computers. UD0, UD1, and UD2 are update domains within the fault domains. You will see this same representation of an availability set within other Azure training as well, but it's a bit misleading because update domains are not tied to a particular fault domain.

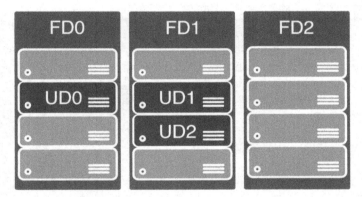

FIGURE 2-17 Microsoft documentation representation of an availability set

Figure 2-18 shows a better representation of an availability set, with five VMs in the availability set. There are two fault domains and three update domains. When VMs were created in this availability set, they were assigned as follows:

- The first VM is assigned Fault Domain 0 and Update Domain 0.
- The second VM is assigned Fault Domain 1 and Update Domain 1.
- The third VM is assigned Fault Domain 0 and Update Domain 2.
- The fourth VM is assigned Fault Domain 1 and Update Domain 0.
- The fifth VM is assigned Fault Domain 0 and Update Domain 1.

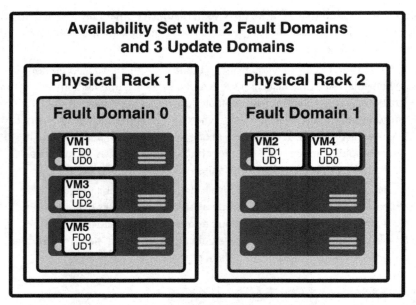

FIGURE 2-18 A better representation of an availability set

You can verify the placement of fault domains and update domains by creating five VMs in an availability set with two fault domains and three update domains. If you then look at the availability set created in the Azure portal, as shown in Figure 2-19, you can see the same configuration depicted in Figure 2-18.

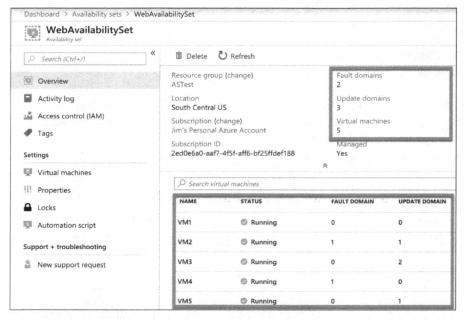

FIGURE 2-19 An availability set in the Azure portal showing fault domains and update domains

Notice in Figure 2-19 that the availability set is named *WebAvailabilitySet*. In this availability set, we run five VMs that are all running a web server and host the website for an application. Suppose you need a database for this application, and you want to host that database on VMs as well. In that situation, you would want to separate the database VMs into their own availability set. As a best practice, you should always separate your workloads into separate availability sets.

Availability sets certainly provide a benefit in protecting from downtime in certain situations, but they also have some disadvantages. First of all, every machine in an availability set has to be explicitly created. While you can use an ARM template to deploy multiple virtual machines in one deployment, you still have to configure those machines with the software and configuration necessary to support your application.

An availability set also requires that you configure something in front of your VMs that will handle the distribution of traffic to those VMs. For example, if your availability set is servicing a website hosted on the VMs, you'll need to configure a load balancer that will handle the job of routing users of your website to the VMs that are running it.

Another disadvantage to availability sets relates to cost. In a situation where your VM needs to be changed often based on things like load on the application, you might find yourself paying for many more VMs than you need.

Azure offers another feature for VMs called *scale sets* that solves these problems nicely. When you create a scale set, you tell Azure what operating system you want to run and then you tell Azure how many VMs you want in your scale set. You have many other options such as creating a load balancer or gateway and so forth. Azure will create as many VMs as you specify (up to 1,000) in one easy step.

> **MORE INFO** **USING A CUSTOM IMAGE**
>
> The default set of templates for VMs are basic and include only the operating system. However, you can create a VM, install all of the necessary components you need (including your own applications), and then create an image that can be used when creating scale sets.
>
> For more information on using custom images, see *https://bit.ly/az900-customvmimages*.

Scale sets are deployed in availability sets automatically, so you automatically benefit from multiple fault domains and update domains. Unlike VMs in an availability set, however, VMs in a scale set are also compatible with availability zones, so you are protected from problems in an Azure datacenter.

As you might imagine, you can also scale a scale set in a situation where you need more or fewer VMs. You might start with only one VM in a scale set, but as load on that VM increases, you might want to automatically add additional VMs. Scale sets provide that functionality by using Azure's auto-scale feature. You define scaling rules that use metrics like CPU, disk usage, network usage, and so forth. You can configure when Azure should add additional instances and when it should scale back and deallocate instances. This is a great way to ensure availability while reducing costs by taking advantage of the elasticity that auto-scale provides.

Microsoft guarantees an SLA of 99.95 percent when you use a multi-VM deployment scenario, and for most production scenarios, a multi-VM deployment is preferred. However, if you use a single-instance VM, and you use premium storage, Microsoft guarantees a 99.9 percent SLA. Premium storage uses solid-state drives (SSDs) that are located on the same physical server that is hosting the VM for enhanced performance and uptime.

Azure App Service

As mentioned in Chapter 1, Azure App Service is a PaaS offering in Azure for hosting websites. In addition to basic web hosting services, App Service also offers many additional features that you can easily add to your web app, often with the flip of a switch within the Azure portal.

When you create a web app in Azure App Service, your app runs on an Azure virtual machine that is preconfigured specifically for App Service. Depending on the tier of service you use when you create your app, it will either run on a VM that is shared among many users or a VM that is dedicated to you.

Figure 2-20 shows a diagram of the basic App Service architecture. This diagram is simplified, but it illustrates the basics of how App Service works. Azure Load Balancer distributes traffic to a special VM within App Service called a *front end*. The front end is running special software that allows it to effectively distribute traffic to the VMs that are actually running your web app. These VMs run inside of an *App Service plan*, a logical container for one or more VMs that are running your web app.

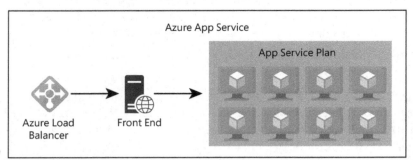

FIGURE 2-20 A high-level representation of Azure App Service

App Service plans

Every web app you create in App Service runs inside of an App Service plan. An App Service plan is created within a specific Azure region, and it specifies how many VMs your app runs on and the properties of those VMs.

In Figure 2-21, an App Service plan named *AZ900-Plan* is being created in the Central US region. The VMs in this App Service plan will run Windows and will be created in the Standard S1 App Service pricing tier. You can click **Change Size** to change the pricing tier before the App Service plan is created, and you can also scale the App Service plan at any point to change the size.

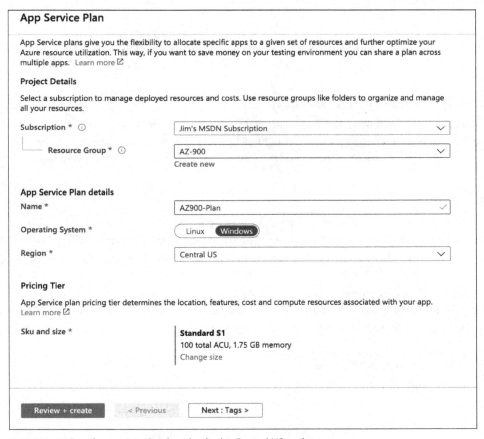

FIGURE 2-21 Creating an App Service plan in the Central US region

The following pricing tiers are available in App Service:

- **Free** A no-cost tier for testing only that runs on VMs shared with other App Service customers.

- **Shared** A low-cost tier for testing only with some additional features not offered in the Free tier. Runs on VMs shared with other App Service customers.
- **Basic, Standard, Premium, and PremiumV2** Higher-cost tiers that offer many additional features. Runs on dedicated VMs that are not shared with other customers.

EXAM TIP

You are charged for App Service plans even when no web apps are running in them. If you do have web apps in your App Service plan, you are still charged if you stop the web apps. The only way to avoid being billed for an App Service plan is to delete it.

When you move from a lower pricing tier to a higher pricing tier, you are scaling up. You can also scale down at any time by moving to a lower pricing tier. If you are running in the Basic, Standard, Premium, or PremiumV2 tier, you can also scale out to multiple VMs. The Basic tier allows you to scale to a maximum of 3 VMs (or *instances*), the Standard tier allows for 10 instances, and the Premium and PremiumV2 tiers allow for up to 20 instances.

> **MORE INFO APP SERVICE VIRTUAL MACHINES**
>
> Creating a web app in App Service is very fast and scaling it out to multiple instances is also very fast. That's because the VMs that are running App Service web apps are already up and running. When you create a web app, you are simply allocating an existing VM for your use.

Web apps

When you create a new web app, you can create it in an existing App Service plan, or you can create a new App Service plan for the app. All apps in an App Service plan run on the same VMs, so if you are already stressing the resources of an existing App Service plan, your best choice might be to create a new App Service plan for your new web app.

App Service allows you to choose between a VM preconfigured with a runtime stack (such as Java, .NET, PHP, and so forth) to run your app or a Docker container. If you choose to run a preconfigured runtime stack, you can choose between multiple versions that App Service provides.

> **MORE INFO DOCKER CONTAINERS**
>
> You'll learn about Docker contains in the next section when we cover Azure Container Instances.

Figure 2-22 shows a web app being created in the AZ900-Plan App Service plan. This new web app will run on a VM that is configured to run .NET Core 3.0 apps on a Windows VM.

Configuring and managing your web app is extremely easy. Because App Service is a PaaS service, you are only responsible for your code. Microsoft manages the features available to you. In Figure 2-23, you can see many of the features available in App Service, including the ability to quickly and easily scale out when needed.

Web App

Project Details

Select a subscription to manage deployed resources and costs. Use resource groups like folders to organize and manage all your resources.

Subscription * ⓘ
> Jim's MSDN Subscription ⌄

    Resource Group * ⓘ
> AZ-900 ⌄
> Create new

Instance Details

Name *
> cheshireaz900 ✓
> .azurewebsites.net

Publish *
> (Code) Docker Container

Runtime stack *
> .NET Core 3.0 ⌄

Operating System *
> Linux (Windows)

Region *
> Central US ⌄
> ⓘ Not finding your App Service Plan? Try a different region.

App Service Plan

App Service plan pricing tier determines the location, features, cost and compute resources associated with your app. Learn more ☑

Windows Plan (Central US) * ⓘ
> AZ900-Plan (S1) ⌄
> Create new

[Review + create] [< Previous] [Next : Monitoring >]

FIGURE 2-22 Creating a web app to run a .NET Core 3.0 website

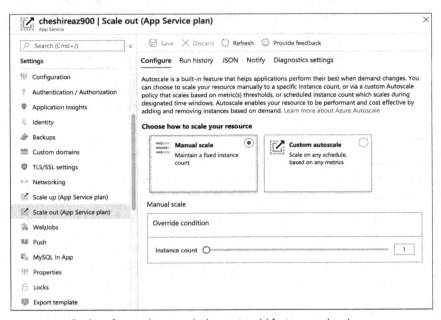

FIGURE 2-23 Settings for a web app make it easy to add features and scale your app

Azure Container Instances (ACI)

Azure Container Instances (ACI) is a PaaS service that offers the ability to run a containerized application easily. In order to understand how ACI works, it's necessary to have a basic understanding of containers.

Containers

It's becoming pretty commonplace for companies to move applications between "environments," and this type of thing is even more prevalent when it comes to the cloud. In fact, one of the most complicated aspects of moving to the cloud is dealing with the complexities of moving to a new environment. To help with this problem and to make it easier to shift applications into new environments, the concept of *containers* was invented.

A container is created using a zipped version of an application called an *image*, and it includes everything the application needs to run. That might include a database engine, a web server, and so on. The image can be deployed to any environment that supports the use of containers. Once there, the image is used to start a container the application runs in.

In order to run an application in a container, a computer needs to have a container runtime installed on it. The most popular container runtime is Docker, a runtime developed and maintained by Docker Inc. Docker not only knows how to run applications in containers, but it also enforces certain conditions to ensure a secure environment.

> **MORE INFO   DOCKER IMAGES**
>
> You aren't limited to your own images. In fact, Docker runs a repository of images that you are free to use in your own applications. You can find it at *https://hub.docker.com*.

Each container typically operates within an isolated environment. It has its own network, its own storage, and so on. Other containers running on the same machine cannot access the data and systems used by another container unless the developer of the image takes explicit steps to allow it. This makes containerized applications an ideal solution when security is a concern.

Running containers in ACI

ACI makes it easy to start a container with minimal configuration. You simply tell ACI where to find the image (using either a Docker tag or a URL to the image) and some basic configuration for the VM you want the container to run on.

Azure creates server resources as needed to run your container, but you're not paying for an underlying VM. Instead, you pay for the memory and CPU that your container uses. That translates into extremely low costs in most cases. For example, if your ACI app is running on a machine with 1 CPU and 1 GB of memory and you use the app for 5 minutes a day, your cost would be less than 5 cents at the end of the month!

> ***NOTE*** **CONTAINERS USE THEIR OWN OPERATING SYSTEM**
>
> **The operating system for a container is actually part of the image. The VM that you are configuring when you create an ACI app is the VM that runs the container runtime. Even so, it's important that you choose an operating system that's compatible with your container. A Docker image that was built for Linux will not run on a Windows host and vice versa.**

ACI is designed to work with simple applications. You can define a container group and run multiple containers within an ACI instance, but ACI isn't a good choice for you if you have an application that is used heavily by many people and that might need to take advantage of scaling. Instead, Azure Kubernetes Service (AKS) would be a better choice.

> ***MORE INFO*** **AZURE KUBERNETES SERVICE**
>
> **You'll learn about Azure Kubernetes Service in the next section.**

When you create a container instance in ACI, you specify a name for the container, the image you want to use, and the size of the VM you want to run your container. If you don't have an image handy, Microsoft provides multiple sample images you can use. In Figure 2-24, an ACI instance named *jimsaciapp* is being created in the East US region using one of the sample Quickstart images.

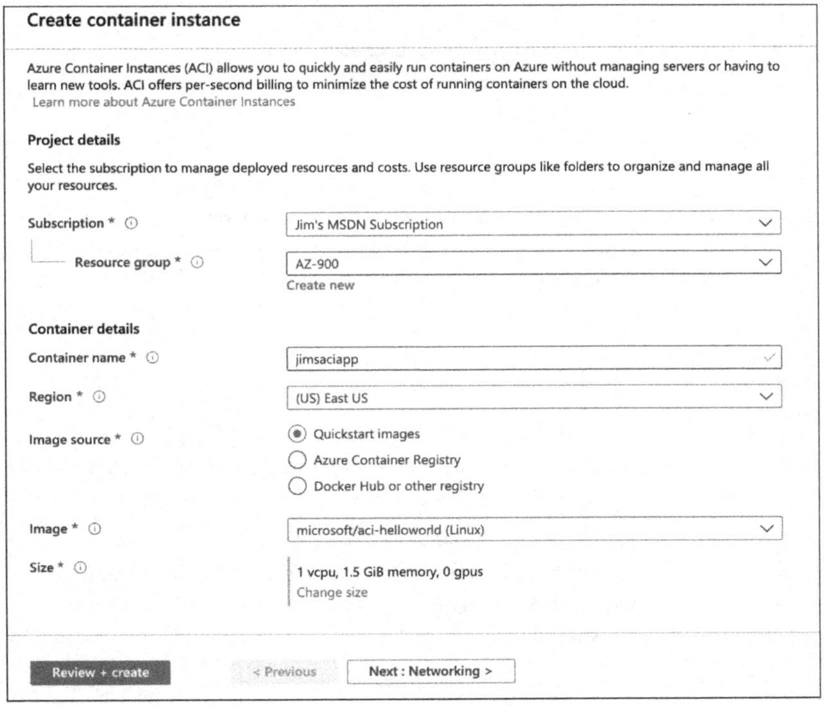

FIGURE 2-24 Creating an ACI instance with a Quickstart image

In order to make this instance accessible on the Internet, you'll need to set the DNS name label for the instance. This setting is accessible by clicking **Next: Networking** at the bottom of the screen, as shown in Figure 2-24. In Figure 2-25, the **DNS Name Label** for this instance is set to *jimsaciapp*. After the instance is created, it can be accessed by browsing to *http://jimsaciapp. eastus.azurecontainer.io*.

Create container instance

Basics   Networking   Advanced   Tags   Review + create

Choose between three networking options for your container instance:

- '**Public**' will create a public IP address for your container instance.
- '**Private**' will allow you to choose a new or existing virtual network for your container instance. This is not yet available for Windows containers.
- '**None**' will not create either a public IP or virtual network. You will still be able to access your container logs using the command line.

Networking type   ◉ Public   ○ Private   ○ None

DNS name label ⓘ   jimsaciapp   ✓
                                                                            .eastus.azurecontainer.io

Ports ⓘ

Ports	Ports protocol
80	TCP

FIGURE 2-25 Setting a DNS Name Label so the instance can be reached using a URL

EXAM TIP

You can't change the DNS Name Label after the instance is created. You also can't change the image your instance uses. If you want to change these settings, you'll need to delete the instance and re-create it. However, doing so might mean that you lose your public IP address, so it's best to plan ahead before you create your instance.

Azure Kubernetes Service (AKS)

Kubernetes is a container orchestration service. This means that it's responsible for monitoring containers and ensuring that they're always running. It can also scale to add additional containers when the needs require it to, and it can then scale back when the needs are reduced.

Kubernetes creates containers in a *pod*. A pod is a group of related containers, and containers within a pod can share resources. This is one of the advantages to using Kubernetes because it releases you from the resource-sharing restriction typically imposed in a multi-container environment. However, a container in one pod is not able to share resources with a container in another pod.

The computer that Kubernetes pods are running on is called a *node* or a *worker*. This computer must have a container runtime such as Docker running on it. In addition to pods, the node also runs several services that are required for Kubernetes to manage the pods and so on. There will typically be multiple nodes within a Kubernetes instance, and they are all controlled by a master node called the Kubernetes *master*. The entire environment of the master and all its nodes is called a Kubernetes *cluster*.

A Kubernetes master contains all of the configuration and services necessary to manage the orchestration of pods and other Kubernetes entities. Configuring a master can be complex, and it is by far the most laborious task of using Kubernetes. For that reason, services such as Azure Kubernetes Service (AKS) are becoming more popular.

AKS offloads the burden of dealing with the Kubernetes master to Microsoft. When you create a Kubernetes cluster in AKS, Azure creates the master and the nodes for you. All you have to do is deploy your containers and you're up and running with a managed Kubernetes cluster.

AKS simplifies the creation of a Kubernetes cluster, but it also makes it extremely easy to manage a cluster (see Figure 2-26). Operations such as upgrading a cluster or scaling a cluster are simple using the Azure portal menu options. You can also get detailed information on your cluster, including each node that's running in the cluster.

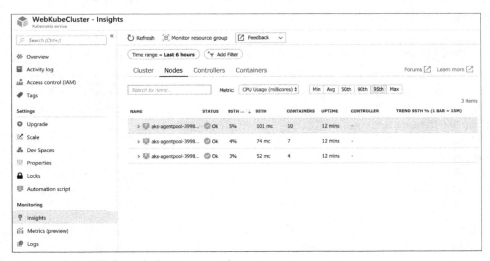

FIGURE 2-26 An AKS cluster in the Azure portal

While AKS makes adopting and managing Kubernetes easier, it doesn't completely obfuscate Kubernetes. In order to deploy your applications, you still need to understand how to use Kubernetes, and in some cases, you'll need to use the Kubernetes command line. Azure, however, makes it far easier than doing all the legwork and maintenance yourself. Even better, AKS in Azure is free. You only pay for the Azure compute resources you use within your cluster.

Windows Virtual Desktop

Most businesses have applications that all their employees need to use. For example, employees might need access to Microsoft Word, Microsoft Excel, Microsoft Outlook, and so on. In many situations, businesses fill this need by purchasing a Microsoft Office license for all employees and installing Office apps on each computer.

This classic model of each employee using one computer with applications installed on it is not only inefficient for businesses, but it's also insecure. First off, it requires that the business purchase operating system and application licenses for each employee. It also requires that the IT department be available to troubleshoot any operating system or application issues. Users of local applications also have data that is stored on the local hard drive, and this represents a security risk if an unwanted person gets access to the machine.

For these reasons and many others, many businesses take advantage of desktop virtualization. In a desktop virtualization model, a business installs an operating system and applications on one central server. The desktop virtualization infrastructure makes it possible for employees to access the operating system and applications from virtually any device, provided it has access to the network. The OS and applications aren't downloaded to the employee's device. Instead, the employee uses the applications in a virtualized environment that makes it feel like the applications are running locally.

> **MORE INFO   DESKTOP VIRTUALIZATION**
>
> If you've ever used Windows Remote Desktop to remote into another computer, you've experienced something similar to desktop virtualization. The difference is that desktop virtualization allows you to virtually access the operating system and applications that an administrator has installed for remote access.

Desktop virtualization might sound like the perfect solution for many businesses, but in fact, it's quite complex to configure, and it requires many components in order to ensure a secure environment. For that reason, Microsoft developed a service in Azure called Windows Virtual Desktop.

Windows Virtual Desktop is a PaaS offering in Azure that provides desktop virtualization that is managed by Microsoft. It requires a bit of advanced configuration, but once you have it configured, the infrastructure is entirely managed by Microsoft.

To use Windows Virtual Desktop (WVD), you first create a WVD *tenant*. A tenant is a collection of one or more *host pools*, and a host pool consists of both *session hosts* and one or more app groups that represent the applications and OS desktops users should be able to access. These session hosts are simply Azure VMs that you've configured for WVD.

Once you've set up the tenant, you can add users from your Azure Active Directory so that they can access the OSes and apps in your tenant and assign permissions to them. Those users can then access WVD using the following methods.

- Using the WVD client app for Windows
- Using the WVD client app for MacOS

- Using the WVD client for iOS
- Using the WVD client for Android
- Using the web-based client from any web browser

> **MORE INFO** **WINDOWS VIRTUAL DESKTOP**
>
> For more information on Windows Virtual Desktop, including requirements for using it and a guide to configuring it, browse to *https://bit.ly/AZ900-winvirtualdesktop*.

Users accessing WVD sees a list of OSes and applications they can use. When they click an OS, they can interact with that OS just as though they were running it on their local machines. When they click an app, the app launches in a virtual session, but it looks exactly as if it's running locally. Better yet, through the use of technology Microsoft acquired called FSLogix, WVD provides for a local profile while the user is using apps. This capability even allows for users to use files in Microsoft OneDrive along with WVD.

> **MORE INFO** **WINDOWS 10 MULTI-USER**
>
> Microsoft actually developed a special version of Windows 10 called Windows 10 Multi-User in order to support the functionality of Windows Virtual Desktop.

Virtual networks

An Azure virtual network (often called a VNet) allows Azure services to communicate with each other and with the Internet. You can even use a VNet to communicate between your on-premises resources and your Azure resources. When you create a virtual machine in Azure, Azure creates a VNet for you. Without that VNet, you wouldn't be able to remote into the VM or use the VM for any of your applications. However, you can also create your own VNet and configure it any way you choose.

An Azure VNet is just like any other computer network. It's comprised of a network interface card (a NIC), IP addresses, and so on. You can break up your VNet into multiple subnets and set up a portion of your network's IP address space for those subnets. You can then configure rules that control the connectivity between those subnets.

Figure 2-27 illustrates an Azure VNet that we might use for a multi-tier application. The VNet uses IP addresses in the 10.0.0.0 address range, and each subnet has its own range of addresses. IP address ranges in VNets are specified using classless inter-domain routing (CIDR) notation, and a discussion of that is far outside the scope of this exam. However, with the configuration shown in Figure 2-27, we have 65,536 IP addresses available in our VNet, and each subnet has 256 IP addresses allocated to it. (The first four IP addresses and the last IP address in the range are reserved for Azure's use, so you really only have 251 addresses to use in each subnet.) This is a typical design because you still have many addresses available in your network for later expansion into additional subnets.

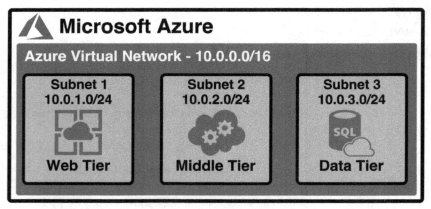

FIGURE 2-27 A multi-tier application in an Azure Virtual Network

In most cases, you create VNets before you create the resources that use them. As I said earlier, when you create a VM in Azure, a VNet is created automatically. Azure does that because you can't use a VM unless there's a network associated with it. While you can connect a VM you are creating to an existing VNet, you can't connect a VM to a VNet after it's been created. For that reason, if you wanted to use your own VNet instead of the one Azure creates automatically, you would create your VNet before you create your VM.

The web tier shown previously in Figure 2-27, on the other hand, is running in Azure App Service, a PaaS offering. This is running on a VM that Microsoft manages, so Microsoft creates and manages the VM and its network. In order to use that tier with the VNet, App Service offers a feature called VNet Integration that allows you to integrate a web app in App Service with an existing VNet.

The IP addresses within the VNet at this point are all private IP addresses. They allow resources within the VNet to talk to each other, but you can't use a private IP address on the Internet. You need a public IP address in order to give the Internet access to your web tier.

> **MORE INFO** **OUTBOUND INTERNET CONNECTIVITY**
>
> A public IP address doesn't have to be assigned to a resource in order for that resource to connect outbound to the Internet. Azure maintains a pool of public IP addresses that can be dynamically assigned to a resource if it needs to connect outbound. That IP address is not exclusively assigned to the resource, so it cannot be used for inbound communication from the Internet to the Azure resource.

Because the web tier is running on Azure App Service (a PaaS service), Microsoft manages the public-facing network for us. You get Internet access on that tier without needing to do anything. If you want to run the web tier on an IaaS VM instead, configure the public IP address for the web tier. In those situations, Azure allows you to create a Public IP Address resource and assign it to a virtual network.

Azure VPN Gateway

In most cases, you'll want to connect your VNet to other networks. You might need to connect your VNet to another VNet in Azure, or you might also want to connect your VNet to on-premises resources. In both of these cases, network traffic is going to travel over the Internet, and that incurs a certain amount of risk. To provide more security for your network traffic, you can use a secure virtual private network (VPN) connection.

A VPN is a network technology that allows connectivity between a private network and a public network. If you ever connect to resources on your company's private network from your home computer, you're likely using a VPN connection that allows your home network to connect to your company's network.

EXAM TIP

You may see VPN Gateway referred to as a virtual network gateway. Keep in mind that when you see the term "virtual network gateway," it's the same thing as VPN Gateway.

Azure VPN Gateway uses VPN connections to enable secure connectivity between an Azure VNet and other networks. VPN Gateway secures these connections using Internet protocol security (IPSec) and the Internet key exchange (IKE) protocol. This ensures that traffic flowing over the public Internet is encrypted and secure.

A VPN Gateway uses two or more VMs that are created inside a subnet (called the *gateway subnet*) that is created explicitly for the VPN Gateway. These VMs run services that implement the functionality of VPN Gateway, and they also have network routing tables that enable them to properly route network traffic. You can't use these VMs for anything other than VPN Gateway, and you also can't remote into them or change their configurations.

Before you can create a VPN Gateway, you create the gateway subnet and specify the IP address range for that subnet. Azure makes this easy for you in the Azure portal. Once you open your VNet in the portal, click **Subnets** in the menu and then click the **+ Gateway Subnet** button, as shown in Figure 2-28.

FIGURE 2-28 Creating a gateway subnet

MORE INFO **GATEWAY SUBNETS**

Microsoft provides more information on the gateway subnet, including some guidance on choosing an IP address range for your subnet. You can find that information by browsing to *http://bit.ly/az900-gatewaysubnets*.

Once you've created a subnet for VPN Gateway, you can create the VPN Gateway. To create a VPN Gateway, you create a new virtual network gateway and specify the gateway type as VPN, as shown in Figure 2-29. Notice that the portal has automatically selected the gateway subnet that exists in the selected VNet.

MORE INFO **CREATING VPN GATEWAYS**

It can take a long time to create a VPN Gateway. Azure must create VMs in the gateway subnet to support the gateway, and it also must configure VPN Gateway services and network routing tables. It can take up to 45 minutes before your VPN Gateway is ready for use.

After you create your VPN Gateway, you can configure a connection to it. There are three connection types supported by VPN Gateway: VNet-to-VNet, site-to-site, and point-to-site.

A VNet-to-VNet connection allows you to connect two Azure VNets to each other. Each VNet must have a VPN Gateway configured, and the VNets don't have to be in the same Azure region or even in the same Azure subscription. Communication between VNets that are using a VNet-to-VNet connection is encrypted and travels over Microsoft's backbone infrastructure, not over the Internet.

FIGURE 2-29 Creating a VPN Gateway

EXAM TIP

VPN Gateway has several pricing tiers, and each pricing tier has an associated bandwidth cap. When connecting two VNets using a VNet-to-VNet connection, make sure you can live with the bandwidth restrictions imposed by the VPN Gateway pricing tier you are using. If you need to avoid a bandwidth restriction, using VNet peering (covered in the next section) might be a better option for you.

A site-to-site connection allows you to connect your VNet to an on-premises network using an encrypted VPN connection. Site-to-site connections require you to configure a VPN device on your on-premises network, and that VPN device must have a public-facing IP address. Network traffic between your VNet and your on-premises network travels over an encrypted VPN connection.

MORE INFO **VPN DEVICES**

For more information on VPN devices you can use with a site-to-site connection, browse to *https://bit.ly/az900-vpndevices*.

A point-to-site connection connects your VNet to a single device. That device can be a computer, but it can also be a mobile device, such as a tablet or a smartphone. When using a point-to-site connection, software on the device establishes a VPN connection to VPN Gateway, and all traffic is encrypted and travels over that connection.

Virtual network peering

You can connect two VNets together using a VNet-to-VNet connection with VPN Gateway, but when you use that method, you might experience some latency because of the two VPN Gateways that are involved. As I pointed out earlier, you are also going to incur a bandwidth restriction based on the VPN Gateway pricing tier you are using.

To avoid both of those situations, you can connect your VNets using virtual network peering. Traffic between two VNets that are peered travels over Microsoft's private backbone infrastructure and not over the Internet; however, unlike a VNet-to-VNet connection, the traffic is not encrypted.

EXAM TIP

You can peer VNets that are in the same region or in different regions. Microsoft refers to peering VNets between two Azure regions as *global virtual network peering*.

To connect two VNets using virtual network peering, open your VNet and click **Peerings** on the menu on the left in the Azure portal. You can then click **+Add** to add a virtual network peering, as shown in Figure 2-30.

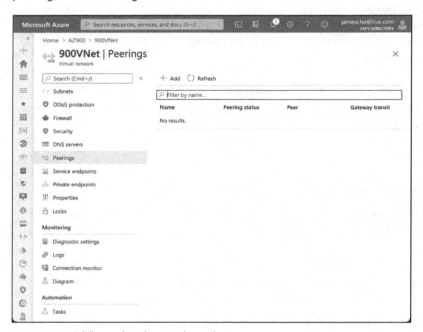

FIGURE 2-30 Adding a virtual network peering

For virtual network peering to work, a peering must be created in both networks. Once you've named your peering and selected the VNet you want to peer, you'll also need to name the peering that will be created in the second network you're peering to, as shown in Figure 2-31.

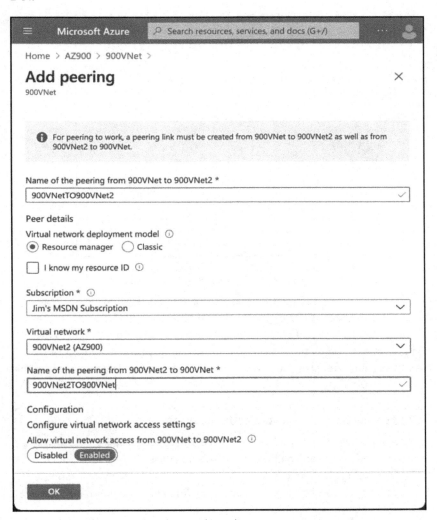

FIGURE 2-31 Configuring a virtual network peering

Once the peering has been added, you can view the status of the peering in the **Peerings** blade in the portal. Figure 2-32 shows the peering created earlier with a status of Connected.

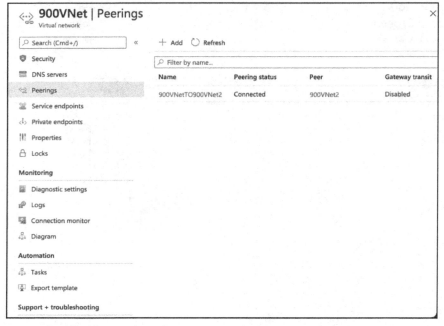

FIGURE 2-32 Virtual network peering status

There is one important limitation related to global virtual network peering. (Remember, global virtual network peering means peering two VNets in different Azure regions.) If you have resources you need to connect to that are behind Azure Load Balancer running in the Basic tier, you won't be able to connect to those resources using the public IP address of the load balancer. If that's a requirement for you, you'll need to change Azure Load Balancer to the Standard tier.

> **MORE INFO   AZURE LOAD BALANCER AND VIRTUAL NETWORK PEERING**
>
> There are some Azure services that can use the Basic tier of Azure Load Balancer under the hood, so you won't be able to connect to those resources using the load balancer's public IP address when you are using global virtual network peering. You can find more information, including a list of those resource types, by browsing to *http://bit.ly/az900-peeringconstraints*.

ExpressRoute

As you've just learned, you can use Azure VPN Gateway to connect your Azure VNet to on-premises resources, and many customers use this method. However, there are some aspects of using a VPN that might not meet the requirements of some customers. For example, a VPN is limited to a maximum of 1.25 Gbps in network speed. If a customer needs more speed than that, VPN isn't a good choice. VPN Gateway also sends all traffic over the public Internet, and that might not be a viable option for some people.

For these reasons, Azure offers a service called ExpressRoute that can offer speeds up to 10 Gbps over dedicated fiber-optic connections. When you use ExpressRoute, you connect from your on-premises network to a Microsoft Enterprise Edge router (MSEE), and that MSEE router then connects you to Azure. The MSEE router sits on the edge of Microsoft's network, and in most cases, your connection will also be from a router in your on-premises network that is on the edge of your network.

> **MORE INFO** **EDGE NETWORK DEVICES**
>
> An edge device on a network refers to a device that operates as the access point into the network. If you think of a network as a circle and devices that are on that network as being inside that circle, you can think of an edge device as sitting on the line that makes up the circle.

In most situations, customers connect to the MSEE router using a third-party service provider. The service provider is a major network service provider, often an Internet service provider. The service provider has network connections directly into the MSEE router, and those connections have dedicated bandwidth. Figure 2-33 shows a typical ExpressRoute configuration.

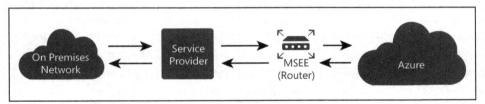

FIGURE 2-33 A typical ExpressRoute configuration

EXAM TIP

Microsoft calls an ExpressRoute connection a *circuit*.

Because data in ExpressRoute doesn't traverse the public Internet, bandwidth is much more reliable. However, the ExpressRoute configuration you see in Figure 2-28 does require that you trust the service provider with the data flowing through the circuit. If you want to remove the service provider from the picture, you can use an offering called ExpressRoute Direct that allows you to connect directly to a physical port on the MSEE router. ExpressRoute Direct also provides for much higher bandwidth if that's a concern for you.

Container (blob) storage

Azure Blob Storage is designed for storing unstructured data, which has no defined structure. That includes text files, images, videos, documents, and much more. An entity stored in Blob Storage is referred to as a *blob*. There are three types of blobs in Azure Storage.

- **Block blobs**   Used to store files used by an application.
- **Append blobs**   They are like block blobs, but append blobs are specialized for append operations. For that reason, they are often used to store constantly updated data like diagnostic logs.
- **Page blobs**   They are used to store virtual hard disk (.vhd) files that are used in Azure virtual machines. We'll cover these in Azure Disk Storage later in this chapter.

Blobs are stored in storage *containers*. A container is used as a means of organizing blobs, so you might have a container for video files, another container for image files, and so on. The choice, however, is entirely up to you.

If you're planning on moving data from on-premises into Azure Storage, there are many options available to you. You can use Azure Storage Explorer, a free tool available from Microsoft, to upload data. You can also use command line tools that Microsoft provides for uploading to Azure Storage.

If you want to move a large amount of data, Microsoft offers a service called *Data Box*. Data Box has an online service called Data Box Edge that makes copying data to Azure Storage as easy as copying it to a hard drive on your system. For even larger amounts of data, Microsoft offers a Data Box offline service where they will ship you hard drives. You simply copy your data to the hard drives, encrypt the drives with BitLocker, and then ship them back to Microsoft. Microsoft even offers Data Box Heavy, a service where they'll ship you a rugged device on wheels that can hold up to 1 petabyte of data!

Disk storage

Disk storage in Azure refers to disks that are used in virtual machines. Azure creates a disk that is automatically designated for temporary storage when you create a VM. This means data on that disk will be lost if there's a maintenance event on the VM. If you need to store data for a longer period of time that will persist between VM deployments and maintenance events, you can create a disk using an image stored in Azure Storage.

Azure disks are available as both traditional hard disks (HDD) and solid-state drives (SSD). HDD disks are cheaper and designed for noncritical data. SSD disks are available in a Standard tier for light use and as Azure Premium Disk for heavy use.

Azure disks are available as either managed disks or unmanaged disks. All Azure disks are backed by page blobs in Azure Storage. When you use unmanaged disks, they use an Azure Storage account in your Azure subscription, and you must manage that account. This is particularly troublesome because there are limitations in Azure Storage, and if you have heavy disk usage, you might end up experiencing downtime because of throttling.

When you move to managed disks, Microsoft handles the storage account, and all storage limitations are removed. All you need to worry about is your disk. You can leave the storage account in Microsoft's hands.

> **MORE INFO** **MANAGED DISKS**
>
> **Microsoft recommends managed disks for all new VMs. They also recommend that all VMs currently using unmanaged disks be moved to managed disks.**

Perhaps an even more important reason to use managed disks is that by doing so, you avoid a possible single point of failure in your VM. When you use unmanaged disks, there is a possibility that the Azure Storage accounts backing up your disks might exist within the same storage scale unit. If a failure occurs in that scale unit, you will lose all your disks. By ensuring that each managed disk is in a separate scale unit, you avoid the situation of a single point of failure.

Azure Files

Azure disks are a good option for adding a disk to a virtual machine, but if you just need disk space in the cloud, it doesn't make sense to take on the burden of managing a virtual machine and its operating system. In those situations, Azure Files is the perfect solution.

> **NOTE** **AZURE FILES AND AZURE STORAGE**
>
> **Azure Files shares are backed by Azure Storage, so you will need a storage account to create an Azure Files share.**

Azure Files is a completely managed file share that you can mount just like any SMB file share. That means existing applications that use network attached storage (NAS) devices or SMB file shares can use Azure Files without any special tooling, and if you have multiple applications that need to access the same share, that will work with Azure Files, too.

One possible problem with using Azure Files is the remote location of files. If your users or applications are using a file share mapped to Azure Files, they might experience longer-than-usual file transfer times because the files are in Azure. To solve that problem, Microsoft introduced Azure File Sync.

Install Azure File Sync on one or more servers in your local network and it will keep your files in Azure Files synchronized with your on-premises server. When users or applications need to access those files, they can access the local copy quickly. Any changes you make to the centralized Azure Files share are synchronized to servers running Azure File Sync.

Storage tiers

Microsoft offers numerous storage tiers for Blob Storage that are priced according to how often the data is accessed, how long you intend to store the data, and so on. The Hot storage tier is for data you need to access often. It has the highest cost of storage, but the cost for accessing the data is low. The Cool storage tier is for data that you intend to store for a longer period and not access quite as often. It has a lower storage cost than the Hot tier, but the access costs are higher. You're also required to keep data in storage for at least 30 days.

Microsoft also offers an Archive storage tier for long-term data storage. Data stored in the Archive tier enjoys the lowest storage costs available, but the access costs are the highest. You must keep data in storage for a minimum of 180 days in the Archive tier or you can be subjected to an early deletion charge. Because data in the Archive tier isn't designed for quick and frequent access, it can take a very long time to retrieve it. In fact, while the Hot and Cool access tiers guarantee access to the first byte of data within milliseconds, the Archive tier only guarantees access to the first byte within 15 hours.

Cosmos DB

Many database systems use relational data. A relational database contains tables of data that are related to each other. Part of the database design defines the relationship between tables, and when new data is added to the database, it must conform to the *schema* (the way the database is set up).

Some database systems, known as *NoSQL databases*, are not relational. In a NoSQL database system, you're not locked into a schema for your data. For example, in a relational system, if you're storing information about some customers and you want to add customer birthdays to your data, you have to edit the schema of your database to allow for the birthday to be added. However, in a NoSQL system, you simply add the birthday to your data and add it to the database. The database doesn't care about the type of data or fields it contains.

There are four types of NoSQL database systems: key-value, column, document, and graph. Table 2-1 lists each of these types and provides some information about each.

TABLE 2-1 NoSQL database systems

System	Description	Common Use
Key-value	Stores data that is tied to a unique key. Pass in the key and the database returns the data.	Because the value can be just about anything, key-value databases have many uses.
Column	NoSQL databases are called *keyspaces*, and a key-space contains column families. A column contains rows and columns like a relational table, but each row can have its own set of columns. You aren't locked into a schema.	Storing user-profile data for a website. Also, because column databases scale well and are extremely fast, they are well-suited to storing large amounts of data.
Document	Data is stored as a structured string of text called a document. This can be HTML, JSON, and so forth. This is similar to a key-value database, except that the document is a structured value.	Same as key-value, but document databases have advantages. They scale well horizontally, and they allow you to query against the value and return portions of the value. A key-value database query returns the entire value associated with the key.
Graph	Stores data and the relationships between each piece of data. Data is stored in nodes, and relationships are drawn between nodes.	Many systems use graph databases because they are extremely fast. A social network might use a graph database because it would be easy to store relationships between people, things those people like, and so forth.

There are many different NoSQL database systems, and most of them are geared toward a particular database model. Microsoft offers a hosted NoSQL database system in Azure called Cosmos DB, which supports all the NoSQL database types. Microsoft has built some custom code around Cosmos DB so that developers can use their existing skills with other database systems with a Cosmos DB database. This makes it easy for existing applications to begin taking advantage of Cosmos DB without engineers having to write new code.

When you create a Cosmos DB database, you choose the API you want to use, which determines the database type for your database. The database API types are

- **Core (SQL)** Creates a document database that you can query using SQL syntax that you might be familiar with from using relational databases.
- **Azure Cosmos DB for MongoDB API** Used for migrating a MongoDB database to Cosmos DB. MongoDB databases are document databases.

- **Cassandra** Used for migrating a Cassandra database to Cosmos DB. Cassandra databases are column databases.
- **Azure Table** Used for migrating data stored in Azure Table Storage to Cosmos DB. This creates a key-value database.
- **Gremlin** Used for migrating Gremlin databases to Cosmos DB. Gremlin databases are graph databases.

Microsoft calls these APIs because they are just that: APIs. They are application programming interfaces that allow developers who are already using an existing NoSQL database technology to migrate to Cosmos DB without having to change their code.

Another huge advantage to Cosmos DB is a feature known as turnkey global distribution. This feature takes advantage of the horizontal scalability of NoSQL databases and allows you to replicate your data globally with a few clicks. In the Azure portal, you can simply click the region(s) where you want data replicated, as shown in Figure 2-34. Once you click **Save**, Cosmos DB will begin to replicate data, which will be available in the selected regions. This makes it easy to ensure that users have the fastest experience possible with an application.

FIGURE 2-34 Easy replication across the globe with Cosmos DB

Azure SQL Database

Azure SQL Database is a PaaS offering for SQL Server database hosting. Microsoft manages the platform, so all you must worry about is your database and the data in it.

SQL Server databases are *relational databases* made up of tables of data, and each table has a schema that defines what the data should look like. For example, the schema might define that your data contains an ID number, a first name, a last name, and a date. Any data that you add to the table must follow the schema, so data you add must not have fields that are not defined in the schema.

A database will contain many tables of data that are related to each other, and by using specialized queries, developers can return data that is a result of joining related data from multiple tables. For example, you might have a Customers table and an Orders table, each with a field that identifies a customer. By querying and joining the data from both tables, you can provide a user with an invoice showing all their orders. This relationship between the tables is how relational databases got their name, as shown in Figure 2-35.

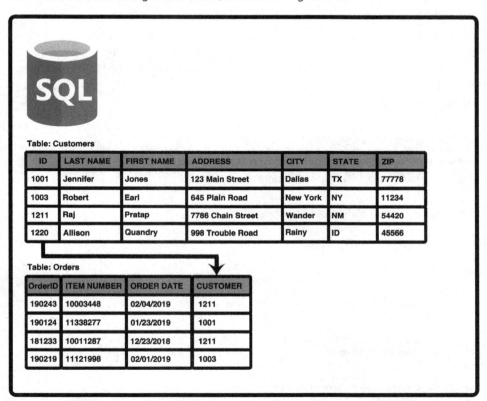

Table: Customers

ID	LAST NAME	FIRST NAME	ADDRESS	CITY	STATE	ZIP
1001	Jennifer	Jones	123 Main Street	Dallas	TX	77778
1003	Robert	Earl	645 Plain Road	New York	NY	11234
1211	Raj	Pratap	7786 Chain Street	Wander	NM	54420
1220	Allison	Quandry	998 Trouble Road	Rainy	ID	45566

Table: Orders

OrderID	ITEM NUMBER	ORDER DATE	CUSTOMER
190243	10003448	02/04/2019	1211
190124	11338277	01/23/2019	1001
181233	10011287	12/23/2018	1211
190219	11121998	02/01/2019	1003

FIGURE 2-35 Two tables in a relational database

NOTE **RELATIONAL DATABASES**

SQL Server isn't the only relational database system. There are many relational database systems, including Oracle, PostgreSQL, and MySQL.

Azure offers three different deployment options for Azure SQL Database: single database, elastic pool, and managed instance.

A single database is simply a database running in a hosted SQL Server instance running in Azure. Microsoft manages the database server, so all you have to worry about is the database itself. Microsoft provides two different purchase models for single databases: Database Transaction Unit (DTU) and virtual core (vCore).

A DTU represents a collection of CPU, memory, and data reads and writes. There are three tiers in the DTU model: Basic, Standard, and Premium. Each tier offers a higher level of CPU, memory, and data transfer.

The vCore model uses a virtual CPU, and it makes it easy to configure the exact hardware configuration you need. It offers a General-Purpose tier and a Business-Critical tier. You can choose between a provisioned tier (where you choose the CPU, memory, and other resources that are always available) and a serverless tier where you choose a range of resource needs so you can control costs more effectively.

> **MORE INFO**   **CHOOSING A PURCHASING MODEL**
>
> For details on the available purchasing models and how you can choose between them, browse to https://bit.ly/az900-sqlpurchasingmodels.

Table 2-2 shows these models and how they differ.

TABLE 2-2 Single database purchase models

DTU Model	vCore Model
Good choice for users who don't need a high degree of flexibility with configuration and who want fixed pricing.	Good choice if you need a high level of visibility and control of individual resources (such as memory, storage, and CPU power) your database uses.
Pre-configured limits for transactions against the database, and pre-configured storage, CPU, and memory configurations.	Flexibility in CPU power, memory, and storage, with storage charged on a usage basis.
Basic and Standard offerings, along with a Premium tier for production databases with a large number of transactions.	General Purpose and Business Critical offerings to provide lower costs when desired and high-performance and availability when required.
Ability to scale to a higher tier when needed.	Ability and flexibility to scale CPU, memory, and storage as needed.
Backup storage and long-term retention of data provided for an additional charge.	Backup storage and long-term retention of data provided for an additional charge.

An elastic pool consists of more than one database (and often many databases) all managed by the same SQL Database server. This solution is geared toward SaaS offerings where you might want to have multiple users (or maybe even each user) to be assigned their own database. You can easily move databases in and out of an elastic pool, making it ideal for SaaS.

In some cases, being able to scale a single database to add additional power is sufficient. However, if your application has wide variations in usage and you find it hard to predict usage (such as with a SaaS service), the ability to add more databases to a pool is much more desirable. In an elastic pool, you are charged for the resource usage of the pool versus individual databases, and you have full control over how individual databases use those resources. This makes it possible to not only control costs, but you can also ensure that each database has the resources it needs while still being able to maintain predictability in expenses. What's more, you can easily transition a single database into an elastic pool by simply moving the database into a pool.

NOTE   PRICING MODELS OF ELASTIC POOLS

The pricing model information in Table 2-2 also applies to elastic pools. However, your resources aren't applied to an individual database; they are applied to the pool.

EXAM TIP

While you can scale up and down easily with Azure SQL Database by moving to a higher tier or adding compute, memory, and storage resources, relational databases don't scale horizontally. There are some options available for scaling out a read-only copy of your database, but in general, relational databases don't offer the capability of scaling out to provide additional copies of your data in multiple regions.

A managed instance is explicitly designed for customers who want an easy migration path from on-premises or another non-Azure environment to Azure. Managed instances are fully compatible with SQL Server on-premises, and because your database server is integrated with an isolated VNet and has a private IP address, your database server can sit within your private Azure VNet. The features are designed for users who want to lift and shift an on-premises database to Azure without a lot of configuration changes or hassle. Both the General Purpose and Business Critical service tiers are available.

Microsoft developed the Azure Database Migration Service (DMS) to make it easier for customers to easily move on-premises databases or databases hosted elsewhere in the cloud to a managed instance. The DMS works by walking you through a wizard experience to tell Azure which database(s) and table(s) you want to migrate from your source database to Azure SQL Database. It will then use the Azure VNet that comes with the managed instance to migrate the data. Once the data has been migrated, DMS sets up synchronization between the source database and Azure SQL Database. This means that as long as the source database remains online, any changes made to it will be synchronized with the managed instance in Azure SQL Database.

MORE INFO   DMS AND ON-PREMISES DATABASES

In order to migrate an on-premises database, you must have connectivity between Azure and your on-premises network over VPN or using a service such as ExpressRoute.

Azure Database for MySQL

Like SQL Server databases, MySQL databases are relational databases. However, MySQL is an open-source system. In fact, MySQL is one of the most popular open-source database system in the world.

Azure Database for MySQL is a fully managed cloud offering of the Community Edition of MySQL. With Azure Database for MySQL, you don't have to worry about managing the database server, dealing with security concerns, or performing complex tasks such as performance tuning. Microsoft takes care of all that for you.

EXAM TIP

Azure Database for MySQL secures your data at rest and in motion. That means that not only are your databases secure, but data is also secure when users are querying your database.

Azure Database for MySQL offers several pricing plans based on your specific needs. The Basic plan is best for users who have light usage; the General-Purpose plan is more suitable for business use; and the Memory Optimized plan is for high-performance requirements. As you move up in pricing plans, you get more CPU cores and more memory, and each pricing plan offers multiple tiers so that you can plan for specifically what your needs require.

Because Azure Database for MySQL is based on the MySQL Community Edition, you can easily move your on-premises MySQL databases to the cloud without worrying about compatibility.

Azure Database for PostgreSQL

PostgreSQL is another relational, open-source database system. While PostgreSQL was initially designed to run on Unix or Linux, it's now available for MacOS, Linux, OpenBSD, FreeBSD, and Windows.

PostgreSQL was designed with the enterprise in mind, and it supports a large number of users performing complex operations. Azure Database for PostgreSQL is a managed version of PostgreSQL in Azure. Like Azure Database for MySQL and Azure SQL Database, Azure Database for PostgreSQL allows you to utilize a powerful database system without having to manage the server, database security, performance, and other administrative tasks.

Pricing for Azure Database for PostgreSQL is similar to Azure Database for MySQL. Basic, General Purpose, and Memory Optimized plans are available, and prices increase as you add additional database resources like CPU and memory.

The Azure Marketplace and its usage scenarios

You've learned about many of the products and services available in Azure, but there are many available products outside of what we've discussed. Not only does Microsoft offer many additional services, but third-party vendors also provide a wide array of resources you can use in Azure. All these resources are available in a single repository called the Azure Marketplace.

To access the Azure Marketplace, click **Create A Resource** in the Azure portal, as shown in Figure 2-36. This will display a list of categories you can choose from. It will also show a list of popular offerings from all categories. You can click a category to see all templates in that category, and you can click a template in the list of popular templates, enter a search term, or even click **See All** to see all templates that are available.

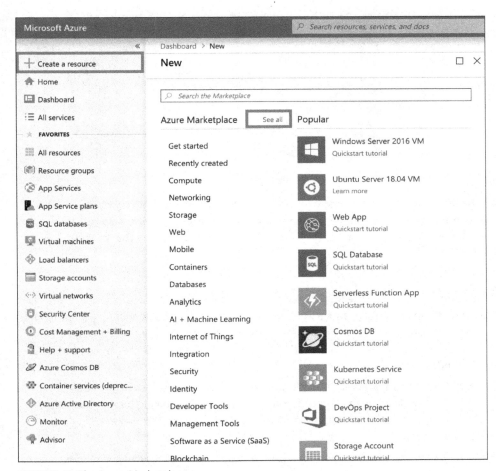

FIGURE 2-36 The Azure Marketplace

If you click **See All**, you'll be taken to the full Marketplace experience where you can filter based on pricing, operating systems, and publisher as shown in Figure 2-37.

FIGURE 2-37 Filtering the Azure Marketplace

EXAM TIP

All the templates in the Azure Marketplace are ARM templates that deploy one or more Azure services. Remember from our earlier discussion of Azure Resource Manager that all ARM deployments are deployed using ARM templates. The Marketplace is no different.

Some of the templates in the Marketplace deploy a single resource. For example, if you click the Web App template, it will create a web app running in Azure App Service. Other templates create many resources that combine to make an entire solution. For example, you can create a DataStax Enterprise database cluster and the template will create between 1 and 40 DataStax Enterprise nodes.

You are billed for each Marketplace offering on your Azure invoice, so if you create a DataStax Enterprise cluster with 40 nodes, you won't see separate billing for 40 VMs, VNETs, and so on. Instead, you'll see a bill for a DataStax Enterprise cluster. This makes billing much easier to understand.

As shown in Figure 2-38, many Marketplace templates provide links to documentation and other information to help you get the most out of the template. If you decide that you don't want to immediately create the resources, you can click **Save For Later** and the template will be added to your saved list that you can access by clicking **My Saved List**, as previously shown in the upper-left corner in Figure 2-37.

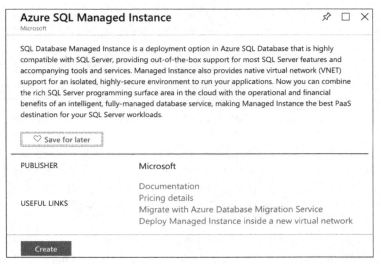

FIGURE 2-38 Marketplace links and Saved List

Thought experiment

Now that you've learned about core Azure services, let's apply that knowledge. You can find the answers to this thought experiment in the section that follows.

ContosoPharm has contacted you for assistance in setting up some Azure virtual machines for hosting their Azure services. They want to ensure that their services experience high availability and are protected against disasters that might occur in a datacenter at a particular Azure region. In addition to that, they want to ensure that a power outage at a particular datacenter doesn't affect their service in that region.

ContosoPharm plans on having a large number of VMs, but they're only going to be hosting three different services in the cloud. Each of these services will have other Azure services associated with them in addition to the VMs. They're very interested in having a way to easily view all the Azure resources associated with a particular service inside the Azure portal.

Two of the services they plan on deploying belong to the marketing department. The other service belongs to the development division. They need a way to report on each of these departments, so they'd like a way to logically group these services.

Along those same lines, the CTO wants to ensure that they can control who has access to the services in each department. He also wants to have control over how those services are configured.

ContosoPharm's VMs will also be using specific configurations for virtual networks, and they want to ensure that they can easily deploy these resources into new Azure regions, if necessary later. It's critical to them that the later deployments have the exact same configuration as all other deployments because any differences can cause application incompatibilities.

The CTO is also worried about VMs in particular from experiencing availability problems due to possible hardware failures. He's also heard that some cloud customers experience issues when the cloud provider must reboot the underlying host computer for some reason. This kind of thing cannot happen in ContosoPharm's case, so you will need to make a recommendation to prevent that.

During some periods of time, ContosoPharm has noticed that their applications can cause extreme CPU spikes. They'd like a system that will account for that and possibly add additional VMs during these peak times, but they want to control costs and don't want to pay for these additional VMs when they aren't experiencing a usage spike. Any advice you can offer for that would be a bonus.

One of ContosoPharm's services has a web portal that was written using PHP. They'll need to move this web portal to the cloud, but they don't want to have to hassle with a lot of configuration. They need it to be available for users reliably and they need to be able to update the code if necessary, but they don't want to worry about anything else. They're looking to you to suggest the best Azure solution for that, and keep in mind that they need to be able to scale this web portal easily when usage increases during busy times of the month.

Another portion of one of their services exists as a Docker image. They want to run this in Azure as well, but the CTO is concerned about costs. This part of their service is only needed for specific operations, so it runs only for a few minutes every month. Even so, it's a critical component, so they need it to be reliable. The CTO wants you to suggest an option that will be the most cost-efficient option in Azure.

One of their other services is also containerized, but it's quite a bit more complex. Usage of this service is all over the place. Sometimes they require a lot of computing resources for it, and other times, they don't require much at all. However, when it's needed, they need to ensure that it's always running.

Sales managers in the ContosoPharm sales department need access to Office applications reliably, but the CIO is greatly concerned about sensitive sales data being stored on laptop hard drives. He'd like for you to recommend a way for these employees to access the applications they need while keeping data secure. Being able to access these applications from any device (or even a web browser) would be a real game-changer.

Much of the infrastructure ContosoPharm is moving to the cloud is made up of multi-tiered applications, and each of these tiers needs to be able to communicate with each other and with the Internet. The on-premises network engineers at ContosoPharm completely understand the on-premises network and how it's configured, but they have no idea how to translate that to the cloud. They'll need you to provide some recommendations in that area as well.

ContosoPharm might need to use two different virtual networks for its marketing department. It's important that ContosoPharm be able to connect the VMs in those networks, but it wants to ensure that no traffic between the VMs flows over the Internet. It's also critical that the company gets maximum network speed between these VMs because ContosoPharm will be transferring some massive files between them. ContosoPharm needs you to recommend options for connecting these VMs.

Some sales associates in the field will need to be able to connect to the marketing VMs, and the information they will be accessing is confidential in nature. These associates might be accessing these VMs from public Wi-Fi hotspots in places like hotels, and it's critical that ContosoPharm keep this data safe when it's accessed using laptops and mobile devices in the field. ContosoPharm needs you to recommend a solution for that.

ContosoPharm also has an on-premises system that cannot be migrated to the cloud, so it will remain on-premises. This system uses 3D animations of cell structures and how different drugs interact with them. The file sizes are very large, and ContosoPharm is concerned that transferring these large files from the cloud is going to make their application slow. Also, ContosoPharm is concerned over privacy implications and would prefer to keep these files from being transferred over the Internet if possible.

ContosoPharm is required to keep a copy of each order invoice from its customers. These invoices are uploaded to the website as a PDF, and ContosoPharm wants to keep them in the cloud. ContosoPharm doesn't need to be able to run any kind of reporting on these invoices, but it does need them in case regulators ask for them in the future.

ContosoPharm also needs to persist data that's stored on any of their VMs, even if a maintenance event happens in Azure or they are moved to another VM for some reason. It's critical data, so ContosoPharm wants to ensure it chooses the right solution.

Another part of their application also needs to persist data, but ContosoPharm needs to be able to access the data from an on-premises server running Windows Server 2016. The company doesn't want to have to install anything special on the server to be able to access these files that are in the cloud.

All ContosoPharm's chemicals and pharmaceuticals are kept in a large research facility. The company would like to integrate a database in that facility with its Azure services and needs that connection to be encrypted and secure. The developers of the current system used the Community Edition of MySQL to develop the database, and ContosoPharm is interested in the easiest solution to have this hosted in the cloud without needing to keep up with configuration and maintenance.

Provide a recommendation to ContosoPharm that meets all its requirements. You don't need to give the company specific technical details on how to implement everything, but you should point ContosoPharm in the right direction if you don't have specifics.

Thought experiment answers

In this section, we'll go over the answers to the thought experiment.

To ensure that their VMs are protected against disasters at a datacenter within a particular Azure region, you should recommend that ContosoPharm use availability zones. By deploying VMs in availability zones, the company can ensure that VMs are distributed into different physical buildings within the same Azure region. Each building will have separate power, water, cooling system, and network.

To easily view Azure resources associated with a particular service, ContosoPharm can create separate resource groups and create the resources for each service within its own resource group. To logically group its services for the marketing and development divisions so the company can report on them, ContosoPharm can create separate Azure subscriptions for each division.

To resolve the CTO's concern over who has access to services and how those services are configured, you can recommend the use of management groups. Because you've already recommended that each division have their own subscription, management groups are a logical choice because each subscription can be moved into a separate management group.

In order to ensure consistent deployments now and in the future, ContosoPharm can create an ARM template for their deployment. By using an ARM template, the company can ensure that every deployment of its resources will be identical.

To protect the application when a VM has a hardware problem or must be rebooted, ContosoPharm should use an availability set. An availability set would provide the company with multiple fault domains and update domains so that if a VM must be rebooted, it would still have an operational VM in another update domain.

To ensure that they ContosoPharm has enough VMs to handle the load when CPU spikes, it should use scale sets. The company can then configure auto-scale rules to scale out when the load requires it and scale back in to control costs.

The best option for hosting the company's PHP web portal in the cloud is Azure App Service. Because it's a PaaS service, ContosoPharm won't have to worry about a lot of configuration, and because App Service offers scaling capabilities, that meets the requirement of needing to react to increases in usage.

The best option for hosting ContosoPharm's Docker image in the cloud is Azure Container Instances. There are other options in Azure for this, but because the CTO is concerned with costs and this component only runs for a very small amount of time each month, ACI is clearly the cheapest alternative.

The second containerized component would benefit better from Azure Kubernetes Service. The fact that it's more complex and sometimes requires a lot of computing resources makes it an ideal candidate for AKS, especially because Kubernetes can ensure that the container is always running and available.

To provide sales managers with access to Office applications without having to worry about the security aspects of storing files on their laptops, you should recommend Windows Virtual Desktop. They would then be able to access these applications from any device or a web browser.

Your recommendation to the network engineers should be to configure an Azure virtual network. They can easily configure subnets within that network exactly like they have on-premises, and all the networking features they're used to will be available to them.

To connect ContosoPharm's two VNets, you have a couple of options. You can either use Azure VPN Gateway with a VNet-to-VNet connection, or you can use virtual network peering. Because ContosoPharm has stated it needs maximum network speed and because employees are transferring huge files and will likely use a lot of bandwidth, virtual network peering is a better choice. This option reduces the latency that can be associated with VNet-to-VNet peering, and it also removes the bandwidth restriction that comes with VPN Gateway connections.

You can recommend that ContosoPharm use Azure VPN Gateway and a point-to-site connection to allow sales associates to securely connect to the marketing VMs from laptops and mobile devices. This will ensure that the network traffic is encrypted, so even if the associates use a public Wi-Fi access point, the data will be secure.

The 3D animation system ContosoPharm uses sounds like it needs a lot of bandwidth. In that scenario, ExpressRoute is likely a good choice, especially because the company would also like to keep files from being transferred over the Internet. With ExpressRoute, data transfers over a private connection, and ContosoPharm can adjust its bandwidth based on the needs of the app, up to a max of 10 Gbps.

To store their invoices in the cloud, ContosoPharm can use Azure Blob Storage. The company could store them in a database as binary blobs, but because they don't need to run any kind of reporting or queries against them, Azure Blob Storage will be cheaper.

To persist the data on the VMs between reboots or VM moves, ContosoPharm should use Disk Storage. You should probably also recommend that they use managed disks for ease of use and reliability. For the part of the app that needs to persist data that's available by a Windows Server 2016 on-premises server, you should recommend Azure Files. The company can then use SMB to access the files, and existing systems on-premises can map to the files without having to install anything extra.

For the company's database needs, the best choice by far is Azure Database for MySQL. Because it's a managed service, ContosoPharm won't have to worry about maintenance or configuration, and because it's based on the Community Edition of MySQL, they should be able to simply transfer the database directly to the cloud and be done with it.

Chapter summary

This chapter covered a lot of ground! Not only did you learn some of the basics of Azure related to regions and resource groups, but you learned about a lot of the core workload services Azure provides.

Here's a summary of what this chapter covered.

- An Azure region is an area within a specific geographical boundary, and each region is typically hundreds of miles apart.
- A geography is usually a country, and each geography contains at least two regions.
- A datacenter is a physical building within a region, and each datacenter has its own power, cooling supply, water supply, generators, and network.

- Round-trip latency between two regions must be no greater than 2ms, and this is why regions are sometimes defined as a "latency boundary."
- Customers should deploy Azure resources to multiple regions to ensure availability.
- Availability zones ensure that your resources are deployed into separate datacenters in a region. There are at least three availability zones in every region.
- Resource groups allow you to separate Azure resources in a logical way, and you can tag resources for easier management.
- All your Azure resources are created within an Azure subscription, and you can create additional subscriptions if you need to group or report on resources more easily.
- Azure subscriptions have limits associated with them.
- Management groups allow you to assign policies and access control to Azure resources.
- Only subscriptions or other management groups can be added to a management group.
- Azure Resource Manager (ARM) is how Azure management tools create and manage Azure resources.
- ARM uses resource providers to create and manage resources.
- An ARM template allows you to ensure consistency of large Azure deployments.
- Azure virtual machines are an IaaS offering where you manage the operating system and configuration.
- Availability sets protect your VMs with fault domains and update domains. Fault domains protect your VM from a hardware failure in a hardware rack. You are protected from VM reboots by update domains.
- Scale sets allow you to set up auto-scale rules to scale horizontally when needed.
- Azure App Service makes it easy to host web apps in the cloud because it's a PaaS service that removes the management burden from the user.
- App Service apps run inside of an App Service plan that specifies the number of VMs and the configuration of those VMs.
- Containers allow you to create an image of an application and everything needed to run it.
- Azure Container Instances (ACI) allow you to run containers for very little cost.
- Azure Kubernetes Service (AKS) is a managed service that makes it easy to host Kubernetes clusters in the cloud.
- Windows Virtual Desktop makes applications and OSes easily available to multiple users from almost any device.
- An Azure virtual network (VNet) allows Azure services to communicate with each other and the Internet.
- You can add a public IP address to a VNet for inbound Internet connectivity. This is useful if a website is running in your VNET and you want to allow people to access it.
- Azure Load Balancer can distribute traffic from the Internet across multiple VMs in your VNet.

- Azure VPN Gateway allows you to establish encrypted connections between Azure VNets and other VNets or on-premises networks. You can configure VNet-to-VNet connections, site-to-site connections, and point-to-site connections.

- Virtual network peering connects two Azure VNets to each other without the bandwidth restriction associated with a VNet-to-VNet connection. Peering VNets in different regions is called global virtual network peering.

- ExpressRoute allows you to have a high-bandwidth connection to Azure of up to 10 Gbps by connecting to a Microsoft Enterprise Edge (MSEE) router.

- Traffic over ExpressRoute does not travel over the Internet.

- Azure Blob Storage is a good storage option for unstructured data such as binary files.

- If you need to move a large amount of data to Blob Storage, Azure Data Box is a good option. You can have hard drives of numerous sizes shipped to you. Add your data to them and ship them back to Microsoft where they'll be added to your storage account.

- Azure Disk Storage is virtual disk storage for Azure VMs. Managed disks allow you to remove the management burden of disks.

- Azure Files allows you to have disk space in the cloud that you can map to a drive on-premises.

- Azure Blob Storage offers Hot, Cool, and Archive storage tiers that are based on how long you intend to store the data, how often the data is accessed, and so on.

- Azure Cosmos DB is a NoSQL database in the cloud for unstructured data.

- Azure SQL Database is a relational database system in the cloud that is completely managed by Microsoft.

- Azure Database for MySQL is based on the Community Edition of the open-source MySQL database system. It's a managed service that removes the burden of management from the user.

- Azure Database for PostgreSQL is a managed service for hosting PostgreSQL databases.

- The Azure Marketplace is a source of templates for creating Azure resources. Some are provided by Microsoft and some are provided by third parties.

CHAPTER 3

Describe core solutions and management tools on Azure

In Chapter 2, you learned about the core services in Azure. In this chapter, we'll dig into a vast array of core solutions in Azure. We'll cover some exciting new technologies, such as artificial intelligence, the Internet of Things (IoT), big data, and serverless computing.

If you're really going to learn how to use Azure, you're also going to need to know about how you can manage your Azure resources. You've seen the Azure portal already, but that's not the only solution for managing and creating resources in Azure. There are several command-line tools that are available, making it easy to script powerful interactions with Azure resources. You can even manage your Azure resources from your phone!

Once you've created and configured your Azure services, it's important to keep up with how they're performing so that you'll know if you need to make changes to get the most out of your cloud resources. However, keeping up with the best practices and recommended configurations can be hard, especially when you're dealing with multiple services. Fortunately, Azure provides Azure Advisor to help you, and by coupling Azure Advisor with Azure Monitor, you can stay on top of all your Azure services.

Tracking the health of your particular cloud applications is only half the story when it comes to making sure your cloud resources are available. While Microsoft Azure is a highly reliable cloud platform, things can still go wrong, and when they do, the Azure Service Health website will keep you informed of what's going on.

Here are the skills that are covered in this chapter.

Skills covered in this chapter:
- Describe core solutions available in Azure
- Describe Azure management tools

Skill 3.1: Describe core solutions available in Azure

Even though cloud computing is a relatively new technology, it's become a key component of many computing solutions. The scope of cloud computing is growing at a tremendous pace, and Microsoft Azure is growing right along with it. Since the first edition of this book published just a few short months ago, new Azure services have been introduced and changes to existing services have been abundant. The ancient Greek philosopher Heraclitus said, "The only thing that is constant is change." It's a certainty that Heraclitus couldn't have predicted Azure thousands of years ago, but he certainly described the constant state of Azure perfectly!

The sheer number of Azure services can be overwhelming, but this chapter should help you make sense of the landscape.

This section covers:

- Azure IoT Hub
- IoT Central
- Azure Sphere
- Azure Synapse Analytics
- HDInsight
- Azure Databricks
- Azure Machine Learning
- Cognitive Services
- Azure Bot Service
- Serverless computing
- Azure Functions
- Logic Apps
- Event Grid
- Azure DevOps
- Azure DevTest Labs
- GitHub and GitHub Actions

Azure IoT Hub

You probably have quite a few devices connected to your home network. Several years ago, you'd probably have a few computers connected to your network, but now you likely have a lot of other types of devices, such as smartphones, streaming media devices, cameras, and even devices such as smart electrical sockets, smart light bulbs, and more. Most of these devices also connect to the Internet so that you can access them from anywhere.

Devices that connect to the Internet and have multiple sensors, such as cameras, light meters, temperature sensors, and so forth, are referred to as Internet of Things (IoT) devices, and the Internet is becoming heavily populated with them. To put it into context, the popular statistics portal Statista reports that there are more than 25 billion IoT-connected devices today, and that number is expected to grow to a staggering 75 billion by the year 2025. There are about 3.2 billion people on the Internet today, and the entire world's population is only around 8 billion. These IoT devices eclipse the human race in number, and the amount of information they collect and share is mind-boggling.

To make more sense out of Azure's IoT services, let's revisit our theoretical company named ContosoPharm, which in this example, is a pharmaceutical company with a large, multi-story building where they store drugs under development, along with sensitive components used in research. These items must be under strict climate control. If the temperature or humidity moves outside of a very tight range, it results in the loss of priceless materials.

To protect their investment, ContosoPharm uses IoT-connected climate-control systems, along with IoT-connected generators and lighting systems. These systems constantly monitor the environment and send alerts if something goes wrong. There are approximately 5,000 IoT devices in the building, and ContosoPharm must meet the following requirements for all those devices.

- ContosoPharm must update firmware on the IoT devices easily and in a staged way so they aren't all updated at the same time.

- ContosoPharm must alter the settings on the devices, such as changing alert levels, but these settings are specific to the physical location of the devices in the building.

- ContosoPharm must ensure that any connectivity to the devices is completely secure.

IoT Hub can easily solve all these problems. IoT devices are added to IoT Hub, and you can then manage them, monitor them, and send messages to them, either individually or to groups that you create. You can add up to 1,000,000 IoT devices to a single IoT Hub.

Figure 3-1 shows an IoT device added to the IoT Hub for ContosoPharm.

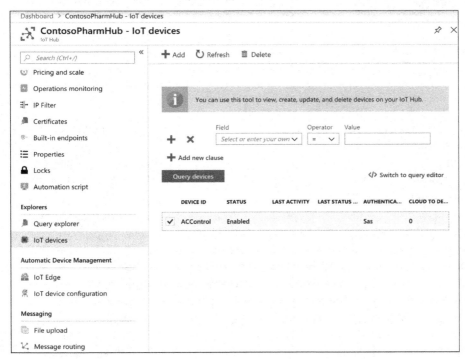

FIGURE 3-1 An IoT device in IoT Hub

From IoT Hub, you can send messages to devices (called cloud-to-device, or C2D messaging) or from your device to IoT Hub (called device-to-cloud, or D2C messaging). You can also intelligently route messages to Event Hub, Azure Storage, and Service Bus based on the content in the message.

When you add a new IoT device, IoT Hub creates a connection string that uses a shared access key for authentication. This key prevents unauthorized access to your IoT Hub. Once connected, messages between your device and IoT Hub are encrypted for additional security.

In addition to messages, you can also use IoT Hub to send files to your devices. This allows you to easily update the firmware on your devices in a secure way. To update the firmware on an IoT device, you simply copy the firmware to the device. The device will detect the firmware and will reboot and flash the new firmware to the device.

One important concept in IoT Hub is the concept of what's called a *device twin*. Every IoT device in IoT Hub has a logical equivalent that's stored in IoT Hub in JSON format. This JSON representation of the device is called a device twin, and it provides important capabilities.

Each device twin can contain metadata that adds additional categorization for the device. This metadata is stored as tags in the JSON for the device twin, and it's not known to the actual device. Only IoT Hub can see this metadata. One of ContosoPharm's requirements was to update firmware in a staged way instead of updating all devices at the same time. ContosoPharm can achieve that by adding tags for the device twins from their devices that might look like the following:

```
"tags": {
    "deploymentLocation": {
            "department": "researchInjectibles",
            "floor": "14"
        }
}
```

ContosoPharm can then choose to send firmware files only to devices on the 14th floor, for instance, or say, to devices in the researchInjectibles department. Figure 3-2 shows the device twin configuration in IoT Hub with tags set for the location of the device. Notice the building tag with a value of null. This is a tag that was previously set on the device twin, and by setting it to null, the tag will be removed.

The device twin also contains the properties for the IoT device. There are two copies of every property. One is the *reported* property, and the other is the desired property. You can change a device property in IoT Hub by changing the desired property to a new value. The next time the device connects to IoT Hub, that property will be set on the device. Until that happens, the reported property will contain the last value the device reported to IoT Hub. Once the property is updated, the reported and desired properties will be equal.

The reason IoT Hub uses this method for setting properties is that it might not always have a connection to every device. For example, if a device puts itself to sleep to save power, IoT Hub can't write property changes to that device. By keeping a desired and reported version of every property, IoT Hub always knows if a property needs to be written to a device the next time the device connects to IoT Hub.

FIGURE 3-2 Device twin showing tags set in the JSON

To help with users who want to add a large number of IoT devices to IoT Hub, Microsoft offers the IoT Hub Device Provisioning Service, or DPS. The DPS uses enrollment groups to add devices to your IoT Hub. The concept is that once the device wakes up (often, for the first time if it's a new device), it needs to know that it should connect to your IoT Hub. In order to do that, the DPS needs to uniquely identify the device, and it does that with either a certificate or via a trusted platform module chip.

Once DPS confirms the identity of the device, it can use the enrollment group details to determine which IoT Hub it should be added to. It will then provide the device with the connection information to connect to that IoT Hub. Also, the enrollment group can provide the initial configuration for the device twin. This allows you to specify properties, such as a firmware version, that the device needs to have when it starts.

As your devices send messages to IoT Hub, you can route those messages to Azure Storage, Event Hub, and various other endpoints. You can choose the type of messages you want to route, and you can also write a query to filter which messages are routed. In Figure 3-3, we have configured a route that sends messages to Azure Blob Storage. You can see in the query that we are only going to route those messages that come from a device with a device twin containing the tag for our `researchInjectibles` department.

Dashboard > ContosoPharmHub - Message routing > Add a route

Add a route ✕

* Name ❶

Event_Hub ✓

* Endpoint ❶

ioTBlob ∨ ＋ Add

* Data source ❶

Device Telemetry Messages ∨

* Enable route ❶

Enable | Disable

Create a query to filter messages before data is routed to an endpoint. Learn more

Routing query ❶

```
1    $twin.tags.deploymentLocation.department = "researchInjectibles"
```

FIGURE 3-3 Adding a message route in IoT Hub

There are two pricing tiers for IoT Hub: Basic and Standard. Each tier offers multiple editions that offer pricing based on the number of messages per day for each IoT Hub unit. When you scale an IoT Hub, you add additional units. This adds the ability to handle more messages at an increased price. Table 3-1 shows the editions and pricing for the Basic tier. Table 3-2 shows editions and pricing for the Standard tier.

EXAM TIP

Pricing for scale in IoT Hub is pretty clear. Most enterprises will choose the Standard tier because of the additional functionality available in that tier. They will then choose an edition that meets their minimal needs for messages. When they need additional messages during spikes, they'll scale to more IoT Hub units.

For example, assume that ContosoPharm message needs are approximately 5,000,000 per day. They would choose the S2 pricing tier and pay $250 US per month if they are running one IoT Hub unit in the North America geography. If the number of messages increases to 8,000,000 (either because of configuration changes or the addition of additional IoT devices), they would likely choose to scale to two IoT Hub units. Doing so would give them 12,000,000 messages per day at a cost of $500 US per month.

TABLE 3-1 IoT Hub Basic tier pricing

Edition	Monthly Price per IoT Hub Unit	Messages per day per IoT Hub Unit
B1	$10 US	400,000
B2	$50 US	6,000,000
B3	$500 US	300,000,000

TABLE 3-2 IoT Hub Standard tier pricing

Edition	Monthly Price per IoT Hub Unit	Messages per day per IoT Hub Unit
Free	Free	8,000
S1	$25 US	400,000
S2	$250 US	6,000,000
S3	$2,500 US	300,000,000

> *NOTE* **CHANGING PRICING TIER**
>
> You cannot change to a lower pricing tier after you create your IoT Hub. If you create your IoT Hub in the Standard tier, you cannot change it to the Basic tier. If you create an IoT Hub in the Standard tier using the S1, S2, or S3 edition, you cannot change it to the free edition.

It's also important to note that the following features are only available in the Standard tier:

- Device Streams for streaming messages in near real-time
- Cloud-to-device messaging
- Device management, device twin, and module twin
- IoT Edge for handling IoT Devices at the edge of the network where they reside

If you use the Device Provisioning Service, there's a charge of $0.123 US for every 1,000 operations.

IoT Central

IoT Hub is a great way to manage and provision devices, and it provides a robust means of dealing with messages. You can even use Azure Stream Analytics to route messages to Power BI for a near real-time dashboard of device messages, but doing that requires a bit of complex configuration. If you're looking for a first-class experience in monitoring IoT devices without having to do complex configuration, IoT Central is a good choice.

IoT Central is a SaaS offering for IoT devices. Unlike IoT Hub, you don't have to create any Azure resources to use IoT Central. Instead, you browse to *https://apps.azureiotcentral.com* and create your app within the web browser interface, as shown in Figure 3-4.

FIGURE 3-4 Azure IoT Central homepage

To create an IoT app, click the plus sign above **My Apps**. This opens the **Create Application** screen shown in Figure 3-5.

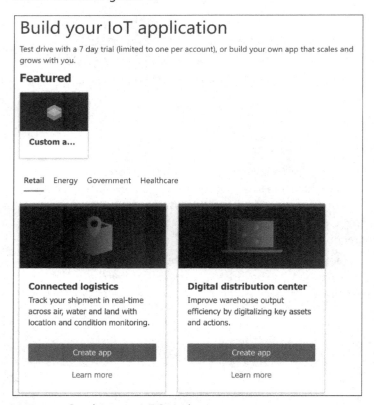

FIGURE 3-5 Creating a new IoT Central app

You have the choice of choosing a template or creating a custom app. For convenience, templates are categorized by Retail, Energy, Government, and Healthcare.

After you select your template, you'll see the New Application screen shown in Figure 3-6. This is where you'll specify the name for your app and the URL. You can use the default names or specify your own, but it's recommended to use your own so you can easily identify your app. Also, once your app has been created, you access it directly by using the URL you specify, so you might want that to be descriptive as well.

Next, you choose your pricing plan. If you're using Pay-As-You-Go, you'll need to specify details about your Azure subscription. If you choose the Free plan, you'll just need to enter some contact information. Scroll to the bottom of the screen and click **Create** to finish the creation of your app.

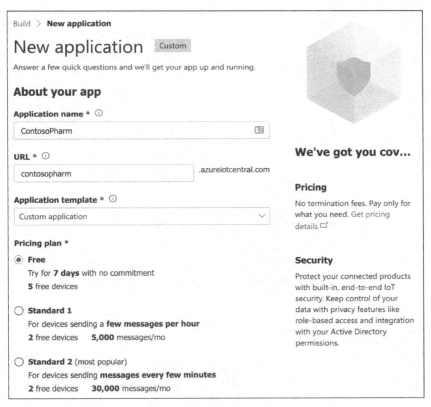

FIGURE 3-6 Specifying an app name, URL, and pricing plan

In Figure 3-4, you can see that we've already created an app called ContosoPharm. When you click that app, you see a menu on the left side of the page, and if you click **Devices**, you can see any devices added, as shown in Figure 3-7.

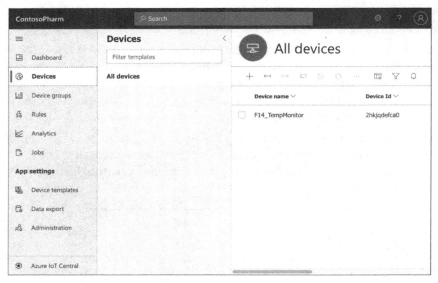

FIGURE 3-7 An IoT device in IoT Central

To add a new device, click the plus sign in the menu bar above your device list to access the **Create New Device** screen shown in Figure 3-8. You have the option of adding a real device if you have one, but you can also add a simulated device. Adding simulated devices is a good way to get everything set up the way you want them in IoT Central, and then you can add real devices at a later time.

> *NOTE* **SIMULATED DEVICES IS AN IOT CENTRAL-ONLY FEATURE**
> The ability to create a simulated device is specific to IoT Central. IoT Hub doesn't offer this capability. If you want to add a simulated device that is based on a real-world device, you can choose a device template from your IoT Central's home page.

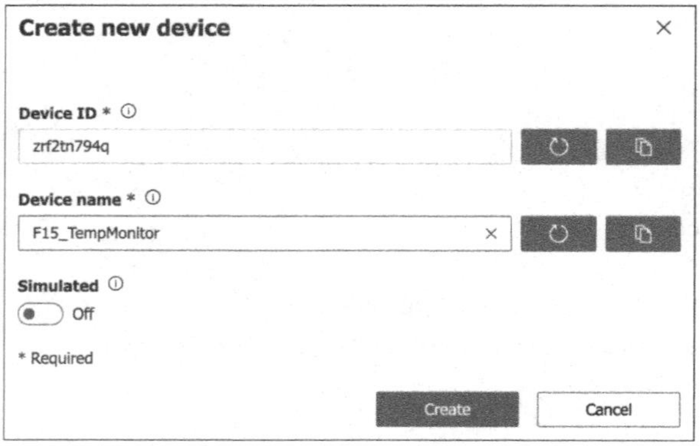

Create new device ✕

Device ID * ⓘ

zrf2tn794q

Device name * ⓘ

F15_TempMonitor

Simulated ⓘ

◉ Off

* Required

Create | Cancel

FIGURE 3-8 Adding a device in IoT Central

Every page within your app can be edited directly in the browser. Figure 3-9 shows the home page for the IoT Central app. If you click the **Edit** button, you can remove tiles, add tiles, and edit information in tiles in a point-and-click interface right within your browser.

FIGURE 3-9 Editing a page in IoT Central

The reason we see an **Edit** button is because this user is set as the administrator of this application. IoT Central gives you control over who can do what using roles. There are three built-in roles to which you can assign a user.

- **Administrator** Users in this role have full access to the application and can edit pages and add new users.
- **Builder** Users in this role can edit pages, but they can't perform any administrative tasks, such as adding users, changing user roles, changing application settings, and so on.
- **Operator** Users in this role can use the application, but they can't edit any pages and they can't perform administrative tasks.

In some situations, these built-in roles might not offer the flexibility you need, so you can also create your own roles with the exact permissions you need.

To administer your application, click **Administration** on the menu on the left, as shown in Figure 3-10. You can then add and remove users, adjust user roles, change the application name or URL, add a custom image for your application, and so on. You can also copy or delete your application from this screen.

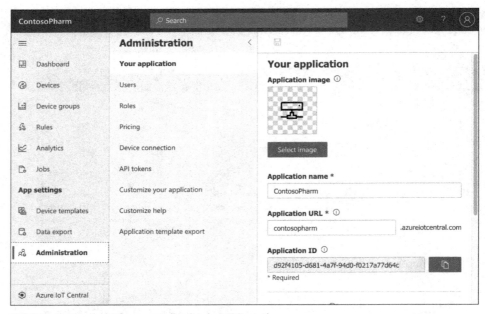

FIGURE 3-10 Administering an application in IoT Central

If you click a device, you can look at information coming from the device's sensors. In Figure 3-11, you can see the **Humidity** and **Temperature** sensors on the *F14_TempMonitor* device.

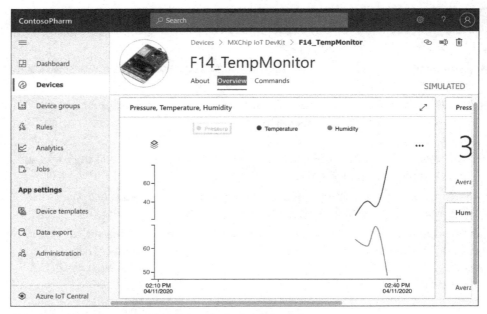

FIGURE 3-11 Reviewing sensor data from a device in IoT Central

IoT Central also allows you to easily configure rules that will monitor your devices and perform an action you choose when your rule is activated. In Figure 3-12, we are configuring a rule that will activate when the Humidity is above 60.

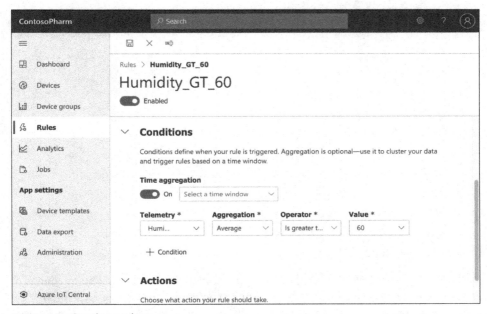

FIGURE 3-12 Creating a rule

When a rule is triggered, IoT Central can send an email to someone with details of what happened. You can also choose to trigger a webhook to call an Azure Function, run a workflow in an Azure Logic App, run a workflow in Microsoft Power Automate, or do something specific in your own app that exposes a webhook.

When you have a large number of devices, it's convenient to group devices into a device group so you can take action on many devices at a time. To create a device group, specify a condition that should be met for a device to be added to the group. In Figure 3-13, we're creating a device group for all devices that have *F14* in the name. If the name contains *F14*, the device is automatically added to the device group. Even when adding a new device later, it will be part of this device group if the name contains *F14*.

FIGURE 3-13 Creating a device group

Once you've created a device group, you can take action on the devices in it by creating a job. Click **Jobs** in the main menu of your application to configure your job. A job can modify properties, change settings, or send commands to devices. In Figure 3-14, we're creating a job that will turn on the LEDs for all devices in our device set.

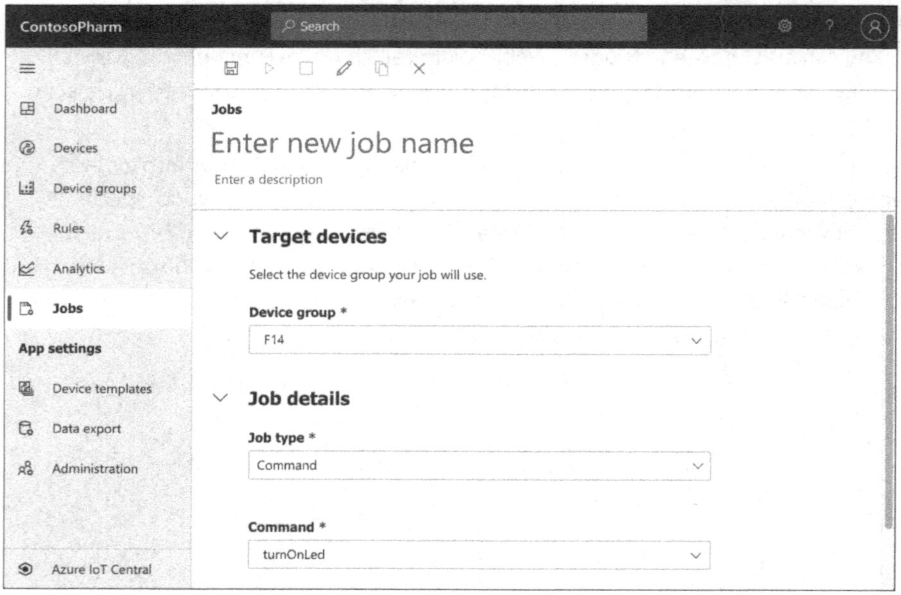

FIGURE 3-14 Creating a job

IoT Central also allows you to perform analytics on metrics from devices in a device set. For example, you can look at all devices that registered temperatures above a certain level. For even richer analytics of data, you can configure IoT Central to continuously export data from your devices to Azure Blob Storage, Azure Event Hubs, or Azure Service Bus.

Azure Sphere

Having your devices connected to the Internet certainly offers a lot of advantages. If you're at the store and you can't remember whether you need milk, your smart fridge can let you know. If you've just left for a trip and think you might have left the oven on, your smart oven can be turned off from your phone. You get the idea. In general, connectivity is a good thing, but it also comes with disadvantages, not the least of which is security. The last thing you want is a hacker to gain control of your Internet-connected door locks on your house!

IoT devices are like any other computing device in that they run software that's designed for a specific purpose. Any device that runs software is susceptible to software bugs, and IoT devices are no different. However, IoT device software is embedded on a chip, and that introduces unique challenges to fixing bugs and updating the software. When you add the fact that there's little to no standardization in the IoT device business, you end up with a possible security nightmare.

To address these security issues, Microsoft developed Azure Sphere. Azure Sphere is based on Microsoft's decades of experience and in-depth research that Microsoft conducted on securing devices.

> **MORE INFO**   **SEVEN PROPERTIES OF HIGHLY SECURED DEVICES**
>
> Microsoft wrote a white paper, "Seven Properties of Highly Secured Devices," which details the research on securing devices. You can read the white paper at *https://aka.ms/7properties*.

Azure Sphere is actually an entire ecosystem, and it starts with the chip, or the microprocessor unit (MCU). Microsoft has developed an Azure Sphere MCU that contains security components embedded in the chip. Third parties can use these MCUs to run code that is specific to their needs, and that code runs on the Azure Sphere operating system, which is a customized version of Linux developed for Azure Sphere.

In Azure, the Azure Sphere Security Service ensures that MCUs are secured, provides for the ability to update the embedded Azure Sphere OS and the applications running on MCUs, and enables reporting on crashes and other analytics. One of the enormous benefits of the Azure Sphere ecosystem is the capability to patch bugs in embedded chips that might create security concerns.

This ecosystem provides a secure environment for running embedded code, but it also enforces secure communication between devices. It's likely that your smart fridge can communicate with other smart devices in your home, and by ensuring strong authentication between these devices, Azure Sphere can help ensure a secure environment for all your smart devices.

As of this writing, there is only one Azure Sphere certified MCU available, but Microsoft expects that smart device manufacturers will continue to adopt Azure Sphere for their MCUs. To make that process easier, Azure Sphere development kits are available at a low price. The development kit includes hardware that is ready for Azure Sphere and an Azure Sphere software developer's kit (SDK) for Microsoft Visual Studio.

> **MORE INFO** **AZURE SPHERE DEVELOPER KITS**
>
> You can see all the Azure Sphere developer kits by browsing to
> *https://aka.ms/AzureSphereDevKitsAll.*

To take advantage of Azure Sphere, you purchase it from a Microsoft distributor. The distributor sells a package that includes an Azure Sphere certified MCU, a license for the Azure Sphere Security Service, and a license for the Azure Sphere OS. The current price for the MediaTek MT3620 AN (currently the only Azure Sphere certified MCU) is less than $8.65. Pricing varies based on how many MCUs you purchase, but the price will not exceed $8.65 per unit.

EXAM TIP

Pricing for Azure Sphere includes operating system and Azure Sphere Security Service updates through July of 2031.

Azure Synapse Analytics

Businesses collect tremendous amounts of data from many different sources. For example, Microsoft offers an SLA on Azure services that is about 99.9 percent or higher in terms of its availability. Microsoft doesn't put that number out there and then just cross their fingers and hope nothing goes wrong. They maintain enormous amounts of data on how the Azure infrastructure is operating, and they use that data to predict problems and react to them before they affect customers.

> **MORE INFO** **USING DATA**
>
> The enormous amount of data that businesses collect is often used for machine learning. You'll learn about machine learning later in this chapter.

Because of the sheer enormity of the Azure infrastructure, you can just imagine how much data is being generated for every single system in that infrastructure, and in order to meet SLAs, they must be able to reliably analyze that data in real time. How exactly do they do that? You can't really throw that amount of data at a VM or a pool of VMs without overloading the system to the point of failure.

The problem of actually doing anything with the vast data we collect is common across all businesses, and this is what we mean by *big data*. Big data means more data than you can analyze through conventional means within the desired timeframe. Analyzing big data requires a powerful system for storing data, the ability to query the data in multiple ways, enormous power to execute large queries, assurance that the data is secure, and much more. That's exactly what Azure Synapse analytics provides.

> *NOTE* **AZURE SYNAPSE**
>
> Azure Synapse is the next evolution of another Azure service called SQL Data Warehouse. While it's true to say that Azure Synapse is the replacement for SQL Data Warehouse, it's also important to note that Azure Synapse adds much more functionality.
>
> SQL Data Warehouse was focused primarily on storage of big data (called *warehousing*), but Azure Synapse provides that functionality in addition to powerful analytics features.

Azure Synapse runs in an Azure Synapse *cluster*. A cluster is a combination of four different components:

- Synapse SQL
- Apache Spark integration
- Data integration of Spark and Azure Data Lake Storage
- A web-based user interface called Azure Synapse Studio

Synapse SQL is the data warehousing portion of Azure Synapse. Using Synapse SQL, you can run powerful queries against your big data. These queries run on *compute nodes*, and multiple compute nodes run at the same time, which allow multiple queries to run in parallel. Each compute node also runs a component called the Data Movement Service (DMS) that moves data efficiently between compute nodes.

Queries are executed on compute nodes in order to separate the query work from data storage. This makes it possible to scale the number of compute nodes easily when more power is needed for your queries. This also allows you to pause the compute power you're using so that you only pay for storage when you don't need to run queries.

Many consumers of big data use a third-party big data processing engine called Apache Spark, and Azure Synapse tightly integrates with the Spark engine. Spark features are automatically incorporated into Azure Synapse when you create a cluster.

Azure Synapse integrates Apache Spark functionality with Azure Data Lake Storage. Azure Data Lake Storage is designed for storing large amounts of data that you'd like to analyze, but Data Lake Storage is designed for a wide array of data instead of relational data. In a data lake, data is stored in *containers*. Each container typically contains related data.

Azure Synapse makes it easy to analyze data and manage your data with a web-based portal called Azure Synapse Studio. Once you've created your Azure Synapse workspace, you simply click a button to launch Synapse Studio, and from there, you can easily manage and analyze your data.

HDInsight

HDInsight makes it possible to easily create and manage clusters of computers on a common framework designed to perform distributed processing of big data. Essentially, HDInsight is Microsoft's managed service that provides a cloud-based implementation of a popular data analytics platform called Hadoop. However, it also supports many other cluster types, as shown in Table 3-3.

TABLE 3-3 HDInsight supported cluster types

Cluster Type	Description
Hadoop	Large-scale data processing that can incorporate additional Hadoop components, such as Hive (for SQL-like queries), Pig (for using scripting languages), and Oozie (a workflow scheduling system)
HBase	Extremely fast and scalable NoSQL database
Storm	Fast and reliable processing of unbounded streams of data in real time
Spark	Extremely fast analytics using in-memory cache across multiple operations in parallel
Interactive Query	In-memory analytics using Hive and LLAP (processes that execute fragments of Hive queries)
R Server	Enterprise-level analytics using R, a language that's specialized for big data analytics
Kafka	Extremely fast processing of huge numbers of synchronous data streams, often from IoT devices.

Building your own cluster is time-consuming and often difficult unless you have previous experience. With HDInsight, Microsoft does all the heavy lifting on its own infrastructure. You benefit from a secure environment—one that is easily scalable to handle huge data processing tasks.

An HDInsight cluster performs analytics by breaking up large data blocks into segments that are then handed off to nodes within the cluster. The nodes then perform analytics on the data and reduce it down to a result set. All this work happens in parallel so that operations are completed dramatically faster than they would be otherwise. By adding additional nodes to a cluster, you can increase the power of your analytics and process more data even faster.

When you create an HDInsight cluster, you specify the type of cluster you want to create and give your cluster a name as shown in Figure 3-15. You will also specify a username and password for accessing the cluster and an SSH user for secure remote access.

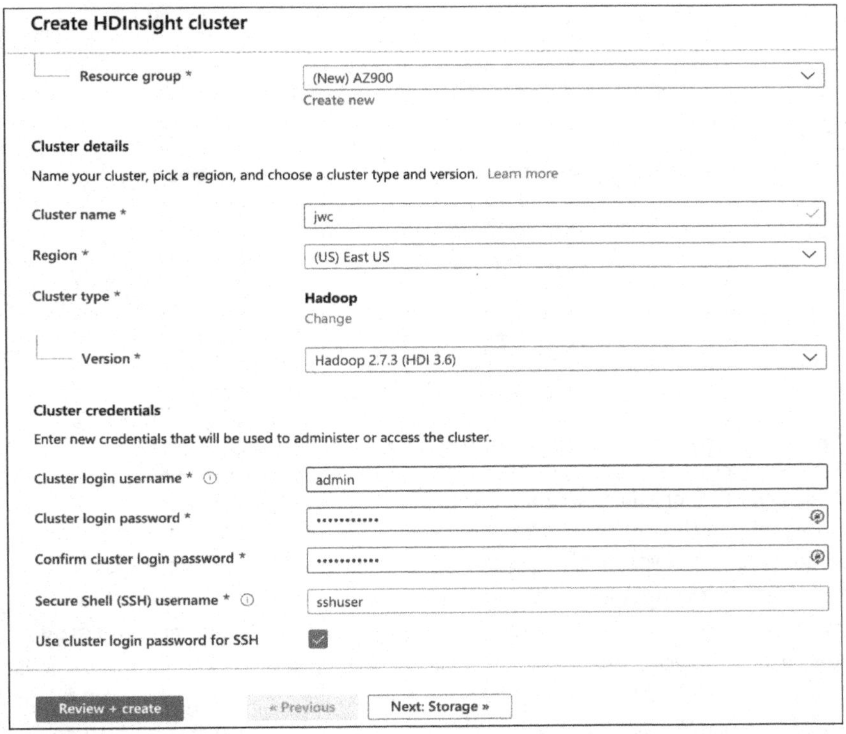

FIGURE 3-15 Creating an HDInsight Hadoop cluster

After you click the **Next: Storage button**, you configure the storage account and Data Lake Storage access if desired. Notice in Figure 3-16 that you only see Data Lake Storage Gen1. To use Data Lake Storage Gen2, you must first create a Data Lake Storage Gen2 account and make a few configuration changes, as documented at *http://bit.ly/az900-datalakegen2*.

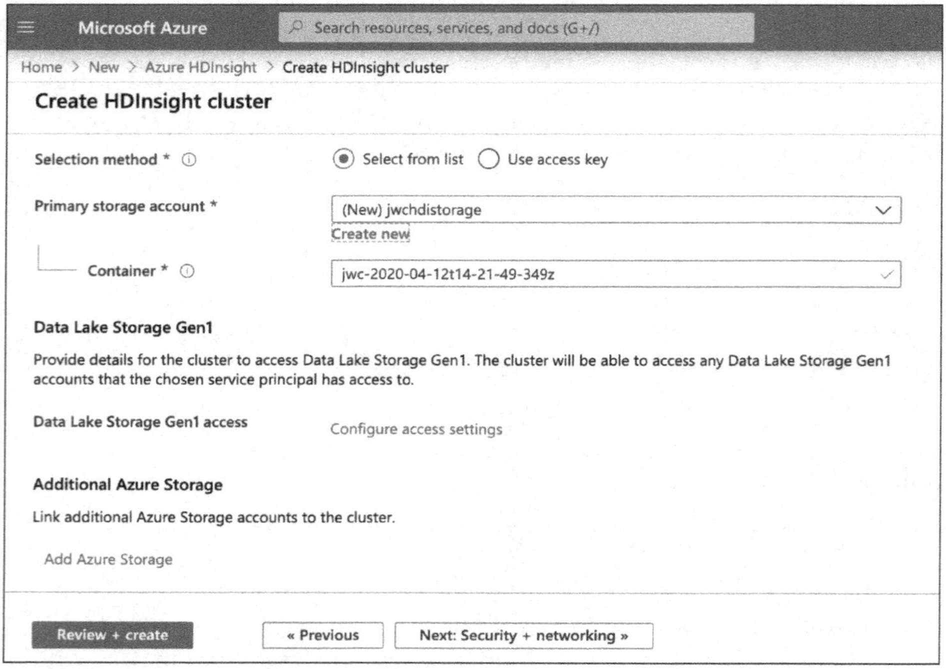

FIGURE 3-16 Configuring an HDInsight cluster's storage account

Once you start the creation of your Hadoop cluster, it might take up to 20 minutes to complete, depending on your configuration. Once your cluster is ready, you can start the analysis of data by writing queries against it. Even if your queries are analyzing millions of rows, HD Insight can handle it, and if you need more processing power, you can add additional nodes as needed.

HD Insight clusters are billed on a per hour basis, and you pay more per hour based on how powerful the machines are in your cluster. See *https://azure.microsoft.com/pricing/details/hdinsight/* for full pricing details.

Azure Databricks

Data that gets stored in a data warehouse or data lake is typically raw data that is often unstructured and difficult to consume. Also, you might need data that comes from multiple sources, some of which might even be outside of Azure. Azure Databricks is an ideal solution for accumulating data and for forming the data (called *data modeling*) so that it's optimal for machine learning models.

> **MORE INFO   MACHINE-LEARNING MODELS**
>
> You'll learn about machine learning models in the next section of this chapter.

Figure 3-17 shows a new instance of an Azure Databricks resource. All your interactivity with Databricks is via the Databricks workspace, which is a web-based portal for interacting with your data. To access the workspace, click the **Launch Workspace** button shown in Figure 3-17.

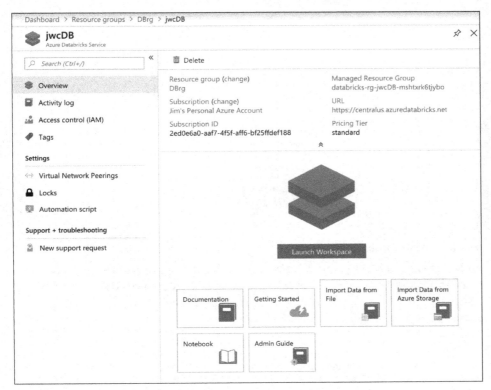

FIGURE 3-17 An instance of Azure Databricks in the Azure portal

> **MORE INFO** **DATABRICKS**
>
> Databricks is actually the name of a company that originally developed Apache Spark. It now operates a data analytics platform called Databricks. You might be tempted to think of Azure Databricks as the Databricks platform running as a service in Azure, but it's much more than that. In fact, Microsoft natively built the Databricks Runtime to run in Azure, and Azure Databricks provides many more unique features outside the Databricks platform developed by Databricks.

When you click **Launch Workspace**, you're taken to the Databricks workspace. Azure will automatically log you in when you do this using your Azure account. In this example, the Databricks instance is empty at this point. Along the left side of the page (as shown in Figure 3-18) are links to access all the Databricks entities, such as workspaces, tables, and jobs. There's also a **Common Tasks** section, which allows you to access these entities; also, you can create new notebooks, which is detailed later in this chapter.

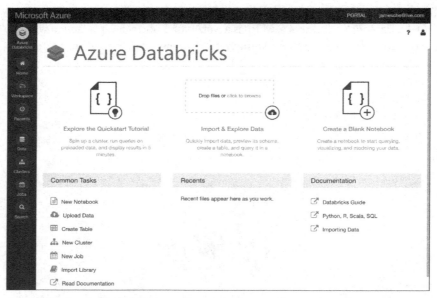

FIGURE 3-18 The Azure Databricks workspace

Now let's create a cluster. Databricks does all its work using clusters, which are the compute resources. To create a cluster, you can click **New Cluster** under **Common Tasks**. You'll now see the **Create Cluster** screen shown in Figure 3-19, where the new cluster has been named `jcCluster` and all other options are set to their defaults.

FIGURE 3-19 Creating a Databricks cluster

Next, we'll create a notebook. Notebooks are a powerful way to present and interact with related data. Each notebook contains data as well as visualizations and documentation to help us understand the data. Once your data is in your notebook, you can run commands against machine learning frameworks in order to build your machine learning model right inside your notebook.

Clicking the **Azure Databricks** button in the menu on the left (shown in Figure 3-18) allows you to then click **New Notebook** to create a notebook. In Figure 3-20, we've created a new notebook that uses SQL as the primary language. Databricks assume that the code written in this notebook will be SQL code unless specified. You can also choose to specify Python, Scala, or R as the language.

> **MORE INFO**   **PROGRAMMING LANGUAGES**
>
> Python, Scala, and R are programming languages that are commonly used to program machine learning models.

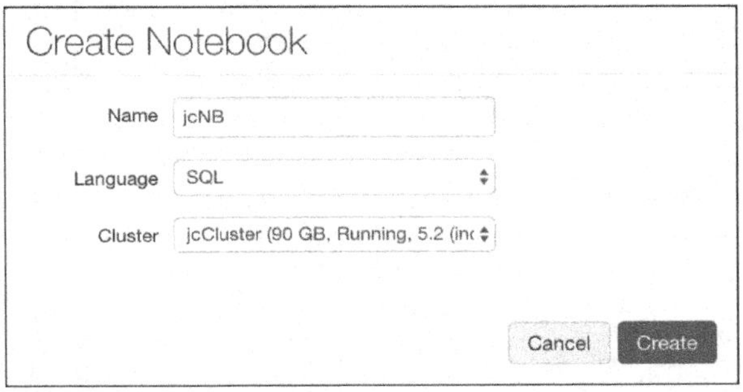

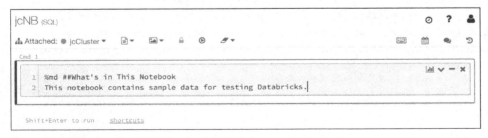

FIGURE 3-20 Creating a notebook

After you create a new notebook, you'll see an empty notebook with one cell. Inside that cell, you can enter any data that you wish. For example, you might want to have some documentation that defines what this notebook contains. Documentation in notebooks is entered using *Markdown*, a language that's well-suited to writing documentation. Figure 3-21 shows the new notebook with some Markdown that documents what's in the notebook. Notice that the Markdown starts with *%md*. This tells Databricks how the content that follows is in Markdown and not in the primary language of SQL.

FIGURE 3-21 Documenting a notebook using Markdown

If you click outside this cell, the markdown code will be rendered in HTML format. In order to add some data to this notebook, you need to create a new cell by pressing **B** on your keyboard or by hovering over the existing cell and clicking the + button to add a new cell.

NOTE **KEYBOARD SHORTCUTS**

Keyboard shortcuts are, by far, the fastest way of working in Databricks. You can find the entire list of keyboard shortcuts by clicking the Shortcuts link shown in Figure 3-21.

After pressing **B** on your keyboard, a new cell is inserted at the end of your notebook. You can enter some SQL code in this cell in order to populate a table with some data, as shown in Figure 3-22. (This code was taken from the Databricks quick start tutorial at *https://docs.azuredatabricks.net/getting-started/index.html*.) After entering your code, you can run it by clicking the **Run** button.

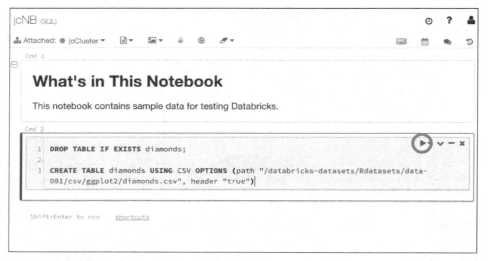

FIGURE 3-22 Adding code and running a command

MORE INFO **WHERE DATA COMES FROM**

Notice that the path entered in Figure 3-22 for the data starts with */databricks-datasets*. When creating a cluster, you gain access to a collection of datasets called Azure Databricks Datasets. Included in these datasets is some sample data in comma-separated values format, and the specified path points to that data. When this command runs, it pulls that data into your notebook.

You can run a query against the data that was added using the command shown in Figure 3-22 by writing a SQL query in a new cell. Figure 3-23 shows the results of a query against the data.

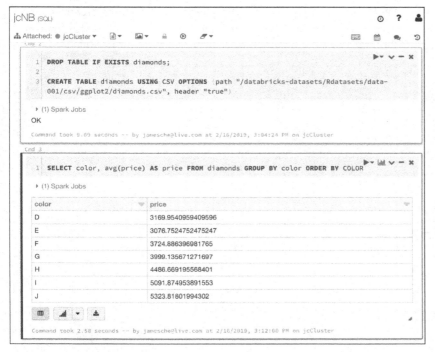

FIGURE 3-23 Querying the data

When you run commands in a cell, Databricks creates a job that runs on the compute resources you allocated to your cluster. Databricks uses a serverless model of computing. That means that when you're not running any jobs, you don't have any VMs or compute resources assigned to you. When you run a job, Azure will allocate VMs to your cluster temporarily in order to process that job. Once the job is complete, it releases those resources.

This example is quite simple, but how does all this relate to machine learning? Azure Databricks includes the Databricks Runtime for Machine Learning (Databricks Runtime ML) so that you can use data in Databricks for training machine learning algorithms. The Databricks Runtime ML includes several popular libraries for machine learning, including: Keras, PyTorch, TensorFlow, and XGBoost. It also makes it possible to use Horovod for distributed deep-learning algorithms. You can use these components without using Databricks Runtime ML. They're open source and freely available, but the Databricks Runtime ML saves you from the hassle of learning how to install and configure them.

EXAM TIP

A discussion of how you program machine learning models is far outside of the scope of the AZ-900 exam, and we won't discuss it here. The important point to remember is that Databricks works with third-party machine learning frameworks to allow you to build machine learning models.

To use the Databricks Runtime ML, you'll need to either specify it when you create your cluster or edit your existing cluster to use it. You do that by choosing one of the ML runtimes, as shown in Figure 3-24.

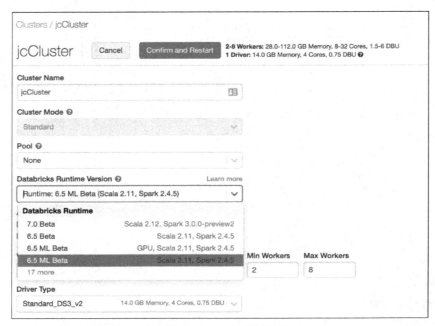

FIGURE 3-24 Databricks Runtime ML in cluster configuration

You're not limited to the libraries included with Databricks Runtime ML. You can configure almost any third-party ML tool in Azure Databricks, and Microsoft provides some pointers on doing that in their documentation located at *https://bit.ly/az900-thirdpartyml*.

EXAM TIP

You might have noticed several references to Spark in Databricks. That's because Databricks is based on Apache Spark.

Once you've built your machine learning model in Databricks, you can export it for use in an external machine learning system. This process is referred to as *productionalizing* the machine-learning pipeline, and Databricks allows you to productionalize using two different methods: MLeap and Databricks ML Model Export.

MLeap is a system that can execute a machine learning model and make predictions based on that model. Databricks allows you to export your model into what's called an MLeap bundle. You can then use that bundle in MLeap to run your model against new data.

Databricks ML Model Export is designed to export your machine learning models and pipeline so that they can be used in other machine learning platforms. It's specifically designed to export Apache Spark-based machine learning models and pipelines.

Azure Machine Learning

Azure Machine Learning is a service that lets you delve into the world of *artificial intelligence*, or *AI*. In order to really grasp Azure Machine Learning, you first need to have a knowledge foundation of AI and machine learning.

Artificial intelligence

Before we go too far into AI, let's first come to an agreement on what we mean by AI. When many people think about computer AI, the image that comes to mind is a human-killing android or some other hostile technology obsessed with ridding the world of humans. You'll be relieved to know that's actually not what AI means in this context.

The AI of today is called Artificial Narrow Intelligence (or sometimes weak AI), and it refers to an AI that is capable of performing one specific task much more efficiently than a human can perform that same task. All the AI that we've developed so far is weak AI. On the other end of the AI spectrum is Artificial General Intelligence, or strong AI. This is the type of AI you see depicted in movies and science fiction books, and we don't currently have this kind of capability.

In many ways, it's a bit misleading to call existing AI technology weak. If you place it in the context of the imaginary strong AI, it certainly has limited capabilities, but weak AI can do extraordinary things, and you almost certainly benefit from its capabilities every day. For example, if you speak to your phone or your smart speaker and it understands what you've said, you've benefitted from AI.

In the 1973 edition of *Profiles of the Future*, the famous science fiction writer Sir Arthur C. Clarke said, "Any sufficiently advanced technology is indistinguishable from magic." While AI was not yet a thing when Clarke made this assertion, the capabilities that AI make possible are certainly applicable, but AI isn't magic. AI is actually mathematics, and as anyone familiar with computers will tell you, computers are very good at math.

In order to develop AI capabilities, computer engineers set out to give computers the ability to "learn" in the same way that the human brain learns. Our brains are made up of neurons and synapses. Each neuron communicates with all the other neurons in the brain, and together, they form what's known as a neural network. While each neuron on its own can't do much, the entire network is capable of extraordinary things.

AI works by creating a digital neural network. Each part of that neural network can communicate and share information with every other part of the network. Just like our brains, a computer neural network takes input, processes it, and provides output. AI can use many methods for processing the input, and each method is a subset of AI. The two most common are natural language understanding and machine learning.

Natural language understanding is AI that is designed to understand human speech. If we were to try to program a computer to understand the spoken word by traditional computing means, it would take an army of programmers decades to come anywhere close to usable recognition. Not only would they have to account for accents and vocabulary differences that occur in different geographic regions, but they'd have to account for the fact that individuals often pronounce words differently even in the same regions. People also have difference speech cadences, and that causes some words to run together. The computer has to know how to distinguish individual words when that might not be easy to do. In addition to all this complexity, the computer must account for the fact that language is an ever-changing thing.

> **MORE INFO   COGNITIVE SERVICES**
>
> Azure offers numerous options for natural language understanding. These services are included in Cognitive Services, and they are covered in the next section.

Given this complexity, how did Amazon ever develop the Echo? How does Siri ever understand what you're saying? How does Cortana know to crack a clever joke when we ask her about Siri? The answer in all these cases is AI. We have millions of hours of audio recordings, and we have millions more hours in videos that include audio. There's so much data available that no human being could ever process all of it, but a computer processes data much more quickly. Not only does it have more analytical pathways than humans do, but it also processes information much more quickly.

> **MORE INFO   COMPUTERS ARE FAST**
>
> When I say that computers can process information more quickly than humans, I really mean it! Information in a human brain travels between neurons at a speed that's just under the speed of sound. While that's plenty fast for our needs, it's nothing compared to computers. The information in an AI neural network travels at the speed of light, and that's what enables computers to process enormous amounts of data. In fact, a computer's AI system can process 20,000 years of human-level learning in just one week.

If we feed all those recordings into a natural language understanding engine, it has plenty of examples in order to determine what words we're speaking when we say something to a smart speaker or smart phone, and determining the meaning of these words is simply pattern recognition. As Apple, Amazon, and Microsoft were working on this technology, they fine-tuned it by getting your feedback. Sometimes, they might actually ask you whether they got it right, and other times, they might assume they got something wrong if you just bowed out of the conversation early. Over time, the system gets better and better as it gets more data.

Machine learning can be used in many applications. One of the common uses of machine learning is image recognition. As it turns out, AI neural networks are particularly good at recognizing patterns in images, and just like audio, we have an enormous amount of data to work with.

We're likely all aware that satellites have been photographing the surface of the earth for quite some time. We have detailed imagery from just about every square inch of our planet, and those images are valuable in many ways. For example, scientists who are working on conservation efforts benefit by knowing how our planet is changing over time. Forest engineers need to know about the health of our forests. Wildlife conservationists need information to focus efforts on where animals are most at risk. By applying an ML model to all these images, Microsoft can serve all these needs.

> **MORE INFO**   **MICROSOFT AI FOR EARTH**
>
> For more information on all the ways Microsoft is using AI for conservation and earth sciences, see *http://aka.ms/aiforearth*.

Image-analyzing AI isn't limited to the planetary scale. It's also helpful when we want to search through our own pictures. Perhaps you want to find all the pictures you've taken of a particular person, or maybe you're interested in finding all your pictures of flowers. Your phone can likely do this kind of thing, and it does it by using AI and ML. In fact, Google Photos is even able to identify specific people in photos when the time between two photos is decades apart. All this uses ML.

ML uses a learning algorithm that is the basis for the AI. Once the algorithm is developed, you feed test data to it and examine the result. Based upon that result, you might determine that you need to tweak the algorithm. Once the algorithm is suitable to your task, you typically deploy it to an environment where it has a vast array of compute resources that you can allocate to it. You can then feed huge amounts of data to it for processing. As the algorithm deals with more data, it can improve itself by recognizing patterns.

Typically, when you're testing an ML model, you set up a scenario where only a portion of your complete dataset is sent to your model for training. Once your model is trained, you send the rest of your data through your model in order to score the results. Because you're dealing with a historical dataset, you already know that which your model is attempting to figure out, so you can accurately determine the accuracy of your model. Once you have achieved the desired accuracy of your model, you can deploy it and begin using it against production data.

Even with careful modeling and scoring, ML algorithms can make mistakes. In a paper on ML published in 2016, Marco Ribeiro, Sameer Singh, and Carlos Guestrin wrote about an ML experiment that was designed to look at pictures and differentiate between dogs and wolves. As it turns out, the algorithm was making plenty of mistakes, but the humans couldn't figure out why.

When they tested the ML algorithm to determine how it was making these incorrect decisions, they found that the algorithm had come to the conclusion that pictures with wolves in them had a snowy background and pictures with dogs had grass in the background. Therefore, every picture with a dog-like creature that was taken on a snowy background was immediately classified (sometimes incorrectly) as a wolf.

Now that you have some foundational knowledge, you're in a better position to understand what Azure offers with Azure Machine Learning.

Machine learning in Azure

Azure Machine Learning is designed to make ML approachable to just about anyone. It offers SDKs for both Python and R, and it also offers a drag-and-drop environment and an automated mode for more easily creating and training ML models in a visual way.

Azure Machine Learning is available in two editions; Basic and Enterprise. The Basic edition offers only access to ML SDKs and notebooks. The Enterprise edition offers the features of the Basic edition, but it adds many additional features, including the visual designers.

To get started with Azure Machine Learning, you first create an Azure Machine Learning workspace. Once you've created your workspace, you can begin to build models, train models, run experiments, and so on. As you can see in Figure 3-25, you're directed to the Azure Machine Learning studio for most operations.

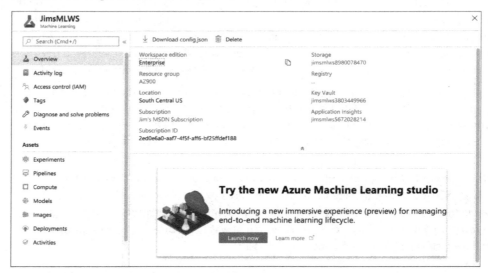

FIGURE 3-25 An Azure Machine Learning workspace

Clicking the Launch Now button shown in Figure 3-25 launches the studio where you can build your ML models. As shown in Figure 3-26, you can also load some samples into the studio so that you can experiment with Azure Machine Learning.

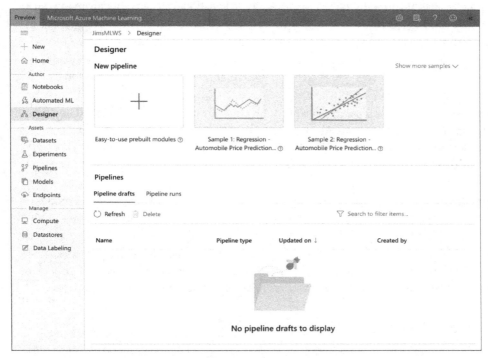

FIGURE 3-26 Azure Machine Learning studio showing the Designer page

Azure Machine Learning is priced based upon your usage. You're billed for a VM where your Azure Machine Learning assets run. You are also charged a machine learning surcharge and a small amount per hour for usage. If you want to save money, you can choose to reserve your usage for one year at a reduced cost or three years at a higher cost reduction.

Cognitive Services

Microsoft offers numerous application programming interfaces (APIs) that can help you to quickly develop machine learning solutions. These offerings allow you to fast-track your ML capabilities by taking advantage of work Microsoft has done to support its own services like Bing, Microsoft 365, and more. You can think of Cognitive Services as SaaS ML models that you can use directly in your ML solutions without the expense of developing your own.

> **MORE INFO COGNITIVE SERVICES ARE MANY**
>
> Microsoft offers many APIs in Cognitive Services, and the number is constantly growing. We'll cover some of them here, but there are too many to cover them all in this book. If you want to read about all them, you can at *https://bit.ly/az900-cognitiveapis*.

Cognitive Services includes an API called Computer Vision that makes it easy to build an ML engine that can extract information from images. Computer Vision can do things like recognize objects or recognize a scene, but it can also recognize inappropriate content so you can moderate images. If you want to see Computer Vision in action, you can enter an image URL or upload your own image for analysis at *https://bit.ly/az900-computervision*.

Along those same lines, the Video Indexer API can analyze video content and extract information from that content. You can easily add closed captioning in multiple languages, recognize people and objects, and search for videos that contain specific words, people, or even emotions.

Numerous speech APIs are also available, from Speech Translation, which offers language translation in real-time to Speaker Recognition, an API that can analyze speech and identify the speaker. Language APIs offer the ability to understand typed commands (useful for creating something like an automated chat agent) or Text Analytics to understand user sentiment in text.

Cognitive Services also provides decision APIs that allow you to do things such as moderate content in images, text, or video. You can also offer users a personalized user experience using the Personalizer API.

Pricing for Azure Cognitive Services is transactional. That means that you pay a small amount for transactions that you process through the service. For a full overview of Cognitive Services pricing, visit *https://azure.microsoft.com/en-us/pricing/details/cognitive-services/*.

Azure Bot Service

One of the common use cases for Cognitive Services is to build AI conversational experiences. These experiences are common throughout the Internet. In fact, most companies that offer some type of chat interaction almost always start you off with an automated agent. Cognitive Services can help to achieve a quality experience in those situations.

To make it even easier to build powerful AI-driven interaction, Microsoft offers Azure Bot Service. Azure Bot Service is a PaaS offering that runs on Azure App Service. That means that it inherits all the features of App Service such as easy scaling and simple configuration.

You create a Bot Service using the Web App Bot template in the Azure portal. As shown in Figure 3-27, you can choose between C# and Node.js for your SDK language, and you can choose between different bot templates for your specific needs.

Once you've created your Bot Service, you have the option of downloading the code so you can customize it, as shown in Figure 3-28. In fact, the Azure portal will walk you through everything you need to do in order to get started with your bot. This includes editing the source code, building the source code, viewing analytics, and so forth. All these tasks are part of the *Bot Framework* that Microsoft developed to streamline the creation of bots.

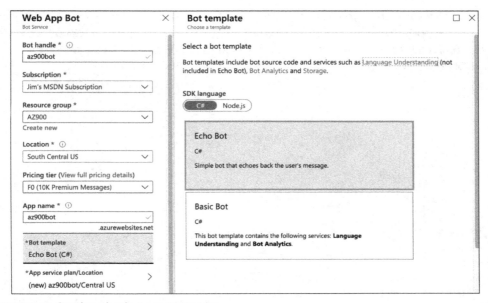

FIGURE 3-27 Creating a bot in Azure Bot Service

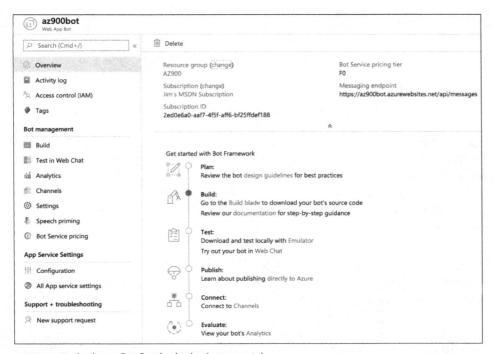

FIGURE 3-28 An Azure Bot Service in the Azure portal

As you're developing your bot, you can use the **Test In Web Chat** menu item on the left side in the portal (shown in Figure 3-28) to test how things are going. After clicking that, you'll be prompted for the type of thing you can say to the bot. In Figure 3-29, you can see the interaction available from the Basic Bot template provided by Microsoft.

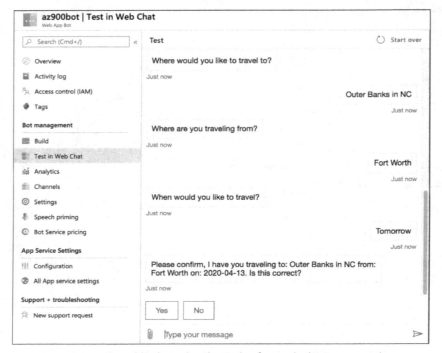

FIGURE 3-29 Interacting with a bot using the testing feature in the Azure portal

Azure Bot Service can be connected to many popular services such as Slack, Facebook Messenger, Microsoft Teams, and more. Each of these is considered a *channel* within the Bot Service, and the channels that Microsoft provides are called *standard channels*. However, you can also use what Microsoft calls *Direct Line* to connect your bot to your own application or website. Direct Line is considered a *premium channel*, and it will cost a small amount for the messages it uses.

EXAM TIP

Because Bot Service runs on Azure App Service, you are also charged for an App Service plan when you create a bot using Bot Service.

Serverless computing

As you've already learned, one of the great advantages of moving to the cloud is that you can take advantage of the large amounts of infrastructure in which cloud providers have invested.

You can create VMs in the cloud and pay for them only when they're running. Sometimes, you just need to "borrow" a computer in order to run a computation or perform a quick task. In those situations, a serverless environment is ideal. In a serverless situation, you pay only when your code is running on a VM. When your code's not running, you don't pay anything.

The concept of serverless computing came about because cloud providers had unused VMs in their data centers and they wanted to monetize them. All cloud providers need surplus capacity so they can meet the needs of customers, but when VMs are sitting there waiting for a customer who might want to use them, it means lost revenue for the cloud provider. To solve that problem, cloud providers created consumption-based plans that allow you to run your code on these surplus VMs, and you pay only for your use while your code is running.

EXAM TIP

It's important to understand that "serverless" doesn't mean that no VMs are involved. It simply means that the VM that's running your code isn't explicitly allocated to you. Your code is moved to the VM, it's executed, and then it's moved off.

Because your serverless code is running on surplus capacity, cloud providers usually offer steep discounts on consumption-based plans. In fact, for small workloads, you might not pay anything at all.

Cognitive Services is an example of a serverless service, but Azure has many other serverless services, many of which don't fit into the categories we've already discussed. They are Azure Functions for serverless compute, Azure Logic Apps for serverless workflows, and Azure Event Grid for serverless event routing.

Azure Functions

Azure Functions is the compute component of Azure's serverless offerings. That means that you can use Functions to write code without having to worry about deploying that code or creating VMs to run your code. Apps that use Azure Functions are often referred to as *Function Apps*.

MORE INFO   **FUNCTION APPS USE APP SERVICE**

Function Apps are serverless, but under the hood, they run on Azure App Service. In fact, you can choose to create your Function App in an App Service plan, but if you do, you won't benefit from the consumption model of paying only when your code runs.

Functions can be created in many different ways. You can create a Function App using:

- Microsoft Visual Studio
- Microsoft Visual Studio Code
- Maven for Java Function Apps
- Python command line for Python Function Apps

- Azure command line interface (CLI) on Windows or Linux
- The Azure portal

Assuming you aren't creating your Function App using a method specific for a particular language, you can choose between .NET Core, Node.js, Python, Java, or PowerShell Core if you're using the Code option. You also have the option to create your Function App using a Docker container on a Linux VM.

In Figure 3-30, we're creating a Function App in the Azure portal, and we've selected .NET Core as the Function App runtime so that we can use the C# language to write functions.

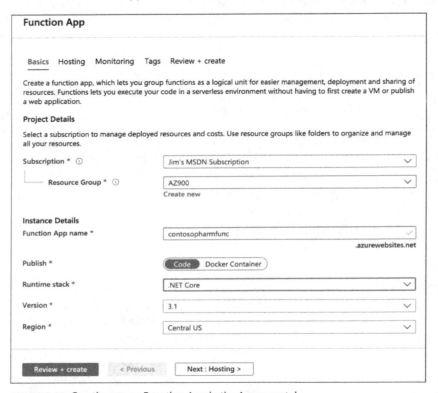

FIGURE 3-30 Creating a new Function App in the Azure portal

After you select your runtime stack and version, you can configure how your Function App is hosted. You can choose between Linux and Windows as your operating system, although some runtime stack selections are valid only for one of the two. You can also choose to run in a serverless plan (which is the default) or run inside of an App Service plan. In Figure 3-31, the Function App is being configured to run on Windows under the Consumption (Serverless) plan type.

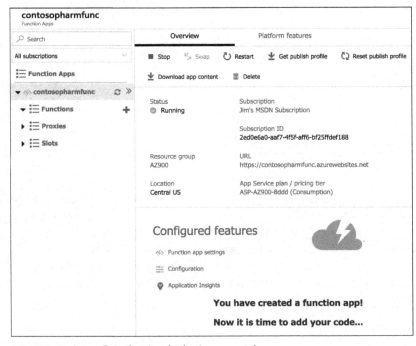

FIGURE 3-31 Configuring hosting options for a Function App

Once your Function App is ready, you can open it in the portal to begin creating functions. Figure 3-32 shows the new Function App in the Azure portal.

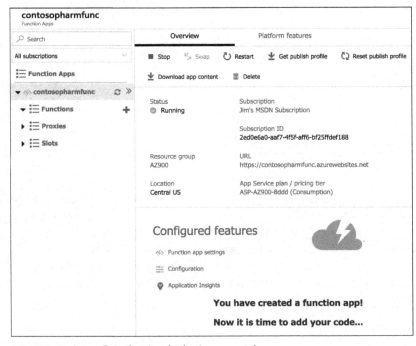

FIGURE 3-32 A new Function App in the Azure portal

From here, you can create a new function, proxy, or slot. A function is code that runs when something triggers it. (We'll look at triggers soon.) A proxy allows you to configure multiple endpoints for your Function App but expose them all via a single URL. Slots allow you to create a copy of your Function App that isn't public facing. You can write code and test this copy, and when you are satisfied that it's ready for production, you can swap it over to production with the click of a button. In App Service, this feature is called Deployment Slots.

If you click **Function App Settings** under **Configured Features** (shown in Figure 3-32), we can change some settings for the Function App, as shown in Figure 3-33.

FIGURE 3-33 Function App settings

From this screen, you can configure a daily quota for your Function App. Once you reach the quota, Azure will stop the Function App until the next day. You can also change the Function App runtime version. This is the runtime version of Azure Functions, and while it's generally advised to use the latest version, if your functions were written in an earlier version, you won't be able to upgrade them by simply changing the version here. Changing major versions can cause your app to break, so Microsoft will prevent you from changing the version if you have existing functions in your Function App.

You can also change your Function App to read-only mode to prevent any changes to it. This is helpful if you have multiple developers writing code for your app and you don't want someone changing something without your knowledge. Finally, you can view, renew, revoke, and add new host keys. A host key is used to control access to your functions. When you create a function, you can specify whether anyone can use it or whether a key is required.

EXAM TIP

Although a key can help protect your functions, they're not designed to offer complete security of Function Apps. If you want to protect your Function App from unauthorized use, you should use authentication features available in App Service to require authentication. You can also use Microsoft API Management to add security requirements to your Function App.

If you click **Configuration** (shown in Figure 3-32), you can configure the settings for the Function App. These are settings specific to App Service. Figure 3-34 shows some of these settings, including whether the app runs in 32-bit or 64-bit, the HTTP version, how you can access your files using FTP, and more.

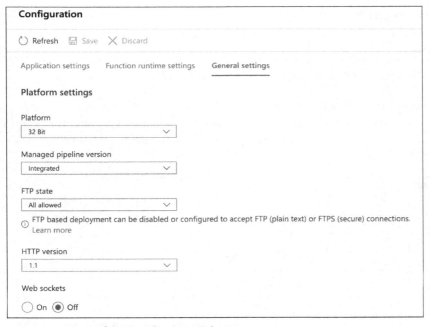

FIGURE 3-34 Some of the Function App settings

Finally, if you click the **Platform Features** tab shown in Figure 3-32, you can see all the features available to you in the App Service platform, as shown in Figure 3-35. From here, you can configure things such as SSL certificates, custom domain names for your Function App, turn-key authentication, and more.

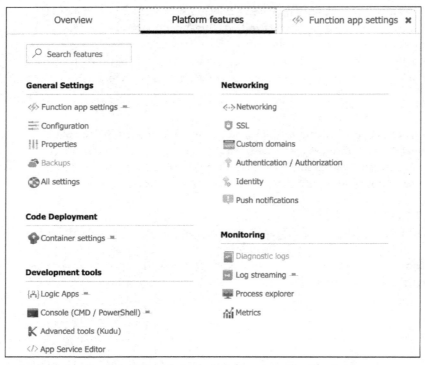

FIGURE 3-35 App Service platform features available to your Function App

To create a new function, click the + sign, as shown in Figure 3-36. You can then choose your development environment. You can choose Visual Studio, Visual Studio Code, or a development environment right inside the Azure portal. Also, you can use a code editor of your choice alongside the Azure Functions Core Tools.

FIGURE 3-36 Creating a function

If you choose any option other than **In-Portal**, you'll need to specify how you want to deploy your function to App Service. Your options depend on which development environment you choose, but typically, it will involve either using features of your environment to send the function directly to App Service or using App Service Deployment Center. Either way, deployment is quick and easy.

Depending on which development environment you choose, you will likely need to complete some prerequisite steps in order to develop your function. You'll see a screen telling you how to make things work correctly. In Figure 3-37, you can see what's required to use VS Code to develop functions. In most cases, you will be required to install the Azure Functions Core Tools.

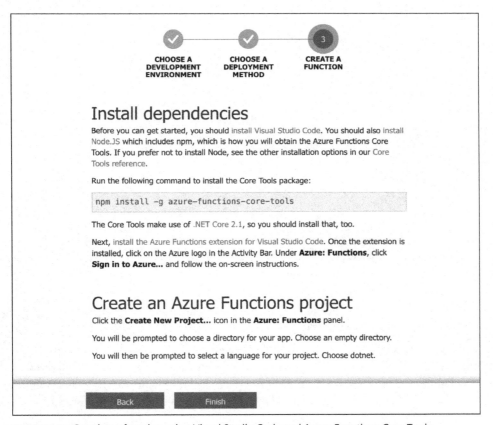

FIGURE 3-37 Creating a function using Visual Studio Code and Azure Functions Core Tools

Functions work using a trigger-based system. When you create your function, you choose a trigger that will kick off your function. When it's triggered, your function code will run. Typically, you will want your function code to do something simple. If you need a more complex function that performs many things, you can use Function Proxies to create several functions that work together to complete a task. This kind of development is referred to as *microservices*, and it allows you to quickly swap out functionality by simply changing a single function.

After your function is triggered and the code runs, you can choose what happens using what's called an *output binding*. The type of bindings you can use are dependent on the type of function you create. Figure 3-38 shows some of the different output bindings available when using an HttpTrigger for a function. This function will run as soon as a particular URL is requested.

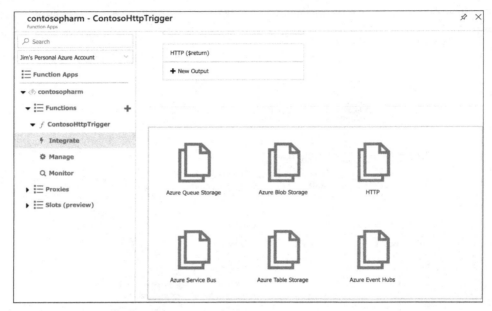

FIGURE 3-38 Output bindings in Azure Functions

MORE INFO **HTTPTRIGGER FUNCTIONS**

HttpTrigger functions are incredibly powerful because they can be called as a webhook. Many online services support webhooks. In a webhook scenario, you can configure a service to make a request to a particular URL in response to events. If you configure that webhook to call your Azure function's URL, you can easily add powerful functionality to your workflow.

You can configure multiple outputs for your function as well. However, for more complex workflows, Logic Apps is often a better choice, and you can integrate Logic Apps directly with Azure Functions.

Logic Apps

Logic Apps are similar to Function Apps in that they are kicked off by a trigger, but what happens after that is completely different. Unlike Function Apps, you don't have to write code to create some powerful workflows with Logic Apps.

> **NOTE POWER AUTOMATE**
>
> You might be familiar with Power Automate, previously called Microsoft Flow. The underlying technology for Power Automate is actually Logic Apps. That's why the Power Automate designer looks very much like Logic Apps.

A workflow simply means that a Logic App reacts to something happening and responds by performing a series of tasks, such as sending an email, transferring data to a database, and so on. It can do these things in order, but it can also do two things at once. For example, when a customer orders a product from your e-commerce site, you might want to

- Update your inventory count of the product
- Generate an invoice for the item
- Email the invoice to the customer
- Sign the customer up for your newsletter
- Generate a shipping label for the item

Logic Apps allows you to create these kinds of complex workflows easily, and because Logic Apps integrates with more than 100 other services (both Azure services and third-party services), you can do just about anything in a Logic Apps workflow.

There are three components in Logic Apps that make workflows possible: connectors, triggers, and actions:

- A connector is a component that connects your Logic App to something, such as another Azure service, a third-party service, an FTP server, and so forth. Each connector will have one or more triggers and actions specific to that connector.
- A trigger is a specific action that will cause your Logic App workflow to run.
- An action is what your Logic App will do as an output.

You can combine multiple actions for a connector, and you can also combine multiple connectors to create complex and powerful workflows.

You create Logic Apps in the Azure portal. Once you create a Logic App, the Logic Apps designer is shown by default. From the designer, you can choose the trigger for your Logic App, as shown in Figure 3-39. The list shown is a brief list of common triggers, but there are many more to choose from. In fact, there's a trigger for Azure Functions as well, so you can trigger a Logic Apps workflow when your function runs.

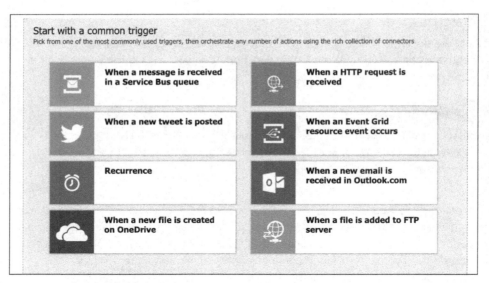

FIGURE 3-39 Common Logic App triggers

EXAM TIP

It's important to understand the difference between connectors and triggers. All the items shown in Figure 3-39 are triggers that are associated with specific connectors. For example, When A New File Is Created On OneDrive is a trigger for the OneDrive connector. Other OneDrive triggers are available as well, including When A File Is Modified and When A File Is Deleted.

If you scroll down, you'll see many templates you can use to create a Logic App, as shown in Figure 3-40. These templates will automatically configure a Logic App that contains a full workflow that you can modify for your own purposes. This is the fastest way to get started. However, the included templates might not be exactly what you want, so you can also create a blank Logic App and start from scratch.

After you create your blank Logic App, you can choose from several ways to start building your workflow. You can select a trigger from the list, search for a trigger or connector, or you can just select a connector from the list and see what triggers are available. As shown in Figure 3-41, there are many options available to get started.

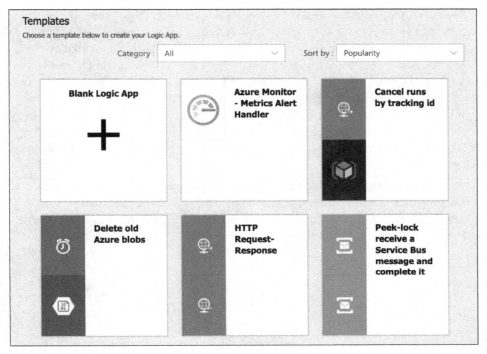

FIGURE 3-40 Logic App templates

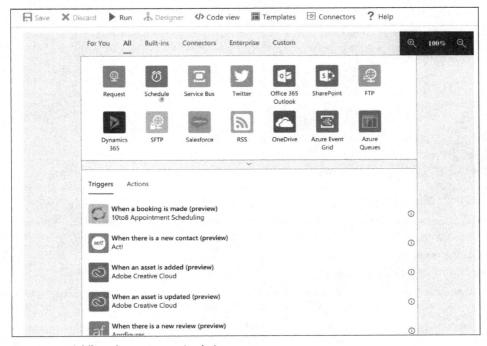

FIGURE 3-41 Adding triggers to your Logic App

Figure 3-41 shows only a small slice of the available connectors in Logic Apps. These connectors span a wide array of complexity, from reacting to file operations in a OneDrive folder to kicking off complex and powerful operations in third-party platforms such as Salesforce. This is the real value of using Logic Apps. Typically, if a development team wanted to integrate an application with a platform like Salesforce, they would have to spend a great deal of time learning Salesforce and learning how to program an application to use it. In fact, many companies would simply hire developers who already have those skills, usually at a high cost. Using Logic Apps, that same company can integrate with platforms like Salesforce and others without even having any developers at all! It's hard to overstate the value of that kind of easy integration.

Not all integration scenarios are complex and involve complicated platforms. In Figure 3-42, we've configured the OneDrive connector to monitor a folder in OneDrive. When a file is modified in that folder, it will start the Logic App workflow. In order to do something when a file is modified, click **New Step** to add an action.

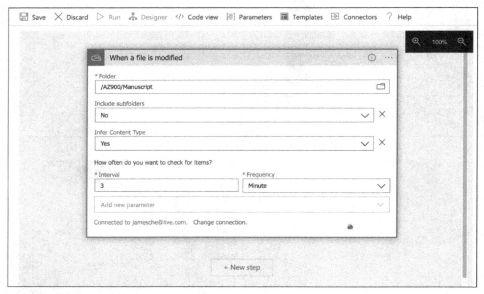

FIGURE 3-42 Using the OneDrive connector

When you click **New Step**, you'll see the same kind of screen that shows when the Logic App starts. Because we added a step to a workflow that already has a trigger, Logic Apps shows the actions you can take when the workflow is triggered. There are many actions to choose from, as shown in Figure 3-43.

In Figure 3-44, we configured the Logic App to call a Function App when a file is modified in the OneDrive folder. (Logic Apps uses an HTTP trigger to call a Function App.) You can pass the filename that was modified to the Function App using dynamic content, so that it will know what has changed. Just click **File Name** from the list. Of course, you can only pass one dynamic content item in your action.

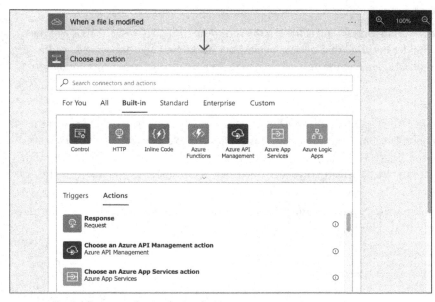

FIGURE 3-43 Adding an action to the Logic App

> **MORE INFO** **PASSING PARAMETERS TO FUNCTION APPS**
>
> When using a Logic App to call a Function App, make sure the Function App was designed to accept the data being passed to it by the Logic App. Otherwise, the Function App will encounter an error when it's triggered by the Logic App.

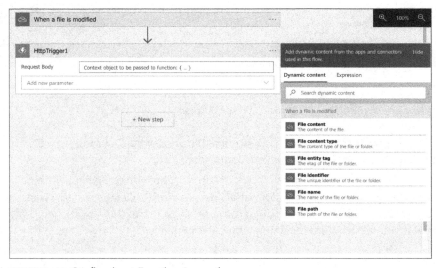

FIGURE 3-44 Configuring a Function App action

You now have a functioning Logic App. You can test the workflow by clicking **Save** at the top of the designer. The OneDrive connector was configured to check for a modified file every three minutes (see Figure 3-42), so you might need to wait a few minutes before the workflow is triggered. You can also click **Run Trigger** at the top of the designer to manually run the trigger.

You can monitor your Logic Apps using the Azure portal. Open the app and click **Overview** to see when your trigger was activated and whether it ran your workflow, as shown in Figure 3-45.

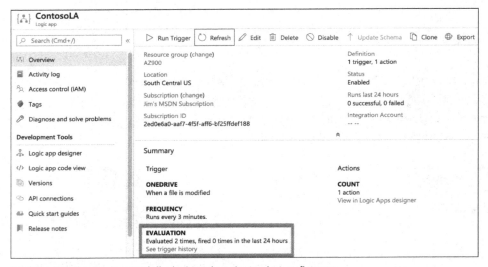

FIGURE 3-45 The Azure portal displaying when the Logic App flow ran

If you click **See Trigger History**, you can see an entire history of when your trigger was evaluated and when it fired the workflow for your Logic App.

In this case, we've used a Logic App to call an Azure Function, but you could have written a log file to Azure Storage or stored some information in an Azure SQL Database. If you want your Logic App to integrate specifically with other Azure services such as this, you can integrate your Logic App with Azure Event Grid for a more optimal experience.

Event Grid

The concept of different Azure services interacting with each other should be pretty familiar to you by now. There are many ways that you can integrate services such as this, and in some cases, you need one Azure resource to know about a change in another Azure resource. You could use a polling method for this, similar to the Logic App checking against OneDrive every three minutes looking for a change. It's more efficient, however, to enable an Azure service to trigger an event when something specific happens and configure another Azure service to listen for that event so it can react to it. Event Grid provides that functionality.

Both Azure Functions and Azure Logic Apps are integrated with Event Grid. You can configure a function to run when an Event Grid event occurs. In Figure 3-46, you can see the list of Azure resources that can trigger Event Grid events. Not all Azure services are represented in Event Grid, but more services are being added over time.

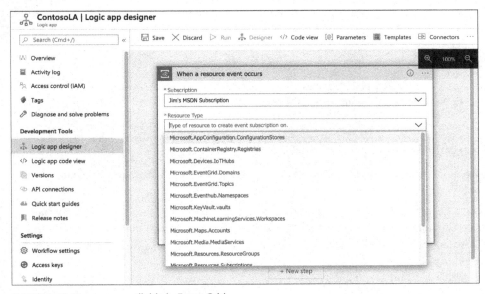

FIGURE 3-46 Resources available in Event Grid

Once you've selected the resource type, configure the event you want to listen for. The events that are available might differ depending on the resource you selected. In Figure 3-47, we are creating an event for an Azure subscription.

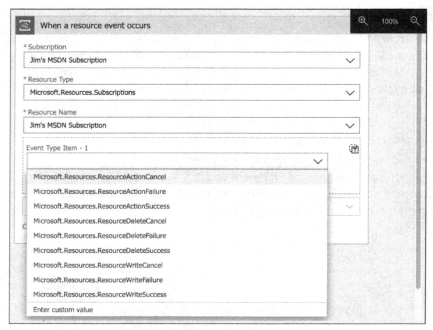

FIGURE 3-47 Events for an Azure subscription

MORE INFO **EVENTS**

For full details on all events and what they mean, see: *https://bit.ly/az900-eventschema*.

When an event occurs, you can take an action against an Azure resource using the Azure Resource Manager connector in a Logic App. You can also run a script that interacts with the Azure resource to do something like tag a resource or configure it in a way that is specific to your organization.

The primary benefit of using Event Grid in this way is the rapid development of solutions. You also benefit from Event Grid reliably triggering your events. If an Event Grid event fails to trigger for any reason, Event Grid will continue to retry triggering the event for up to 24 hours. Event Grid is also extremely cost effective. The first 100,000 operations per month are free, and after that point, you pay 60 cents for every million operations.

Azure DevOps

Keeping track of work can be a daunting task, especially if that work is delegated to individuals on a large team. Add the complexity involved when that team is developing a complex applica-tion (or even a simple application), and the challenges can grow exponentially. Azure DevOps offers a collection of tools that make it much easier to plan, track, and manage such projects.

Azure DevOps is made up of multiple services for helping you with your work. They are:

- **Azure Boards**   A visual way to manage and track work for your team using tiles displayed in a drag-and-drop interface
- **Azure Repos**   Source and version control using either Team Foundation Version Control or Git
- **Azure Pipelines**   Manage software releases through build, test, and release automation
- **Azure Test Plans**   Create and track tests to ensure reliable software releases
- **Azure Artifacts**   Use popular package feeds from both public and private sources

Azure Boards makes it easy to track and manage not only software releases, but just about any project that involves work. You can easily create new tasks with a mouse click, and you have the flexibility of configuring how each task's tile looks based on powerful formatting rules. Figure 3-48 shows a simple Azure Boards project I created to track work I was doing while writing this book.

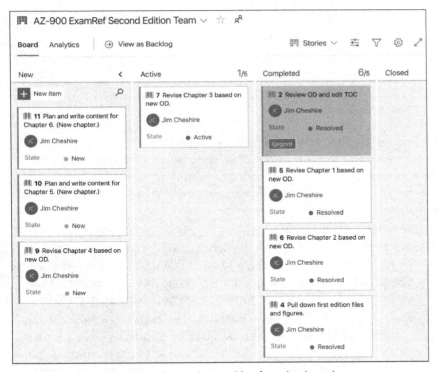

FIGURE 3-48 Azure Boards showing project tracking for a simple project

Each tile in Azure Boards is backed by a DevOps work item that includes quite a bit more detail. Opening a tile displays the underlying work item as shown in Figure 3-49.

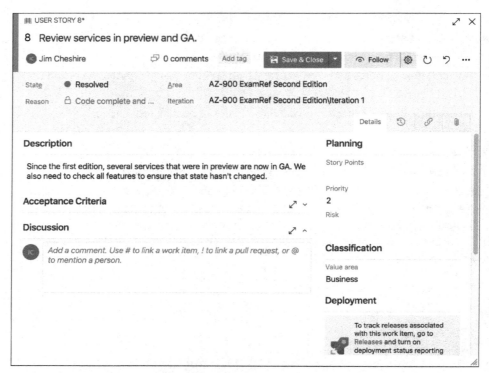

FIGURE 3-49 A work item for a tile in Azure Boards

Azure Repos provides source and version control for a team of developers using either Git (an open source solution for source control) or Team Foundation Version Control (TFVC). Developers who are using Git will have all versions of the repo's files on their local machines, and they can see the history of every change. Developers using TFVC will only have one version of a file on their machines, and everything else is on the server.

A typical application that a development team might be working on consists of thousands of files containing source code. As the application is developed, many developers are working on modifying those files with new code and changing existing code. A source control system allows the development team to keep track of all changes, and if a change causes a problem, it's easy for them to roll back changes, even if those changes involve a large number of source files.

There are also times when development teams want to add substantial new features to an existing application, but they want to keep all the code intact for the existing version. Source-control systems allow them to work on the new functionality separate from the existing source, and when they're confident that everything's working as designed and they're ready to incorporate the new feature, they can merge it back into the existing version.

In Figure 3-50, a development project's files are shown in Azure Repos. A source file is open, so that the source code is visible. Because **History** has been clicked at the top of the source view, all historical changes can be seen. By clicking **Compare**, a view is displayed showing the differences between two versions.

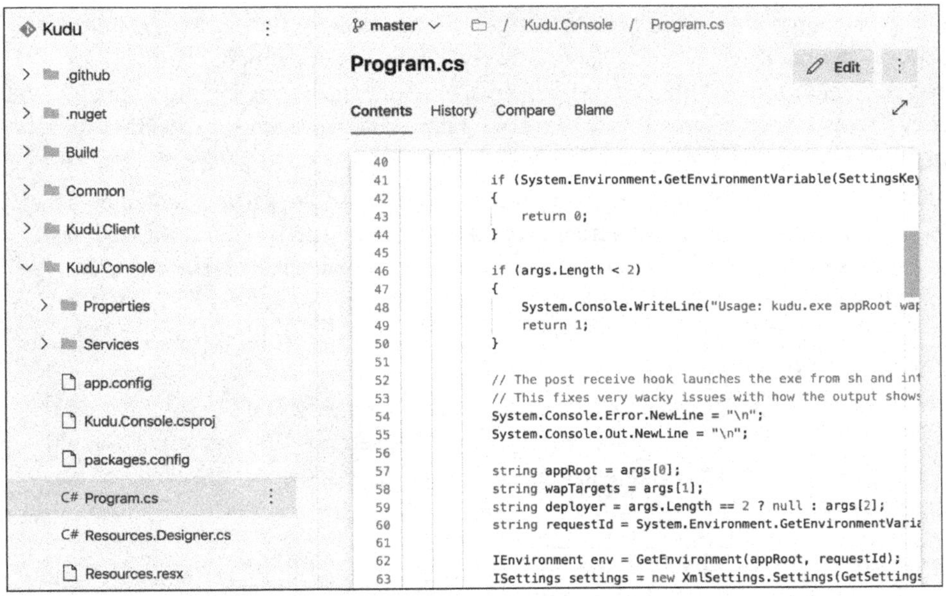

FIGURE 3-50 A repo in Azure Repos showing a source file's contents

Azure Pipelines provides continuous integration and deployment services for projects. You can configure Azure Pipelines to automatically integrate changes into source code and create a new build of the software for deployment. You can also configure your build process so that tests are run as soon as the build completes, allowing you to find problems before they make it into customers' hands.

Azure Test Plans provides features that make it easier to test software for problems. Developers can create complex tests. Tests are often based on work items that might contain details on a bug in the software. Once a test has been created, it can be run from within Azure Test Plans from within the web browser, so tests can be run on any device.

Many software applications use packaged components from third parties or from within the developer's own organization. These packaged components are frequently referred to as *artifacts*, and Azure Artifacts provides an easy way to keep these artifacts organized. Azure Artifacts also provides the ability to integrate these packages into the build process, including builds that happen within Azure Pipelines.

Azure DevTest Labs

As we were looking at Azure DevOps, we talked a little bit about the concept of testing. A typical test scenario might involve a developer creating an Azure VM in order to run some testing tools and development tools. That developer might also need to configure the VM with various packages that the application they're testing needs in order to run. In even more complex scenarios, the application might require multiple VMs with multiple configurations.

There are a couple of concerns with developers creating VMs for testing. First, creating a VM manually might take quite a bit of time, especially if the developer needs to install some required packages onto that VM. Second, a developer might end up costing the company a lot of money if they happen to create a VM that's more powerful than necessary or if they forget to stop or remove the VM after they've finished testing.

Azure DevTest Labs solves both problems nicely, and it adds quite a few other features that developers and IT departments will both find to be helpful. VMs can be created in a DevTest Lab that are preconfigured for specific purposes. When developers need to use a VM for testing, they simply look at a list of available VMs and claim the VM they need. That VM is then allocated to them until they unclaim it. Claiming a VM takes only seconds because the VM doesn't have to be created again when it's claimed.

As shown in Figure 3-51, creating a DevTest Lab is quick and easy. You simply give your lab a name, select the Resource Group, and specify a couple of settings. The DevTest Lab would usually be created by the IT department, the lead developer, or someone else in charge of a particular project.

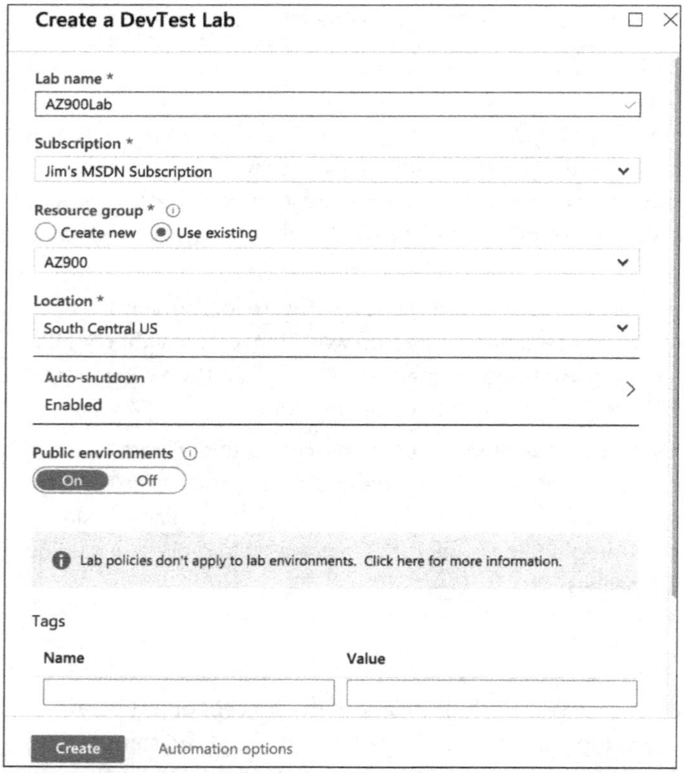

FIGURE 3-51 Creating a DevTest Lab in the Azure portal

Once a DevTest Lab is created, VMs will need to be created inside it so that developers can use them for testing. To create a VM, click the **Add** button, as shown in Figure 3-52.

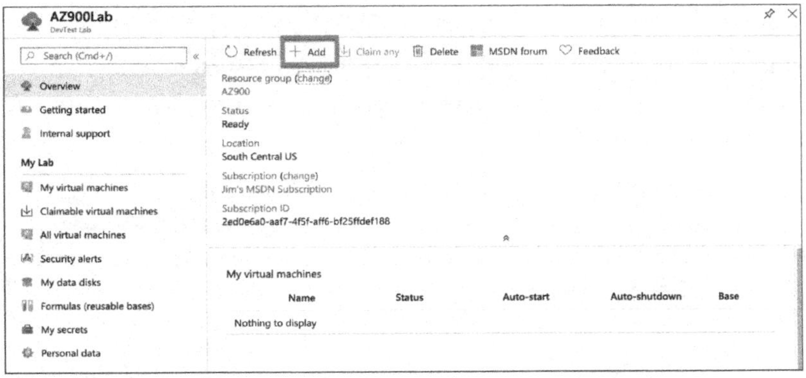

FIGURE 3-52 Click Add to add a new VM to a DevTest Lab

When you add a VM to a DevTest Lab, you first select the base for the VM. The base can be a VM template from the Azure Marketplace or other sources. It can also be a VM that has been specially configured for a particular project and saved out as a *formula* or a *custom image*. We'll talk more about formulas and custom images later in this section.

In Figure 3-53, a VM is being created that uses the Windows Server 2016 Datacenter base image. You can choose to create the VM with just the base image installed, but you can also add additional components to an image by adding an *artifact*. Just as we discussed earlier related to Azure DevOps, artifacts are packaged components that might be necessary for a particular configuration. You can add artifacts to a VM by clicking **Add Or Remove Artifacts** at the bottom of the screen, as shown in Figure 3-53.

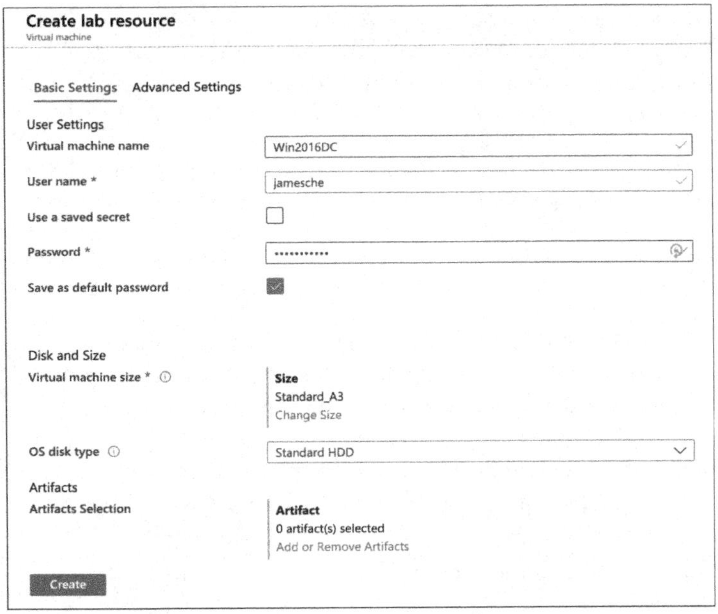

FIGURE 3-53 Adding a new VM to a DevTest Lab

It's very important to understand that when a VM is created in DevTest Labs, it defaults to being dedicated to a single user and is not claimable. If you are creating a VM that you want others to be able to claim and use, you must click **Advanced Settings** at the top of the screen shown previously in Figure 3-53 and configure the machine to be claimable, as shown in Figure 3-54.

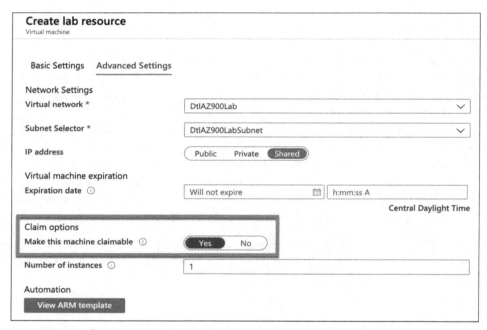

FIGURE 3-54 Configuring a VM to be claimable by others

EXAM TIP

You can't easily add one of your existing VMs into a DevTest Lab. In order to do that, you have to jump through some hoops to copy the VM's VHD image into the Azure Storage container that the DevTest Lab is using and then create a new VM from the custom image.

In some cases, the base images won't contain the configuration you need, even with artifacts added. For example, you might have a proprietary software package your company uses that you want to be included in your VM image, or you might have a specific OS configuration that you need for your VM. In these cases, you can create a custom image or a formula on which to base your new VMs.

Custom images and formulas are similar, but there is one key difference. A custom image is an image that is based on a VHD from an existing VM. A formula is also based on a VHD, but a formula also contains settings that are specific to DevTest Labs, such as VM size, included artifacts, and so forth. A formula, however, often uses a custom image as a base.

To create a custom image, configure the VM the way you want it and then select it from the list of VMs in the DevTest Lab. Click **Create Custom Image** and fill out the necessary fields, as shown in Figure 3-55.

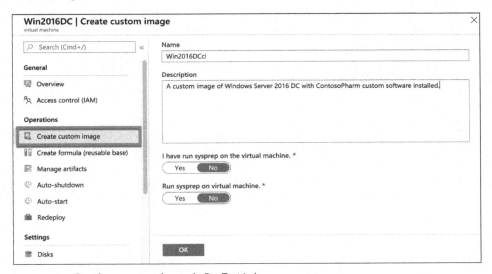

FIGURE 3-55 Creating a custom image in DevTest Labs

After you click **OK** to create the custom image, it will take a few minutes before the image is available as a base for other VMs.

To create a formula, click **Formulas** in the menu shown previously in Figure 3-52 and then click **Add** to create a new formula. Select a base for your formula. In Figure 3-56, the first base image listed is a custom image created earlier from a VM in a DevTest Lab.

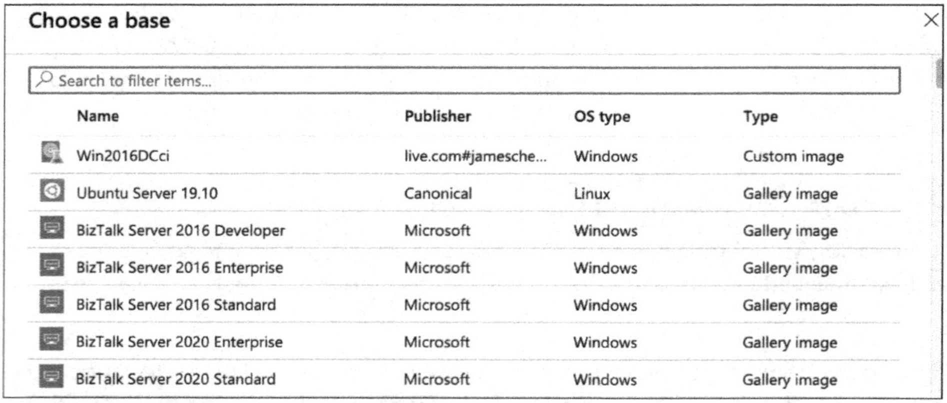

FIGURE 3-56 Choosing a base image for a formula

Once you've selected a base for your formula, you can configure the DevTest Lab settings you want for your formula, as shown in Figure 3-57. VMs created with this formula will have these settings preconfigured.

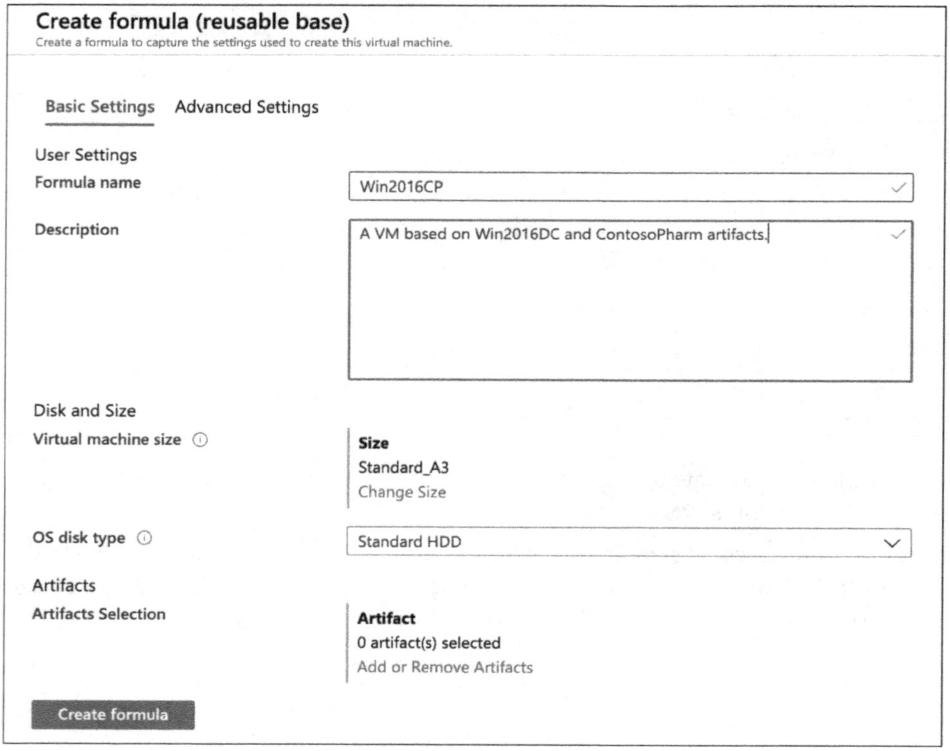

FIGURE 3-57 Specifying settings for a DevTest Lab formula

Another cost-saving feature of DevTest Labs is the auto-shutdown property for VMs. By default, all VMs are created with auto-shutdown enabled, and this means that after a certain period of time, unused VMs will be shut down so that you won't have to pay for them.

IT administrators or others also can define policies in DevTest Labs. These policies allow you to control VM sizes that can be created, the number of VMs per user and per lab, and so forth. To configure policies, click **Configuration And Policies** on the menu for your DevTest Lab.

Policies can be configured by clicking the desired policy on the menu and then configuring the policy. In Figure 3-58, a policy is being configured that limits the available VM sizes to Standard_A0, Standard_A1, and Standard_A2. Once this policy has been saved, users will not be able to create VMs unless they are one of these three sizes.

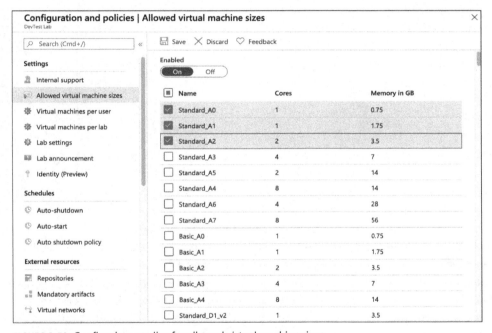

FIGURE 3-58 Configuring a policy for allowed virtual machine sizes

GitHub and GitHub Actions

We talked about Azure DevOps earlier and how it can be used by developers for collaborative work. Another option commonly used by developers is GitHub. GitHub is a web portal for repositories managed by a popular open-source system called Git.

Git was developed in 2005 by Linus Torvalds, the developer of the Linux kernel. It was designed to be a fast and efficient way for teams of developers to collaborate on software development. In 2008, a group of developers released GitHub as a hosting platform for Git repositories, and the largest catalog of source code repositories in the world was born. In fact, there are currently more than 40 million users of GitHub, and it hosts almost 200 million repositories!

To access GitHub, browse to *https://github.com*. From there, you can create a free GitHub account, which gives you access to unlimited repositories. There are a few limitations with the free account, but nothing that would affect most casual users.

Figure 3-59 shows my home page on GitHub. Any repositories I've created appear on the left side of the screen.

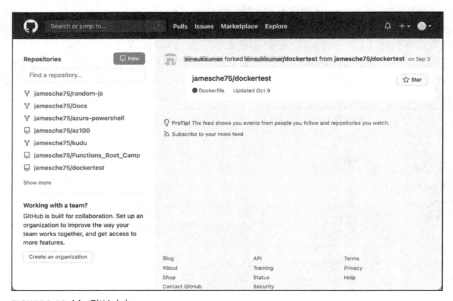

FIGURE 3-59 My GitHub home page

If I click one of my repositories, I can see the files in that repository. Also, clicking a file allows me to see and edit the contents of that file, as shown in Figure 3-60.

Editing a file directly in GitHub isn't commonplace. It's much more common for a developer to create a local copy of the repository and make changes to that local copy. (This is called *forking* the repository.) Changes can then be merged back to the source repository once they are ready—often when you're ready to test changes you've made to source code.

Most software development tools integrate with GitHub to make it easy to take advantage of source control features. Figure 3-61 shows my repository open in Visual Studio Code, and I've opened the same file in the repository. After I make changes to this file, I can push those changes to my original GitHub repository when I'm satisfied with my changes.

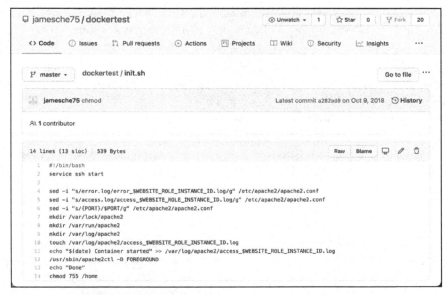

FIGURE 3-60 Editing a file in GitHub

FIGURE 3-61 Source file open in Visual Studio Code

As you've seen, using GitHub as a repository for source code allows developers to edit that code using their favorite editor, but what happens after that? After changes are made to source code, a developer will typically check that code back into the repository. At that point, the new code will usually be compiled and tested to ensure that it works correctly.

Testing the application might also involve things like building a Docker image, publishing some code to a website that the application uses, and so on. Not only is it inconvenient for a developer to have to manually do those tasks each time, but any manual operation introduces the possibility of error that can affect the software testing. For that reason, development teams prefer to have automated workflows that run each time a new version of their software is compiled.

In GitHub, these automated workflows are implemented using a feature called GitHub Actions. GitHub Actions provide you with the ability to create event-driven workflows in GitHub. In other words, they make it possible to automatically perform certain actions as a result of an event such as a developer pushing source code changes to GitHub.

You can define your own workflows using text files that are written in YAML, a format that is similar to JavaScript object notation (JSON) or extensible markup language (XML). However, you can also use one of the many preconfigured GitHub Actions available in the GitHub Marketplace.

EXAM TIP

The example I gave of running a GitHub Action when a push of new source code occurs is only a fraction of what's possible with GitHub Actions. Using Actions, you can start a workflow for a huge number of events in a repository, including when a developer forks a repository, when someone uses a *pull request* to recommend a change to a source file, and much more.

You can see all of the events that Actions support at *https://bit.ly/az900-githubevents*.

To access the GitHub Marketplace and get started with GitHub Actions, open a repository and click the **Actions** tab at the top of the page, as shown in Figure 3-62. As you can see, there are some suggested actions based on the repository that's open, and to use one of these Actions, I can click the **Set Up This Workflow** button displayed on the Action.

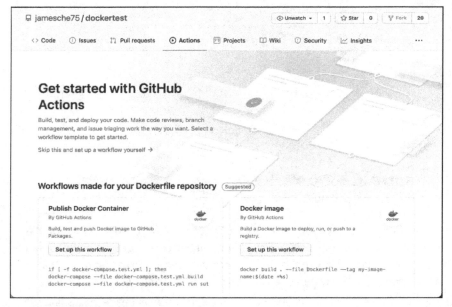

FIGURE 3-62 GitHub Actions

You're certainly not limited to using the suggested actions. You can scroll down to browse for other actions you might be interested in. You can also click the **Set Up A Workflow Yourself** link shown in Figure 3-62 to open an editor where you can manually edit your own YAML file and build your own workflow.

GitHub Actions are often used to integrate with Azure. In fact, if you scroll down on the Actions page shown in Figure 3-62, you'll likely see an action that can help to deploy to Azure, but that's only a small taste of what's available. To discover many more possibilities, you can visit the GitHub Marketplace.

To access the GitHub Marketplace, click **Marketplace** at the top of the page in GitHub. Then click **Actions** in the menu to find the actions that are available. In Figure 3-63, I've done just that, and I've also entered **Azure** as a search term, which enables me to see all the GitHub Actions that can help me to integrate my repository with Azure.

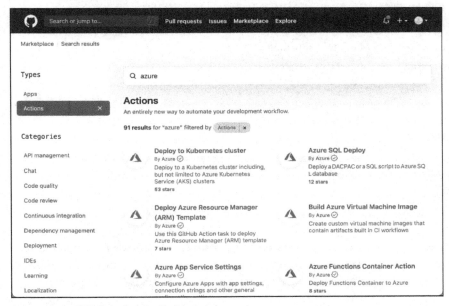

FIGURE 3-63 GitHub Actions in the Marketplace

Skill 3.2: Describe Azure management tools

We've talked a lot about the Azure portal, and you've had the opportunity to use it when interacting with several different Azure services. However, there are many other ways that you can create and manage your Azure services.

Many Azure users want to script interactions with their Azure services, especially when they have a need to interact with a large number of VMs or other Azure resources. For those situations, Azure offers command line tools to help.

Azure users also want to make sure they are getting the most out of their Azure services, and tools such as Azure Advisor and Azure Monitor can help to keep users up-to-date and compliant with Azure best practices and aware of how their Azure resources are performing. When there's a problem, Azure Service Health can also be helpful in determining if the problem is with your app or with Azure itself.

This section covers:
- Azure portal
- Azure PowerShell
- Azure CLI
- Azure Cloud Shell
- Azure Mobile app
- Azure Advisor
- Azure Resource Manager (ARM) templates
- Azure Monitor
- Azure Service Health

Azure portal

The Azure portal that is in use today is the third major iteration of the Azure portal, and it came about when Microsoft moved to ARM. Everything that you do in the Azure portal calls ARM on the back end.

EXAM TIP

For the AZ-900 exam, you probably don't need to know that the Azure portal is just making calls to ARM on the back end, but it doesn't hurt to know it. For the rest of this section, however, we'll cover only the different parts of the portal and how to navigate and customize it. That information is on the AZ-900 exam.

The first time you open the Azure portal, you'll be prompted to take a tour of the portal. If you're completely unfamiliar with the portal, taking a tour will help you to get a feel for how it works. If you choose not to and change your mind later, you can click the question mark in the top toolbar to access the guided tour at any time.

The default view in the portal is Home, as shown in Figure 3-64. From here, you can see icons for various Azure services, and if you click one of those icons, it will show you any resources of that type that you've created. Clicking the **Settings** button at the upper left displays a menu on the left side that includes these same icons and more.

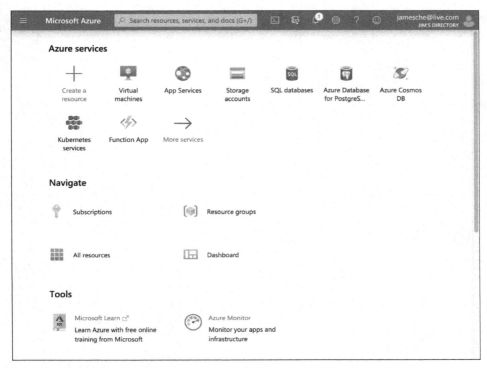

FIGURE 3-64 The Home screen in the Azure portal

If you already have Azure resources you've created, you can navigate to them by clicking one of the links in the **Navigate** section. If you've recently viewed one of your resources, you'll see another section with your recently accessed resources, so you can easily access them again with one click.

Along the top colored bar, you'll find a search bar where you can search for Azure services, docs, or your Azure resources. To the right of the search box is a button that will launch Azure Cloud Shell. Cloud Shell is a web-based command shell where you can interact with Azure from the command line. You can create Azure resources and more. As you're reading through Azure documentation, you might see a **Try It** button, and those buttons use Cloud Shell to help you test out different services and features.

To the right of the **Cloud Shell** button is a **Filter** button that allows you to configure the portal to only show resources in a certain Azure subscription or Azure Active Directory. To the right of that is the **Notification** button. This is where you'll see notifications from Azure that are related to your services and subscription.

To the right of the notifications button is the Settings button. Clicking **Settings** brings up a panel where you can alter portal settings, as shown in Figure 3-65.

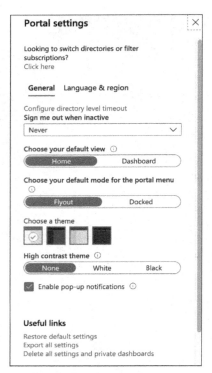

FIGURE 3-65 Portal settings

From **Settings**, you can change your default view, choose whether the menu is docked or flies out when you click the menu button, alter the theme of the portal, and disable toast notifications, which are pop-up notifications that Microsoft might display from time to time. Links are also provided that allow you to restore default settings, export your settings, or delete all your settings and dashboards. (We'll talk about dashboards later in this section.)

If you click your name in the upper-right corner (shown previously in Figure 3-64), you can log out or switch to other Azure accounts. You can also change the Azure Active Directory to access resources in another directory. This is helpful if your company has a corporate directory and you also have a personal directory.

> **MORE INFO   AZURE ACTIVE DIRECTORY**
>
> Azure Active Directory is covered in Chapter 5, Skill 5.1, "Describe core Azure identity services."

As mentioned earlier, if you click the Settings icon in the upper-left portion of the portal, you'll see a menu that contains a default list of Azure resources. Clicking one of those will display all resources of that type. If you'd like to add an Azure service to the list, click **All Services**, as shown in Figure 3-66.

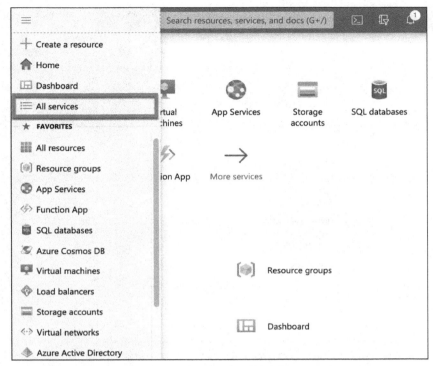

FIGURE 3-66 The Azure portal menu showing the All Services menu item

---

> **NOTE MOVING MENU ITEMS**
> You can reorder items on the menu. Click and hold an item, and then drag it to a new location in the menu.

From the list of all Azure Services, locate the service you want to add to the list and click the star to the right of the service to mark it as a favorite, as shown in Figure 3-67.

In Figure 3-68, we clicked **App Service Plans** on the menu to see all the App Service plans. From this list, you can click a resource to see that resource. You can also click a column header to sort by that column, assuming you have more than one resource of that type. Click **Manage View** to edit the columns that are displayed here, save the current view, and more. To create a new resource of this type, click **Add**.

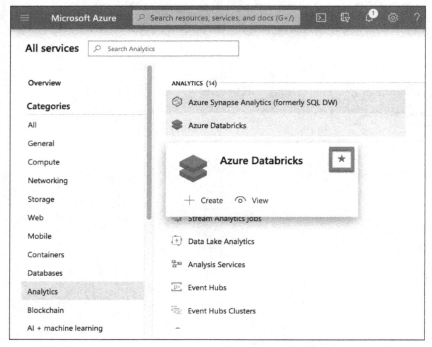

FIGURE 3-67 Making an Azure service a favorite so it will appear on the main menu

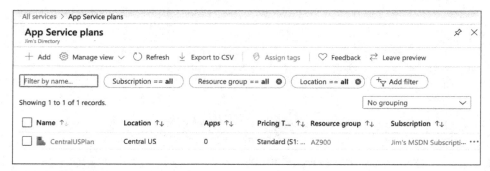

FIGURE 3-68 Viewing an App Service plan in the portal

When you click a particular resource, it will open that resource in the portal. Along the left side will be a menu that's specific to the type of resource you opened. In the main window, you'll see different items based on the type of resource you're viewing. These window areas in the portal are often referred to as blades.

In Figure 3-69, you'll see an App Service web app in the portal. The **Overview** blade is a blade that's common to most Azure resources, but the information that appears there will differ based upon the resource. In a web app, you can see the resource group it's in, the status, the location, and more. In the upper right is a pin button. If you click that pin, it will add this web app to the portal dashboard.

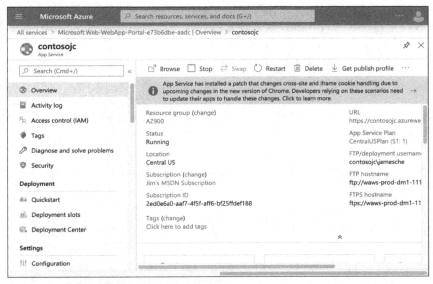

FIGURE 3-69 Viewing a web app in the portal

Along the top of the blade for the web app are several buttons for interacting with the resource. For a web app, you have a **Browse** button that will open the app in a browser, a **Stop** button to stop the web app, a **Swap** button to swap deployment slots, and so on. Each resource type will have different buttons available to you so you can easily interact with the resource from the **Overview** blade.

If you click an item in the menu at the left, the content from the **Overview** blade is replaced with the selected new item. In Figure 3-70, we have clicked **Diagnose And Solve Problems**, which replaces the **Overview** blade with new content from the **Diagnose And Solve Problems** blade.

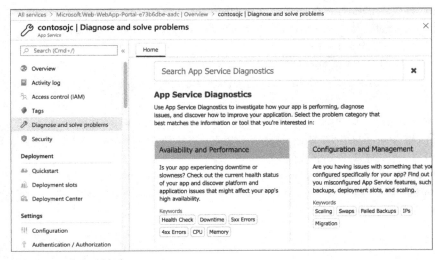

FIGURE 3-70 A new blade

As you use the portal, you'll find that there is inconsistency between different services. Each team at Microsoft has their own portal development team, and they tend to design portal interfaces that make sense for their own team. For that reason, you might see buttons on the top in some blades and buttons on the bottom in other blades.

You can customize your portal experience using the dashboard. If you click Dashboard from the portal menu, you'll see your default dashboard. As you're managing your resources, click the pin icon (as shown in the upper-right portion of Figure 3-69) to pin tiles to your dashboard. You can then move these tiles around and customize them in other ways to create a view that's unique to your needs.

To customize your dashboard, click **Dashboard** in the menu to show the dashboard and then click **Edit**, as shown in Figure 3-71.

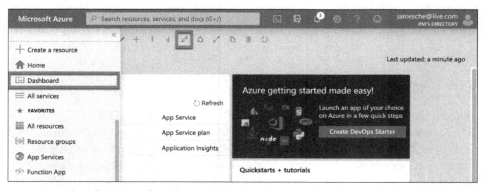

FIGURE 3-71 The Edit button allows for customization of your dashboard

From the customize screen shown in Figure 3-72, you can change the name of your dashboard by clicking inside the current name and changing it to a new name. You can add tiles to the dashboard by choosing from one of the hundreds of tiles available in the **Tile Gallery** on the left side of the portal, and you can search and filter the list if necessary. If you hover over an existing tile, you'll see a **Delete** button and a menu button that is represented by three dots. Click the **Delete** button to remove the tile from the dashboard. Click the menu button to access a context menu where you can resize the tile.

When you're satisfied with your dashboard, click **Done Customizing** to close the customization screen.

You can create new dashboards for specific purposes by clicking the plus sign shown previously in Figure 3-71. This takes you into a customization screen for your new dashboard, just like the one shown in Figure 3-72.

In Figure 3-73, we've created a dashboard specific to web apps. You can easily switch between this dashboard and the default dashboard by clicking the down arrow next to the dashboard name.

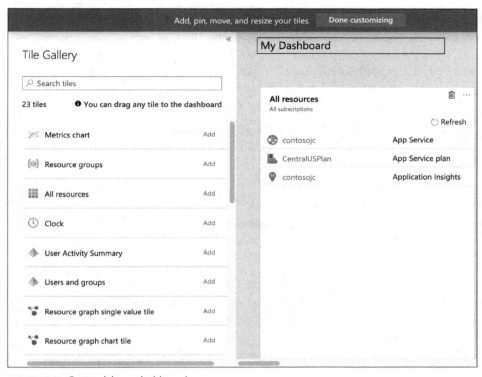

FIGURE 3-72 Customizing a dashboard

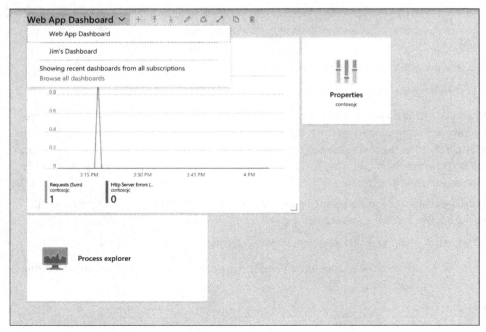

FIGURE 3-73 Switching between dashboards

Azure PowerShell

If you're a PowerShell user, you can take advantage of that knowledge to manage your Azure resources using the Azure PowerShell Az module. This module offers cross-platform support, so whether you're using Windows, Linux, or macOS, you can use the PowerShell Az module.

> **MORE INFO** **AZURERM AND AZ**
>
> The PowerShell Az module is relatively new. Prior to it, all PowerShell commands used the AzureRm module. The commands that you use with both are identical. The only difference is the module name.

> **MORE INFO** **INSTALL POWERSHELL ON LINUX OR MACOS**
>
> If you're running Linux, you can find details on installing PowerShell at *https://bit.ly/az900-powershellonlinux*. MacOS users can find steps at *https://bit.ly/az900-powershellonmac*.

EXAM TIP

The PowerShell Az module uses the .NET Standard library for functionality, which means it will run with PowerShell version 5.x, 6.x, or 7.x. PowerShell 6.x and 7.x are cross-platform and can run on Windows, Linux, or macOS.

If you're running Windows 7 or later and you have PowerShell 5.x, you'll also need to install .NET Framework 4.7.2.

Before you can use the PowerShell Az module, you'll need to install it. To do that, you first need to run PowerShell elevated. In Windows, that means running it as an Administrator. In Linux and macOS, you'll need to run it with superuser privileges using Sudo.

To install the module, run the following command.

```
Install-Module -Name Az -AllowClobber
```

When you install a new PowerShell module, PowerShell checks all existing modules to see if they have any command names that are the same as a command name in the module you're installing. If they do, the installation of the new module fails. By specifying -AllowClobber, you are telling PowerShell that it's okay for the Az module to take precedence for any commands that also exist in another module.

If you are unable to run PowerShell elevated, you can install the module for your user ID only by using the following command:

```
Install-Module -Name Az -AllowClobber -Scope CurrentUser
```

Once you've installed the module, you need to sign in with your Azure account. To do that, run the following command:

```
Connect-AzAccount
```

This command will display a token in the PowerShell window. You'll need to browse to *https://microsoft.com/devicelogin* and enter the code in order to authenticate your PowerShell session. If you close PowerShell, you'll have to run the command again in your next session.

> **MORE INFO** **PERSISTING CREDENTIALS**
>
> It is possible to configure PowerShell to persist your credentials. For more information on doing that, see *https://docs.microsoft.com/powershell/azure/context-persistence*.

If you have more than one Azure subscription, you'll want to set the active subscription so that commands you enter will affect the desired subscription. You can do that using the following command:

```
Set-AzContext -Subscription "subscription_id"
```

Replace `subscription_id` with the subscription ID of your Azure subscription you want to use with the Az module.

All Az module commands will have a common syntax that starts with a verb and an object. Verbs are things like `New`, `Get`, `Move`, or `Remove`. The object is the thing that you want the verb to affect. For example, the following command will create a resource group called `MyRG` in the South Central US region:

```
New-AzResourceGroup -Name MyRG -Location "South Central US"
```

If this succeeds, you'll see a message letting you know that. If it fails, you'll see an error. To remove the resource group, run the following command:

```
Remove-AzResourceGroup -Name MyRG
```

When this command is entered, you'll be asked to confirm whether you want to delete the resource group. Type a **y** and the resource group will be removed, as shown in Figure 3-74.

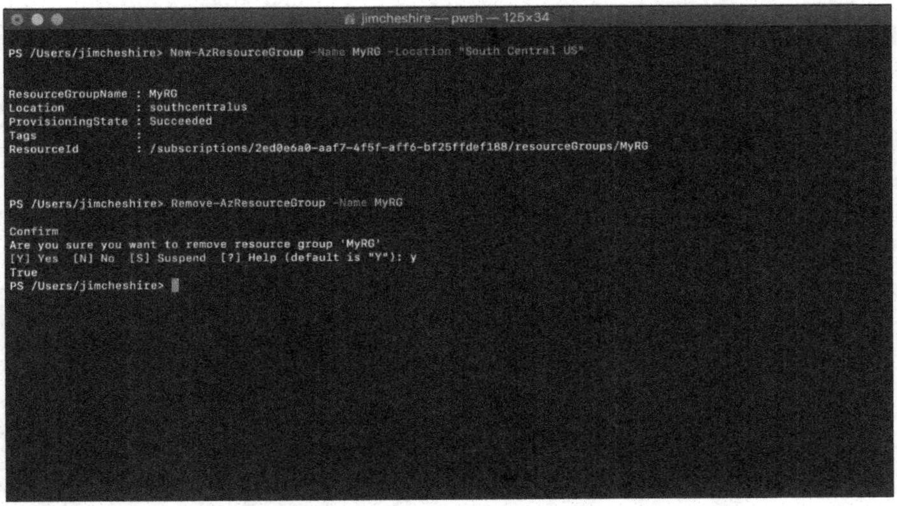

FIGURE 3-74 Creating and deleting a resource group with the Az module

In many situations, you will be including PowerShell commands in a script so that you can perform a number of operations at once. In that case, you won't be able to confirm a command by typing **y**, so you can use the -Force parameter to bypass the prompt. For example, you can delete the resource group using the following command and you won't be prompted.

```
Remove-AzResourceGroup -Name MyRG -Force
```

You can find all the commands available with the PowerShell Az module by browsing to *https://bit.ly/az900-powershellaz*. and clicking Reference in the left menu.

Azure CLI

As I pointed out earlier, one of the main benefits of PowerShell is the ability to script interactions with Azure resources. However, if you want to script with PowerShell, you'll need someone who knows PowerShell development. If you don't have anyone who can do that, the Azure command-line interface (Azure CLI) is a great choice. Azure CLI can be scripted using shell scripts in various languages like Python, Ruby, and so on.

Like the PowerShell Az module, the Azure CLI is cross-platform and works on Windows, Linux, and macOS as long as you use the 2.0 version or later. Installation steps are different depending on your platform. You can find steps for all operating systems at *https://bit.ly/az900-installcli*.

Once you install the Azure CLI, you'll need to log in to your Azure account. To do that, run the following command:

```
az login
```

When you run this command, the CLI will open a browser automatically for you to log in. Once you log in, if you have multiple Azure subscriptions, you can set the default subscription by entering the following command:

```
az account set --subscription "subscription_id"
```

Replace *subscription_id* with the subscription ID you want to use.

To find a list of commands you can run with the CLI, type **az**, and press Enter. You'll see a list of all the commands you can run. You can find detailed help on any command by entering the command and adding a *--help* parameter. Figure 3-75 shows the help for *az resource*.

You can take this a step further if you aren't sure what the commands do. You can, for example, run the following command to get help on the syntax for *az resource create*:

```
az resource create --help
```

This provides you with help and example commands to understand the syntax.

EXAM TIP

Like PowerShell, most commands in the Azure CLI have a --force parameter that you can include so that no prompts are displayed. When scripting PowerShell or the CLI, you need to include this parameter, or your script won't work. Watch out for examples in the AZ-900 exam that test for this kind of knowledge.

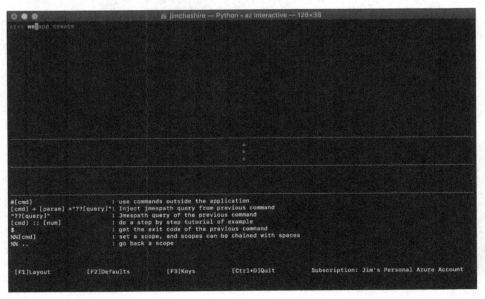

```
                            jimcheshire — pwsh — 116×28
PS /Users/jimcheshire> az resource --help

Group
    az resource : Manage Azure resources.

Subgroups:
    link           : Manage links between resources.
    lock           : Manage Azure resource level locks.

Commands:
    create         : Create a resource.
    delete         : Delete a resource.
    invoke-action  : Invoke an action on the resource.
    list           : List resources.
    move           : Moves resources from one resource group to another(can be under different
                     subscription).
    show           : Get the details of a resource.
    tag            : Tag a resource.
    update         : Update a resource.
    wait           : Place the CLI in a waiting state until a condition of a resources is met.

PS /Users/jimcheshire>
```

FIGURE 3-75 Azure CLI help

An even easier way to learn the CLI is to switch into interactive mode. This provides you with auto-complete, the scoping of commands, and more. To switch into interactive mode, enter **az interactive** at the command prompt. The CLI will install an extension to add this functionality. Figure 3-76 shows the Azure CLI with interactive mode active. At the command prompt, **we** has been typed, and it's displaying the rest of the command in dimmed text. You can press the right arrow key to enter the dimmed text in one keystroke.

```
                            jimcheshire — Python · az interactive — 128×38
az>> we app create



                                         .
                                         .
                                         .

#[cmd]                          : use commands outside the application
[cmd] + [param] +"??[query]"    : Inject jmespath query from previous command
"??[query]"                     : Jmespath query of the previous command
[cmd] :: [num]                  : do a step by step tutorial of example
$                               : get the exit code of the previous command
%%[cmd]                         : set a scope, and scopes can be chained with spaces
%% ..                           : go back a scope


  [F1]Layout        [F2]Defaults        [F3]Keys        [Ctrl+D]Quit       Subscription: Jim's Personal Azure Account
```

FIGURE 3-76 CLI interactive mode

You can install additional extensions for added functionality. Because the CLI uses an extension architecture, Azure teams can provide support for new functionality without having to wait for a new CLI release. You can find a list of all available extensions that Microsoft provides by running the following command:

```
az extension list-available --output table
```

This will not only show you available extensions, but it will show you if you already have the extension installed and whether there's an update you should install. To install an extension, run the following command:

```
az extension add --name extension_name
```

Replace *extension_name* with the name of the extension you want to install.

Azure Cloud Shell

As we've already seen, command line access to your Azure resources with PowerShell and the Azure CLI is powerful and flexible, and we also learned that you can install extensions to add more power to your command line. However, if you use multiple machines, you'll need to install those extensions on each machine and that might be a hassle. You're also limited to running these command line tools on your computer. You can't run them on your phone or your tablet when you're away from your computer.

The natural solution to these problems is to have your command line tools available to you in the cloud, and that's exactly what Microsoft did with Azure Cloud Shell.

To access Cloud Shell, click the **Cloud Shell** button in the Azure portal, as shown in Figure 3-77.

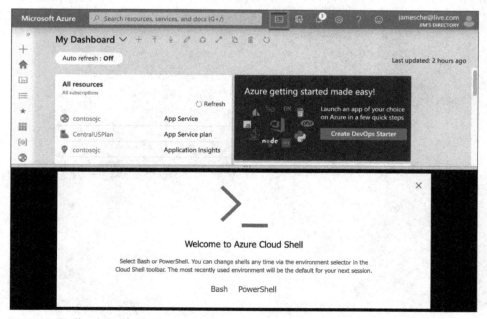

FIGURE 3-77 Cloud Shell in the Azure portal

The first time you launch Cloud Shell, you'll need to select the environment you want to use. You can choose between Bash and PowerShell, but if you change your mind later, you can change it at any time. Once you select an environment, you'll also need to create an Azure storage account. Cloud Shell persists anything you install and your settings throughout all your devices, so you need a storage account to persist those. In Figure 3-78, a storage account is being created for Cloud Shell.

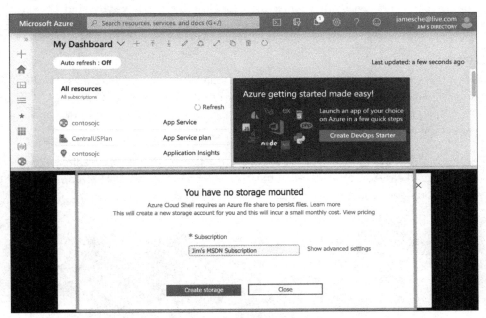

FIGURE 3-78 Creating a storage account for Cloud Shell

Once the storage account is created, Cloud Shell will launch a session as shown in Figure 3-79.

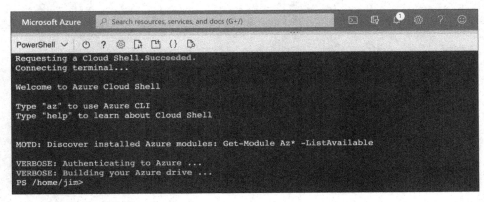

FIGURE 3-79 A Cloud Shell session

From Cloud Shell, you can run any of the commands you can run in the Azure CLI. If you're in PowerShell, you can also use commands from the Az PowerShell module. At the top of the Cloud Shell window is a toolbar. To change between PowerShell and Bash, select the desired environment from the drop-down menu. Next to that drop-down menu is the "power" button that restarts the Cloud Shell session, followed by a **Help** button and a **Settings** button for changing the text size and the font. To the right of the **Settings** button is a button that allows you to upload or download files into your file share for Cloud Shell, followed by a button that opens a new session of Cloud Shell in a new browser tab.

EXAM TIP

Any files that you upload will be available to you in Cloud Shell on any of your devices. That's because your files are stored in your Azure storage account. When you open Cloud Shell, Azure will pick a Cloud Shell instance for you to connect to and it will copy files from your storage account to that Cloud Shell instance.

The **Open Editor** button on the toolbar will open an instance of the Monaco Editor, a code editor that makes it easy to edit scripts and other files. In Figure 3-80, a JSON file is open in the editor and file browser is shown at the left.

FIGURE 3-80 The file editor in Cloud Shell

NOTE CLOSING THE EDITOR

To exit the editor, right-click in the window and click Quit.

The last button on the toolbar is the **Web Preview** button. This button allows you to run a web application using the files in the current folder inside of your web browser. This is a powerful tool for developers who might be developing web applications using Cloud Shell.

In Figure 3-81, I'm running a .NET Core web app in Cloud Shell using the `dotnet run` command. (The dotnet application is used to start applications written for .NET Core.) After I do that, I can see that the app is running on the Cloud Shell instance on port 5000.

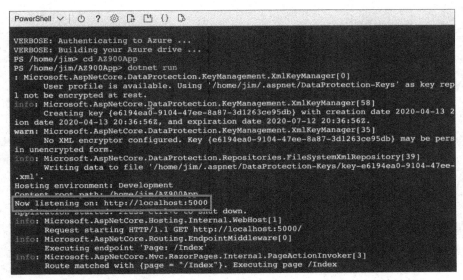

FIGURE 3-81 Running a .NET Core web app from Cloud Shell

If you want to open that in a browser and view it, click **Web Preview** in Cloud Shell and choose **Configure**. Enter the port number (**5000** in this case), as shown in Figure 3-82.

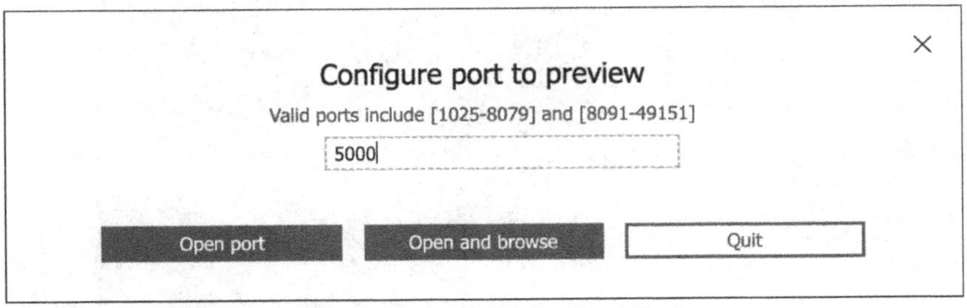

FIGURE 3-82 Configuring a port for Web Preview in Cloud Shell

I can then click **Open And Browse** and see my web app in my browser, as shown in Figure 3-83. It's clear from my site that I have some styling issues with a CSS file, and previewing it allows me to troubleshoot that problem and any other problems with my app.

> *NOTE* **WEB PREVIEW**
>
> Why would someone want to preview an app in Cloud Shell instead of just debugging it locally? Many developers write applications that interact with other Azure services, and they might want to debug these applications while they're running in Azure. For command line developers, this technique in Cloud Shell is a powerful way to enable that.

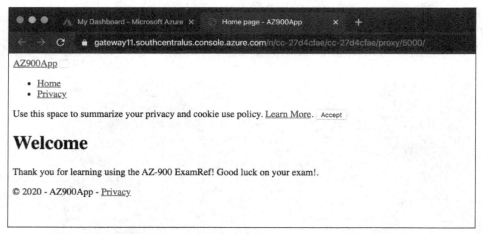

FIGURE 3-83 Browsing a web app using Web Preview

So far, we've only looked at using Cloud Shell from the Azure portal, but that's not the only way to access Cloud Shell. The Azure documentation provides many examples of PowerShell and Azure CLI scripts, and in many cases, there's a **Try It** button that you can click to try the script from within your browser. When you click the **Try It** button, an instance of Cloud Shell will open so that you can easily enter the script and run the commands, as shown in Figure 3-84.

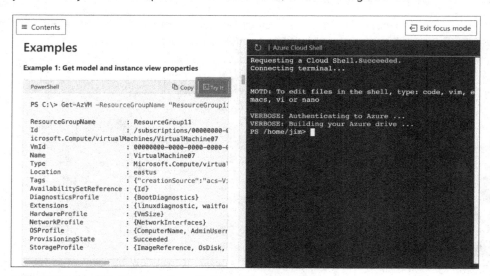

FIGURE 3-84 Cloud Shell's integration with Microsoft documentation

Azure mobile app

If you own an Android or iOS device, you can download the Azure mobile app to manage your Azure resources from your device. You can always browse to the Azure portal on your device, and you'll get an experience customized for smaller screens. However, just as with other websites you might use, an app provides a better first-class experience on a mobile device.

When you first launch the Azure mobile app, you'll be asked to log in to your Azure account. You'll then see a screen like the one shown in Figure 3-85.

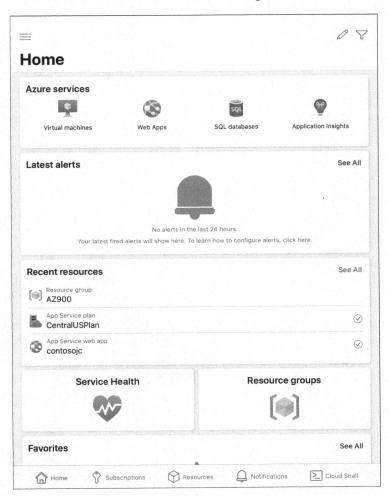

FIGURE 3-85 The Azure mobile app

From the home screen, you can review your Azure services, look at **Service Health** to determine if there's an Azure outage, and more. If you tap an Azure service, you'll see a list of all resources of that service type. Tapping a resource allows you to interact with it. You won't have the full functionality of the Azure portal, but you will be able to see details of the resource and perform basic functions against it.

In Figure 3-86, an Azure virtual machine is displayed in the Azure mobile app. At the bottom, **Stop**, **Restart**, and **Connect** links are shown.

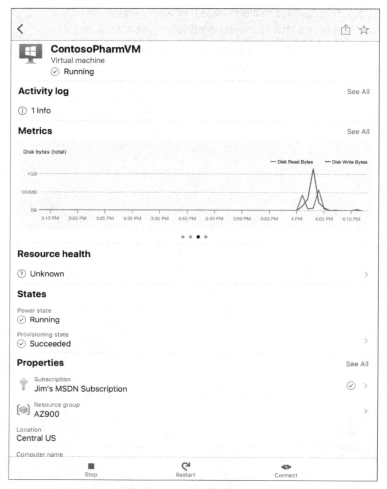

FIGURE 3-86 An Azure VM in the Azure mobile app

NOTE   CONNECTING TO A VM

Connecting to a VM requires that you have the Microsoft Remote Desktop app installed. You can download it free from the Apple Store or the Google Play store.

Even though you don't have the full Azure portal experience in the Azure mobile app, there's still a lot of power under the hood. If you click the **Cloud Shell** button in the lower right (shown previously in Figure 3-85), an instance of Cloud Shell will launch, as shown in Figure 3-87. From here, you can run the same commands you can run in Cloud Shell on your computer. You can switch from PowerShell to Bash, run Azure CLI and Az PowerShell commands, and so forth.

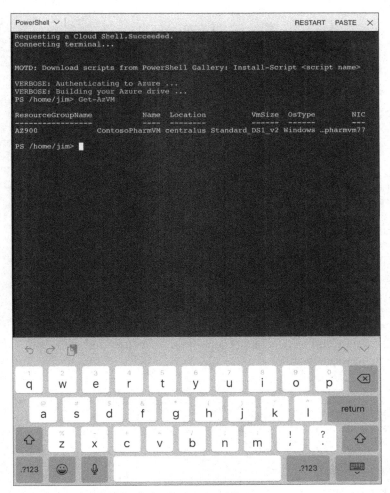

FIGURE 3-87 Cloud Shell running in Azure mobile app

Azure Advisor

Managing your Azure resources doesn't just include creating and deleting resources. It also means ensuring that your resources are configured correctly for high availability and efficiency. Figuring out exactly how to do that can be a daunting task. Entire books have been written on best practices for cloud deployments. Fortunately, Azure can notify you about problems in your configuration so you can avoid problems. It does this via Azure Advisor.

Azure Advisor can offer advice about high availability, security, performance, and cost. To access Azure Advisor, log in to the Azure portal and click **Advisor** in the menu on the left. Figure 3-88 shows Azure Advisor with two high impact recommendations for security.

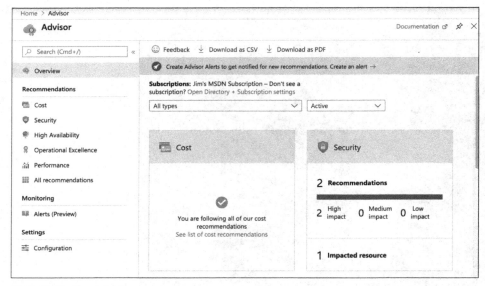

FIGURE 3-88 Azure Advisor

To review details on a recommendation, click the tile. In Figure 3-89, we have clicked the **Security** tile, and you can see a recommendation to enable MFA (multifactor authentication) and add another owner to my subscription.

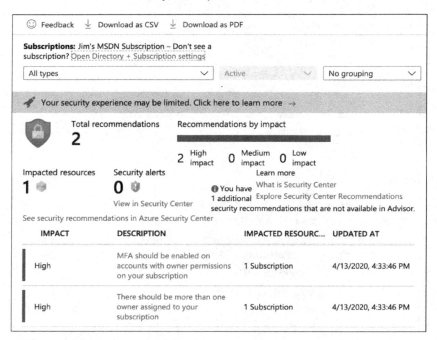

FIGURE 3-89 Advisor recommendations

You don't have to do what Azure Advisor recommends. If you click the description, you can decide to postpone or dismiss the alert, as shown in the lower-right corner in Figure 3-90. If you choose to postpone the alert, you have the option of being reminded in 1 day, 1 week, 1 month, or 3 months.

FIGURE 3-90 Acting on a recommendation

If you have a large number of recommendations, or if you're not the right person to take action on the recommendations, you can download Azure Advisor recommendations as either a comma-separated values file or a PDF. Click Download As CSV or Download As PDF, as shown previously in Figure 3-88. You can also download a file with specific recommendations by clicking the appropriate download button while reviewing details, as shown in both Figure 3-89 and Figure 3-90.

Azure Resource Manager (ARM) templates

In Chapter 2, you learned about Azure Resource Manager (ARM) and how it's involved in helping to create and manage Azure resources. As I said in that chapter, ARM uses a declarative syntax, and you tell ARM what you want it to do using a JSON file called an *ARM template*.

In the most basic sense, an ARM template contains a list of resources that you want to either create or modify. Each resource is accompanied by properties such as the name of the resource and properties that are specific to that resource. For example, if you were using an ARM template to deploy a web app in App Service, your ARM template would specify the region you want your app to be created in, the name of the app, the pricing plan for your app, any domain names you want your app to use, and so forth. You don't have to know how to set all those properties. You simply tell ARM to do it (you declare your intent to ARM), and ARM takes care of it for you.

> *MORE INFO*   **MORE ON ARM TEMPLATES**
>
> ARM templates are incredibly powerful, but they're also pretty simple. If you want to read more about how to use ARM templates, check out the documentation at *https://bit.ly/ az900-armtemplates*.

There's one more important aspect to ARM template deployment. When you're deploying multiple resources (which, as pointed out, is a typical real-world scenario), you often have service dependencies. In other words, you are deploying one or more services that rely on other services already being created.

For example, think of a situation where you're deploying a certificate to be used with a web app. One of the properties you need to set on the web app is the certificate that you want to use, but if that certificate hasn't been deployed yet, your deployment will fail. ARM allows you to specify dependencies so you can avoid issues like this. You simply tell ARM that the web app depends on the certificate and ARM will ensure the certificate's deployment is completed before it deploys the web app.

If you want to see an example of an ARM template, you can see a real-world example using the Azure portal. Open any resource and click on Export Template in the menu as shown in Figure 3-91. The ARM template displayed in the portal can be used to deploy that exact resource.

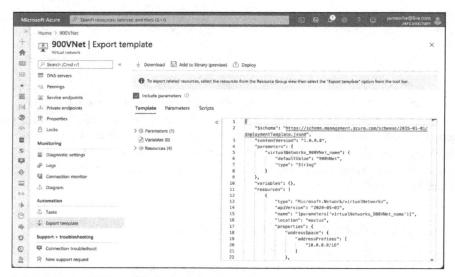

FIGURE 3-91 An ARM template in the Azure portal

Azure Monitor

Azure Monitor aggregates metrics for Azure services and exposes them in a single interface. You can also create alerts that will notify you or someone else when there are concerns you might want to address.

To access Azure Monitor, click **Monitor** in the Azure portal to display the Azure Monitor blade, as shown in Figure 3-92. Azure Monitor is customizable, so you can see exactly what interests you the most. For that reason, it doesn't show any metrics until you configure them. To view metrics, click **Metrics** and then select a scope.

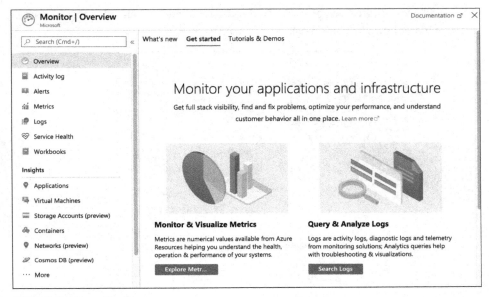

FIGURE 3-92 Azure Monitor

In Figure 3-93, a VM in the AZ900 resource group has been selected for monitoring.

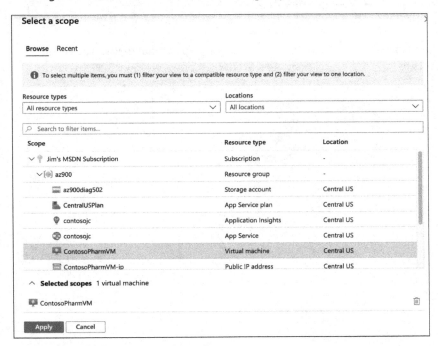

FIGURE 3-93 Selecting a resource to monitor

Once you select a resource, you are presented with a list of metrics related to that resource. Metrics for VMs are shown in Figure 3-94.

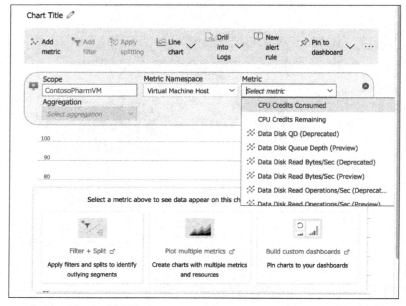

FIGURE 3-94 Metrics for VMs

When you select a metric, the chart updates to show a graph of that metric. You can add additional metrics to your chart by clicking **Add Metric**, as shown in Figure 3-95.

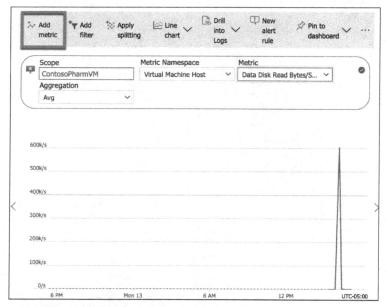

FIGURE 3-95 Monitoring VM disk usage

When adding multiple metrics, you'll want to include only those metrics that share a common unit of measurement. For example, if you were to add a CPU metric to the chart shown in Figure 3-95, it wouldn't make a lot of sense because Percentage CPU is measured as a percentage and disk units are measured in bytes.

In Figure 3-96, we've added **Disk Write Bytes** to the chart. Azure Monitor color codes each metric automatically to distinguish between them. We've also selected **Area Chart** as the type of chart to more clearly see the patterns.

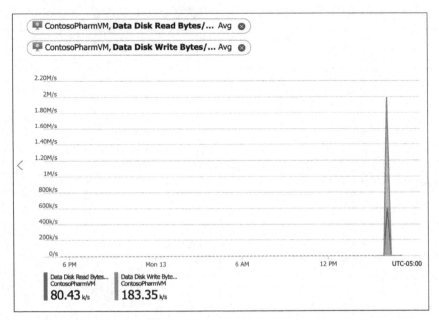

FIGURE 3-96 Chart showing disk usage

By default, charts are shown for the past 24-hour period, and the real-time value is shown at the right edge of the chart. However, you can customize the timeframe that is shown by clicking the timeframe and adjusting it as you like, as shown in Figure 3-97.

Once you have a chart that you find useful, you can pin that chart to the portal dashboard by clicking **Pin To Dashboard**. As shown in Figure 3-98, you can choose **Pin To Current Dashboard**, or you can pin it to a specific dashboard by choosing **Select Another Dashboard** to create a monitoring dashboard in the portal customized for a specific use.

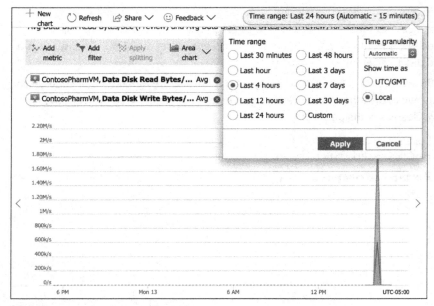

FIGURE 3-97 Changing the chart timeframe

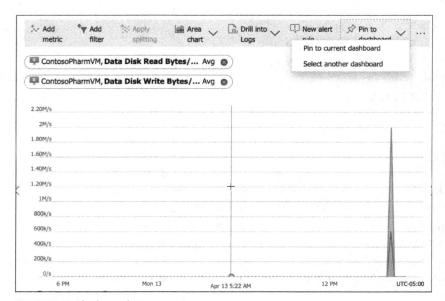

FIGURE 3-98 Pinning a chart

Azure Monitor Alerts can notify you or others with email or SMS text message, run a Logic App flow, call a Function App, make a request to a webhook, and more, when a certain condition is met. Alerts are based on rules that you define, and when a rule's condition is met, an alert performs the action you specify.

You can create an alert rule that is automatically configured for the metrics you've selected in your chart by clicking N**ew Alert Rule** at the top of your chart. You can also start from scratch by clicking **Alerts** in the menu for Azure Monitor, as shown in Figure 3-99, and then clicking **New Alert Rule**.

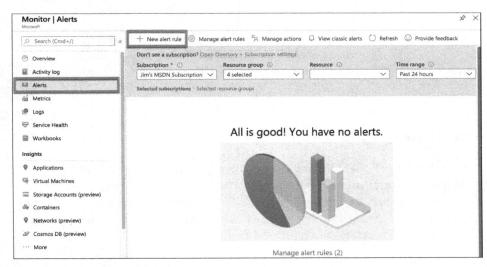

FIGURE 3-99 Creating an alert rule

To start your rule, click **Select** and select the resource for which you want to configure an alert. In Figure 3-100, a VM is selected for a new alert rule.

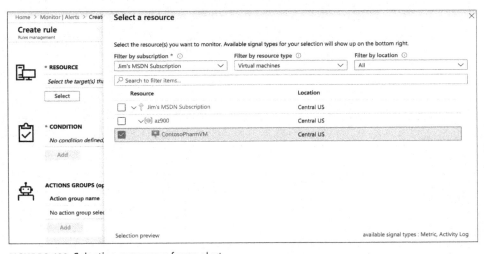

FIGURE 3-100 Selecting a resource for an alert

Next, you'll need to specify the condition for your alert. Click **Add Condition**, and then select the signal you want to monitor for your alert. In Figure 3-101, an alert has been configured based on the Percentage CPU signal of the VM.

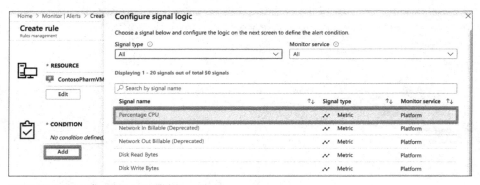

FIGURE 3-101 Configuring a condition

Once you select a signal, the logic for the signal is configured. As shown in Figure 3-102, Monitor displays an interactive graph of the signal you've chosen, which helps you get a feel for how your resource has been performing historically. By default, this shows the last six hours, although you can adjust the chart period. You can specify an operator, aggregation type, and threshold, or click **Done** to create the logic for the alert.

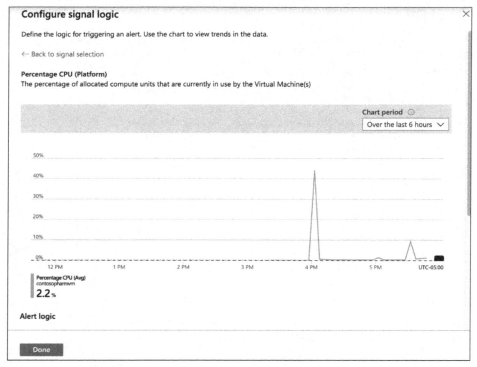

FIGURE 3-102 Alert rule logic

When an alert is triggered, it performs an action that you specify using an *action group*. An action group contains a list of actions to take when an alert is triggered. To create a new action group, click **Create**, as shown in Figure 3-103.

FIGURE 3-103 Creating an action group

In Figure 3-104, we are creating an action to notify the IT director. In this case, the action will send a text message to the IT director, and it will also send a push notification using the Azure mobile app.

Action groups are designed to contain several actions that are executed by an alert being triggered. To add a new action, click **Manage Actions** (shown previously in Figure 3-99) and then select your action group. In Figure 3-105, we've added an additional action to the action group. This action calls a Function App that runs some code to reboot the VM.

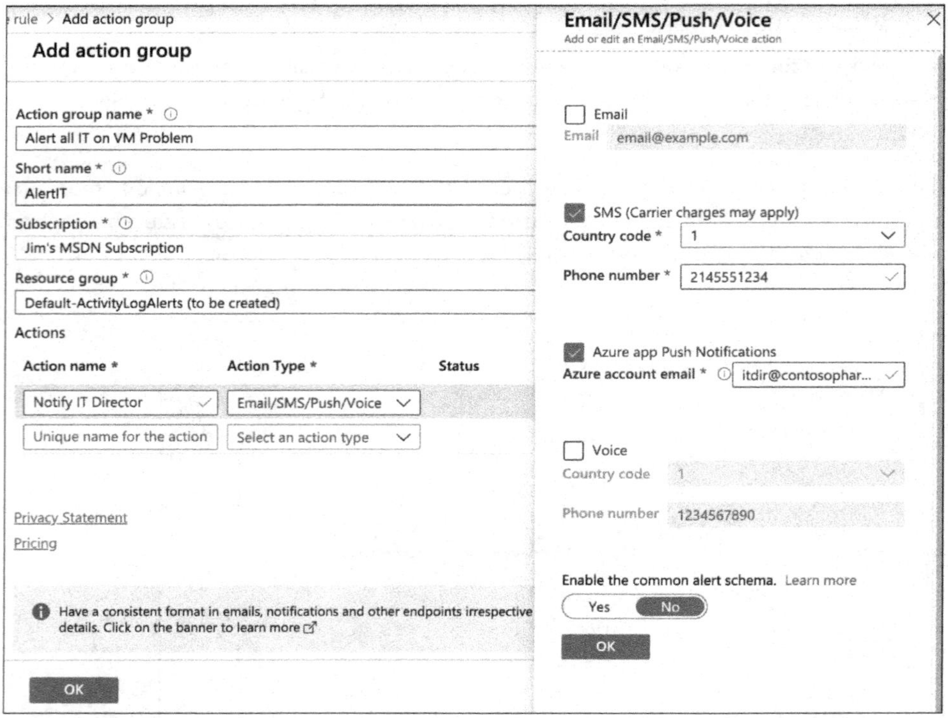

FIGURE 3-104 Creating an action

FIGURE 3-105 Adding another action

Azure Service Health

Microsoft operates an Azure Status web page where you can view the current status of Azure services in all regions where Azure operates. While it is a helpful view of overall Azure health, the enormous scope of the web page doesn't make it the most effective way to get an overview of the health of your specific services. Azure Service Health can provide you with a view specific to your resources.

To access Service Health, click **All Services** > **All** > **Service Health**, as shown in Figure 3-106.

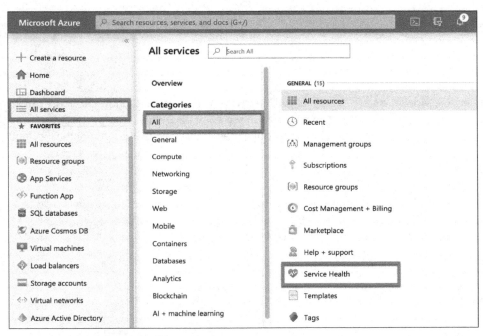

FIGURE 3-106 Azure Service Health

Figure 3-107 shows the **Service Health** blade showing the health and status of the resources. The map shown has three green dots representing the health of the three Azure regions where resources are deployed. This map is specific, and by clicking the pin icon, you can have a quick reference of Azure health for just the regions where you have resources.

You can also view any upcoming planned maintenance that might affect you by clicking **Planned Maintenance** in the menu on the left. By clicking **Health Advisories**, you can see health information that might be related to your own configuration and not a problem somewhere in Azure.

FIGURE 3-107 Service issues in Service Health

When a service issue is affecting you, you'll see details on the issue, as shown in Figure 3-108. In addition to full details on the incident, you also see a link that refers to details on the incident. You can also download a PDF that contains an official Microsoft notice of the incident.

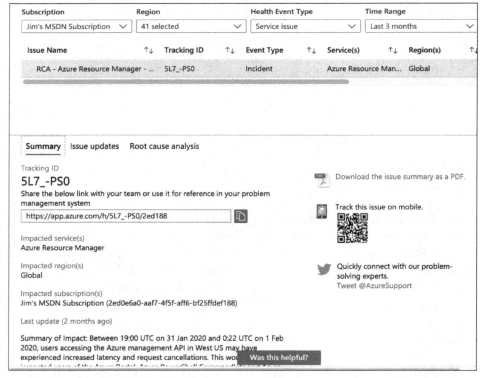

FIGURE 3-108 Azure Service Health incident

Both Azure Monitor and Azure Service Health are critical to the overall view of your Azure resources. Azure Monitor is geared toward monitoring the cost and performance of your resources and alerting you and others when conditions warrant. Azure Service Health, on the other hand, is the single-point-of-truth for information on the health of Azure itself and how Azure incidents are affecting your resources. The combination of these two services provides you with all the tools you need to keep up with your Azure resources and how well they're performing.

Thought Experiment

You've learned about quite a lot in this chapter, so let's apply some of that knowledge in a thought experiment. Answers to this thought experiment can be found in the section that follows.

ContosoPharm is interested in modernizing their systems, and they've turned to you for advice. They want to monitor the environmental conditions in their storage areas, so they've installed some Internet-enabled thermostats. One of their requirements is to be able to alert maintenance staff if there's a defined variance in temperature and humidity. The IT department also wants a way to efficiently upgrade the firmware on these thermostats if necessary, and because there are hundreds of devices, they are concerned about allocating expensive engineer resources to do that work, but they also want to ensure that all thermostats are updated, even when Internet access is temporarily unavailable. Recommend a good solution that fills these needs.

One additional ask they have related to these devices is related to keeping them secure. The IT director is concerned with connecting these systems to the Internet because of the risk that a hacker might be able to gain control of climate-control systems. Make a recommendation for them that can help with securing these devices.

ContosoPharm is also interested in taking advantage of machine learning to make their research more efficient. They've got a large amount of data already in Data Lake Storage, and they need an efficient way to analyze that data and build some machine learning models. They have huge amounts of data, so they need a solution that is scalable and able to handle millions of rows of data. If you can also provide a solution for them to bring some unstructured data into the equation, that would be a bonus. During your preliminary discussions with them about this, they mentioned that their data scientists are interested in taking advantage of their knowledge of Jupyter Notebooks. Make a recommendation for the best way they can do this in Azure.

While ContosoPharm has some skilled data scientists and developers who plan on using R to build some machine learning models, they also want to allow a few other folks who don't know R or Python to develop some models. If there's a suggestion you can make to enable those people, that would be a great selling point.

The IT director realizes that all these tasks are going to strain IT resources, and he's worried about the fact that sales managers in the field can keep IT people tied up providing basic computer support. The problems they encounter aren't complicated, but they do require a lot of time from IT personnel. He's asked that you recommend a way that they can provide some basic support to the field without having to use precious IT resources.

One thing that causes some support issues is related to an Azure VM that is running a custom application ContosoPharm developed a long time ago. This app leaks memory, and that eventually causes the app to slow to the point where it triggers support calls. They don't have the resources available right now to troubleshoot and fix the problem, so when they get calls on it, they reboot the VM to temporarily resolve the issue. If you can recommend some way for them to monitor the memory that's being used and reboot the VM automatically without user interaction, that would help a lot to reduce the number of support calls.

The VM that hosts the app does have to be resized occasionally because of an increase in usage. When that VM gets scaled to a larger size, it means greater expense for ContosoPharm. The CIO is willing to accept this increase in cost, but she wants to be notified via a text message when it happens so she is aware of the change. She suggested that to the IT director, but he's not able to offer a solution due to a limitation in the number of developers who would be able to build such a solution. If you can unblock them on this in a way that doesn't require someone who can write code, that would be a tremendous benefit.

Along with the recommendation to build a solution for the CIO, ContosoPharm would like a good way to track that work as it's being done. They're concerned that they might not be able to adhere to schedules since the people working on the project likely have a lot of other duties. Provide a recommendation on a way for them to track this work and ensure it gets done.

One of ContosoPharm's developers believes he might be able to do some work on the app that is leaking memory, but he can't allocate much time to it. One of the problems in working on that app is that he needs a couple of other VMs with some specific tools installed on them, and he needs debugging symbols installed on them as well. Getting the symbols installed can take a couple of hours after he spins up a new VM. If you can recommend a way that he can save some time on this, it might enable ContosoPharm to get some work done to fix the app and solve that problem long-term.

The development team for the app wants to ensure they are able to incorporate changes in the source code quickly, but they also want to make sure they can test those changes to ensure they aren't going to cause problems. That's going to require them to be able to easily deploy the updated app to Azure after changes are made by the developer working on the memory leak. ContosoPharm would like a solid recommendation on how to address that need.

Another major problem in fixing the problem app is that it relies on three different web apps running in Azure App Service. The developer doesn't want to troubleshoot the app using the live web apps, so he needs to be able to create new apps for testing easily. Because these web apps are billed to ContosoPharm whether they're running or not, they'll have to delete the apps when the developer isn't actively working on the issue. That means the developer has to take the time to recreate the web apps all over again when he returns to work on the problem app. Recommend a solution for ContosoPharm to easily create these web apps when they're needed and then delete them when they're not needed anymore.

The developer who'll be working on the app has informed you that the app relies on a large collection of Bash scripts that are installed on the VM. These scripts interact with Azure resources, so they have to run within the Azure environment. His feeling is that these scripts might be part of the issue with the app, so he'd like a way to easily edit these scripts in an Azure environment. The problem is that he might not always be at the office where his computer is available. In fact, the developer told you that a lot of the work he does on scripting is done while he's commuting around town on the train, and the only device he has with him is an iPad. If you can help make the developer productive while he's on the train, that would be a huge plus for ContosoPharm.

The IT director has been reading up on the cloud, and he's concerned that part of ContosoPharm's problems is that they aren't following Azure best practices. He's asked you to discuss best practices with them so they can be better prepared to avoid problems. You feel that this might not be the best use of your time, and you're concerned that best practices might evolve over time. Provide a better recommendation for ensuring that ContosoPharm complies with best practices in Azure.

Once ContosoPharm has confidence the company's problems have been corrected, they want to ensure they can redeploy this application to other Azure regions as they continue to grow. The company is concerned that they might not be able to re-create these Azure resources correctly in another region, so it would be helpful if you can provide some guidance to help ease those concerns.

As ContosoPharm makes any changes, they'd also like to know if there's any way for them to carefully monitor the performance of their VMs and other resources. In order to save wasted time, they also want to ensure that they're aware of any incidents in Azure that are impacting their resources.

Thought experiment answers

In this section, we'll go over the answers to the thought experiment.

The best option for managing ContosoPharm's thermostat devices is to use IoT Hub. They could use IoT Central to do much of what they want to do, but one of their requirements is being able to update firmware for the devices even if the Internet isn't available temporarily. The device twin feature of IoT Hub is specifically designed for situations like that, so IoT Hub is a better option.

To keep the thermostats secure, you can recommend Azure Sphere. However, they will need to use devices that incorporate MCUs that are designed for Azure Sphere, and if those devices aren't yet available, it might be something that they can't implement right away. Even so, Azure Sphere is the best solution for keeping IoT devices secure, and ContosoPharm would be appreciative of knowing about it.

The best way for ContosoPharm to analyze their big data and build models is to use Azure Synapse analytics. This is an end-to-end solution that works well with Data Lake Storage. Since they need a scalable solution that can also handle millions of rows of data, HDInsight is also a good recommendation for them. They also mentioned they want to work with some unstructured data. Azure Databricks is an ideal solution for using unstructured data, and its support of notebooks fits in well with the desire to use knowledge of Jupyter Notebooks.

To enable users who don't know how to program to build ML models, you can recommend Azure Machine Learning to ContosoPharm. They'll need to use the Enterprise edition so they have access to visual designers, but this will allow them to build ML models in a drag-and-drop interface.

To relieve the IT support strain on the IT department, you can recommend Azure Cognitive Services and Azure Bot Service in order to build an AI support agent. Using this method, they can easily understand natural language and offer suggestions using a chat bot.

In order to monitor the memory usage of the VM and reboot it when necessary, ContosoPharm can use Azure Monitor and configure alerts to call a Function App to run some code to reboot the VM. Since the CIO wants to be informed when the VM is resized to account for memory pressure, you could also suggest that they use Logic Apps to create a workflow. You can use Event Grid to listen for an event when the VM resizes, and Logic Apps can then run a flow that sends a text message to the CIO.

To track the work that's being done on their leaking app, you can recommend Azure DevOps and Azure Boards. This would make it easy to track different tasks and their current status.

The developer who needs access to VMs with specific tools installed can use Azure DevTest Labs. By creating a custom image that includes all the tools and debug symbols he needs, he can always access a VM with what he needs very quickly.

To add some agility to their ability to manage their source code and easily test and deploy their app when a new version is compiled, you can recommend that ContosoPharm's development team use GitHub as a source code repository and GitHub Actions to deploy to Azure automatically when a new version is built.

To create and delete web apps quickly and easily, you can recommend that the developer use the Az module in PowerShell or the Azure CLI. Using these, the developer can script these operations so he can easily create web apps and configure them the way he needs them and then easily delete them all.

For working on his Bash scripts, the developer should use Azure Cloud Shell. Because Cloud Shell uses a mounted file system, any files he uses will be available in any Cloud Shell session, and the built-in Monaco editor makes it easy to edit and develop his scripts. Cloud Shell also solves the problem of making the developer productive while he's on the train. By installing the Azure mobile app on his iPad, he can access a Cloud Shell session on that device and get his work done.

To ensure they are keeping up with best practices, ContosoPharm can use Azure Advisor. Advisor will show them where they aren't following best practices, along with remediation steps to follow.

ARM templates would be an ideal choice to ensure they can redeploy their environment in another Azure region.

They can keep track of any possible service incidents in Azure using Azure Service Health in the Azure portal.

Chapter summary

We covered a lot of ground in this chapter. You learned about some of the latest technologies in cloud computing, and you learned how you can interact and manage Azure resources in multiple ways.

Here's a summary of what this chapter covered.

- The Internet of Things (IoT) refers to devices with sensors that communicate with each other and with the Internet.
- Azure IoT Hub allows you to manage IoT devices and route messages to and from those devices.
- Azure IoT Hub Provisioning Service makes it easy to provision a large number of devices into IoT Hub.
- Azure IoT Central is a SaaS offering for monitoring IoT devices.
- Azure Sphere is a service for securing IoT devices.
- Azure Sphere is composed of the Azure Sphere MCU, the Azure Sphere OS, and the Azure Sphere Security Service.
- Big data refers to more data that you can analyze through conventional means within a desired timeframe.
- Azure Synapse is the replacement for SQL Data Warehouse.
- Azure Synapse stores big data and also provides for data analysis in a cluster.
- An Azure Synapse cluster consists of Synapse SQL, Apache Spark integration, data integration of Apache Spark and Azure Data Lake Storage, and a web-based user interface called Azure Synapse Studio.
- Data Lake Storage is good for any type of data because it stores unstructured data.
- HDInsight is Microsoft's solution for clustered Hadoop processing of big data.
- Azure Databricks is a good solution for modeling data from a data warehouse so that it can be effectively used in ML modeling.
- Databricks clusters are made up of notebooks that can store all types of information.
- The process of AI decision-making at several points along the neural network is referred to as the ML pipeline.
- Azure Machine Learning uses cloud-based resources to train ML models much faster.
- The Enterprise edition of Azure Machine Learning offers designers that allow you to build, train, and score ML models in a drag-and-drop interface.
- Cognitive Services provide numerous APIs that allow you to quickly develop machine learning solutions.

- Azure Bot Service runs on Azure App Service and makes it easy to build powerful AI-driven interaction.
- Serverless computing refers to using surplus VMs in Azure to run your code on demand. You pay only for when your code runs.
- Azure Functions is the compute component of serverless in Azure.
- Azure Logic Apps is a workflow serverless solution that uses connectors, triggers, and actions.
- Azure Event Grid makes it possible to raise and handle events as you interact with your Azure resources.
- Azure DevOps is an easy way to plan, track, and manage projects and work with teams.
- Azure DevTest Labs makes it easy to access ready-made VMs that are configured exactly the way you need them to be.
- GitHub is a source code repository and a web portal for working with those repositories.
- GitHub Actions allow you to add event-driven workflows to events in GitHub using either preconfigured Actions in the Marketplace or Actions you build with YAML files.
- The Azure portal is a web-based interface for interacting with your Azure services. It uses ARM API calls under the hood to talk to Azure Resource Manager.
- Azure PowerShell Az is a cross-platform PowerShell module that makes it easy to manage Azure resources in PowerShell.
- The Azure CLI is a command line tool that is cross-platform and can be scripted in multiple languages.
- Azure Cloud Shell provides command line access to Azure from just about any device.
- Cloud Shell persists any files copied to it by using an Azure storage account.
- The Azure Mobile app allows you to manage your Azure resources from your iOS or Android device.
- Azure Advisor provides best practice recommendations in the area of high availability, security, performance, and cost.
- ARM templates are JSON files that can be used to create and modify Azure resources using Azure Resource Manager.
- Azure Monitor aggregates metrics for Azure resources. You can create alerts based on those metrics.
- Azure Service Health provides information related to incidents in Azure that impact your resources.

CHAPTER 4

Describe general security and network security features

So far, we've wandered into the neighborhood of security in Azure, but we haven't really dived in. That's going to change in this chapter. Naturally, security is of great interest to anyone moving to the cloud. After all, it's not just applications that businesses move to the cloud. They also move large amounts of data—some of which is highly sensitive—and they want to ensure their data is safe from people on the outside. They also want to ensure their own employees don't have access to resources and data they don't need. Also, many businesses have legal requirements for data handling, and they need to trust that their cloud providers meet those requirements.

Azure can help with all these requirements. Azure Security Center can provide confidence that security best practices are being met; Azure Key Vault can ensure secrets are encrypted; Azure Sentinel can watch your Azure resources for threats and respond to them; and Azure Dedicated Host can help you ensure compliance by hosting your VMs on a dedicated host computer.

Also, security threats against networks are a great concern for most businesses and Azure has you covered there as well. In this chapter, we'll talk about defense in depth and how it can help to protect your data. We'll also cover Network Security Groups (NSGs) as a way to control the traffic within your network, Azure Firewall as a means of protecting your network from bad actors, and Azure DDoS Protection as a solution that can prevent a malicious attack that affects access to network resources.

Skills covered in this chapter:

- Describe Azure security features
- Describe Azure network security

Skill 4.1: Describe Azure security features

Ask anyone moving to the cloud what their concerns are, and most will mention security. But what exactly does "security" mean? Security is multi-faceted, and it starts with making sure your resources are configured correctly for security. However, even when you have done everything right, you can still be at risk from bad actors. There's also risk from the inside as employees gain access to sensitive data and systems. Malicious employees can breach security, and there's also the risk of a well-intentioned employee unintentionally creating a security concern.

> **This section covers:**
> - Azure Security Center
> - Key Vault
> - Azure Sentinel
> - Azure Dedicated Host

Azure Security Center

Most companies have someone whose job is to learn best practices and ensure the company complies with them. When it comes to Azure, learning those best practices can be a tough job because of the large number of services available. Because Azure is always changing and evolving, this job is made even tougher.

Fortunately, Azure Security Center can help you keep up with best practices, but it also can help with providing the steps you need to take to keep your resources configured in a way that makes them more secure. Security Center can even help you with keeping your on-premises resources secure.

Security Center offers two tiers of service:

Free tier The free tier provides general assessment and recommendations for securing your Azure resources and also provides a secure score showing you the overall security of your resources.

Azure Defender tier The Azure Defender tier adds functionality for securing VMs, applications, and networks. It also offers additional features such as advanced threat detection, analysis from Microsoft Threat Intelligence, the ability to manage the regulatory compliance of your Azure resources, and Microsoft Defender for Endpoint for your servers. The Azure Defender tier is billed by the hour, and full details on pricing can be found at *https://azure.microsoft.com/en-us/pricing/details/security-center*.

To get started with Security Center, click **Security Center** in the menu on the Azure portal homepage. This will take you to the **Overview** blade where you can see an overview of all your resources being protected by Security Center, as shown in Figure 4-1.

There are four primary areas of coverage in Security Center.

- **Secure Score** Provides a Secure Score, which shows the security of your resources. This area also shows a breakdown of completed controls (broad categories that are broken out into security recommendations) and recommendations that exist within the controls.
- **Regulatory Compliance** Provides a high-level overview of the regulatory compliance of your Azure resources.

- **Azure Defender** Shows you the percentage of protection provided by Azure Defender. (Azure Defender requires the Azure Defender pricing tier of Security Center.)
- **Inventory** Provides an overall view of the health of your Azure resources.

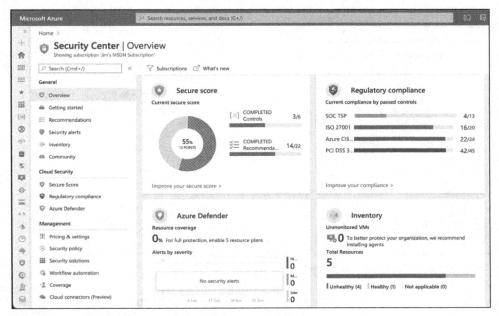

FIGURE 4-1 Azure Security Center

To the right of these four main areas, you'll find further insights into your resources, including resources with the most prevalent recommendations and controls that offer the highest potential increase of your secure score. Figure 4-2 shows insights for my Azure resources, and it clearly shows that I can increase my secure score by 45% percent by enabling multi-factor authentication.

To see a full list of all Security Center recommendations, click **Recommendations** in the menu on the left side of the portal. This provides a view of all Security Center controls, and you can expand a control to see all the recommendations in each control, as shown in Figure 4-3.

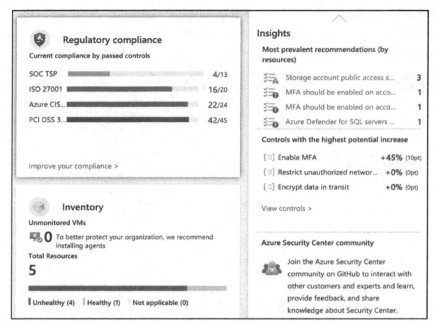

FIGURE 4-2 Azure Security Center Insights

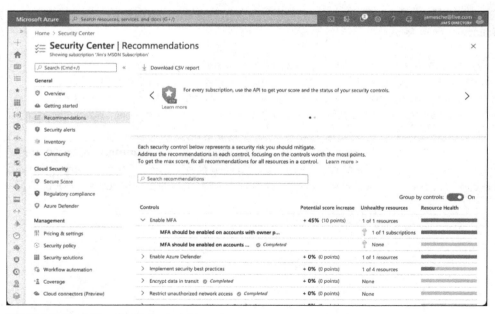

FIGURE 4-3 Azure Security Center Insights

If you're not sure how to address a particular recommendation, you can click the recommendation to get more information. After clicking the recommendation, you'll see remediation steps that you can perform to comply with the recommendation, as shown in Figure 4-4.

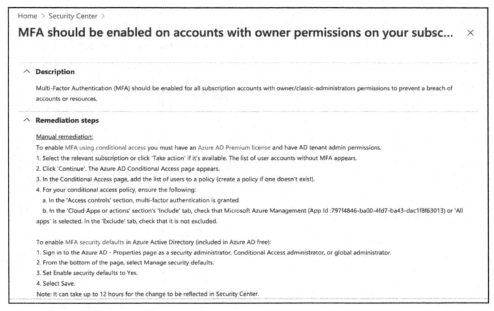

FIGURE 4-4 Remediation steps for a recommendation

The Inventory view is helpful for keeping your resources secure. When you click **Inventory** in the menu on the left side in the portal, you'll see a list of all your Azure resources, along with the health of each resource, as shown in Figure 4-5.

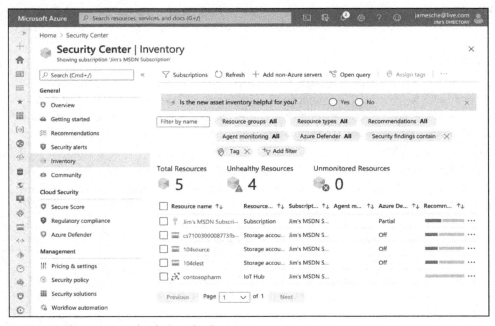

FIGURE 4-5 The Inventory view in Security Center

To see more detail on the secure state of any resource, click the resource. In Figure 4-6, I've clicked a storage account, and this view shows me that I should disallow public access on the storage account. Security Center also provides a **Quick Fix** button that will automatically fix this issue for me.

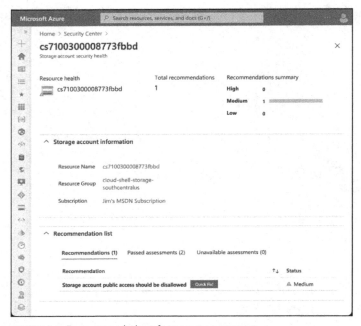

FIGURE 4-6 Recommendations for a storage account

Key Vault

Most applications use sensitive or secret information. For example, an application that uses a database needs to know how to connect to that database, and that connection information is stored in a connection string. The connection string might contain a username and password that protects the database and storing that username and password in a clear text file would be an obvious security risk.

Azure Key Vault provides a secure way to store secrets, keys, and certificates. Once an item is stored in Key Vault, you can apply security policies that define which users and applications can access it. Key Vault is encrypted using encryption keys, but Microsoft has no visibility into the encryption keys or the encrypted data.

Key Vaults are created in the Azure portal, as shown in Figure 4-7.

There are two pricing tiers available in Key Vault: Standard and Premium. The only difference between the two is that keys are stored in hardware security modules (HSMs) in the Premium tier. An HSM is a separate piece of hardware that is designed for securely storing encrypted content, and it's also specialized for processing cryptographic data.

Create key vault   ✕

Azure Key Vault is a cloud service used to manage keys, secrets, and certificates. Key Vault eliminates the need for developers to store security information in their code. It allows you to centralize the storage of your application secrets which greatly reduces the chances that secrets may be leaked. Key Vault also allows you to securely store secrets and keys backed by Hardware Security Modules or HSMs. The HSMs used are Federal Information Processing Standards (FIPS) 140-2 Level 2 validated. In addition, key vault provides logs of all access and usage attempts of your secrets so you have a complete audit trail for compliance. Learn more

Project details

Select the subscription to manage deployed resources and costs. Use resource groups like folders to organize and manage all your resources.

Subscription *	Jim's MSDN Subscription	⌄
└── Resource group *	AZ900	⌄

Create new

Instance details

Key vault name * ⓘ	CPVault	✓
Region *	(US) East US	⌄
Pricing tier * ⓘ	Standard	⌄
Soft delete ⓘ	(Enable) Disable	
Retention period (days) * ⓘ	90	
Purge protection ⓘ	Enable (Disable)	

| Review + create | | < Previous | Next : Access policy > |

FIGURE 4-7 Creating a Key Vault

EXAM TIP

Keeping encryption keys in an HSM boundary is required for Federal Information Processing Standard (FIPS) 140-2, so companies that need to maintain compliance with FIPS 140-2 can do so by using the Premium tier of Key Vault.

You can import a key, secret, or certificate into Key Vault, but Key Vault can also generate security keys and certificates for you. For example, you might want to generate a security key that your company can use to sign certificates. If you want to generate a 4,096-bit security key for this purpose and store it in Key Vault, click **Keys** and then click **Generate/Import**, as shown in Figure 4-8.

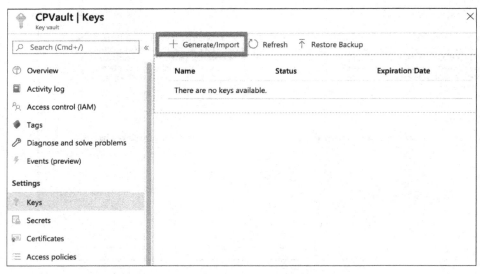

FIGURE 4-8 Adding a key to Key Vault

In Figure 4-9, a 4,096-bit RSA key is being generated and stored in Key Vault.

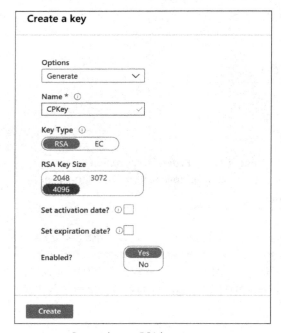

FIGURE 4-9 Generating an RSA key

As shown in Figure 4-10, once the key has been stored, you can view the entry to get the key identifier, which is a URL that can be used by authorized users or applications to retrieve the key. However, you cannot view the key because it's encrypted and not available except through the key identifier.

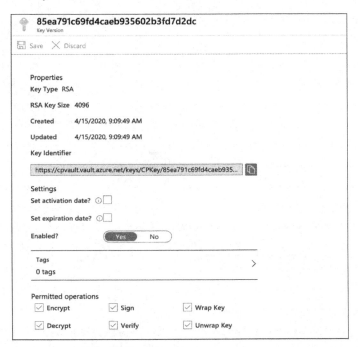

FIGURE 4-10 Details on a key

Another common use scenario for Key Vault is to store encryption keys for Azure VMs. One of the security recommendations offered by Security Center is to encrypt VM disks. A VM disk is stored as a VHD file, and when it's encrypted, the host operating system that runs the VM must be able to access the security key in order to decrypt the VHD and run the VM. Key Vault offers capabilities that are specifically targeted for this kind of scenario.

In order to use Key Vault for disk encryption keys, the access policies must be configured to allow the vault for disk encryption. If this wasn't done when the vault was created, you can change it by clicking **Access Policies**, and checking the **Azure Disk Encryption For Volume Encryption** option, as shown in Figure 4-11.

FIGURE 4-11 Setting access policies to allow access to Azure Disk Encryption

Azure Disk Encryption is enabled on your VMs using Azure PowerShell, the Azure command-line interface (CLI), or an ARM template.

> **MORE INFO   ENABLING ENCRYPTION**
>
> In order to enable encryption and store the keys in Key Vault, your VMs and Key Vault must be in the same Azure subscription, and they must be in the same Azure region. For more details on disk encryption requirements and steps to enable encryption, see: *https://bit.ly/az900-keyvaultvm*.

Azure Sentinel

When it comes to securing data and resources, many businesses use tried and proven frameworks that are designed to focus on what's most important, such as SOAR (Security Orchestration, Automation, and Response) or SIEM (Security Information and Event Management). Many companies, in fact, use SOAR and SIEM in combination.

Implementing SOAR and SIEM can be challenging. Many companies hire security experts to implement them in their businesses. Microsoft wanted to make SOAR and SIEM easy to implement, even for people who aren't security experts. The result of their work is Azure Sentinel.

> **EXAM TIP**
>
> Azure Sentinel isn't only for Azure. It can also provide threat reporting and analysis for on-premises resources and for resources on other clouds.

To start using Azure Sentinel, you first create a Sentinel workspace. Once you do that, you'll see the Azure Sentinel Workspaces screen shown in Figure 4-12. Click the **Connect Workspace** button to create an instance of Azure Log Analytics and add it to your Sentinel workspace. If you already have an instance of Log Analytics, you can choose it to add it to Azure Sentinel.

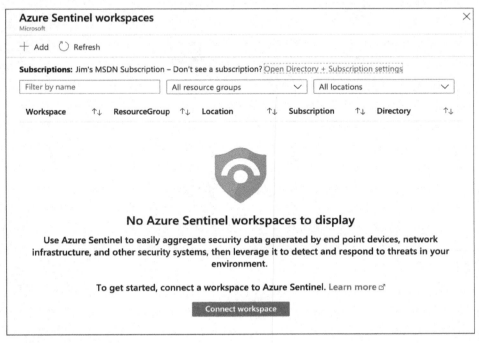

FIGURE 4-12 Creating an Azure Sentinel workspace

> **NOTE   AZURE SENTINEL AND LOG ANALYTICS**
>
> Azure Sentinel sits on top of Log Analytics. As Log Analytics collects information from your Azure resources, Azure Sentinel watches that information for threats.

After you add Log Analytics to Azure Sentinel, you connect data sources to Sentinel using *connectors* by clicking the **Connect** button, as shown in Figure 4-13.

Microsoft provides connectors for Azure and other Microsoft products, but there are also connectors for third parties. In Figure 4-14, you can see a connector for Amazon Web Services.

FIGURE 4-13 Collecting data using Azure Sentinel

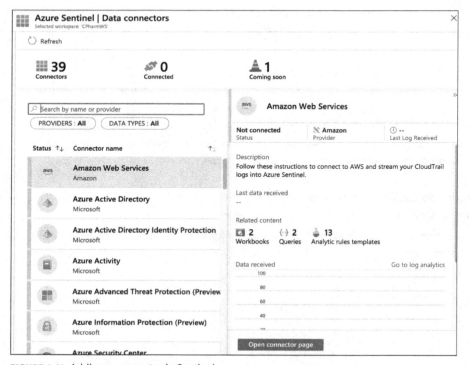

FIGURE 4-14 Adding a connector in Sentinel

Once you add a connector, you'll see prerequisites for the connector, as well as next steps you need to take. In Figure 4-15, we've added a connector for Azure Active Directory.

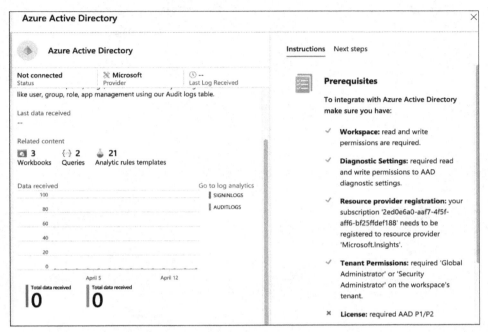

FIGURE 4-15 The Azure Active Directory connector in Sentinel

The list of prerequisites is an active list that shows the current status of all prerequisites. In Figure 4-15, all prerequisites have been met except for the Azure Active Directory license requirement that is showing an X icon.

Clicking **Next Steps** allows you to take the steps necessary to complete adding your connector. In Figure 4-16, Next Steps for configuring the Azure Active Directory connector are shown.

After you add your connector, you'll save the configuration inside an Azure Monitor Workbook. Workbooks make it easy to aggregate data so that it's easier to consume.

Azure Sentinel can also search for specific security threats. Many queries are provided that search for threats of all kinds. By clicking **Hunting**, you can select a query you want to run against your resources, as shown in Figure 4-17.

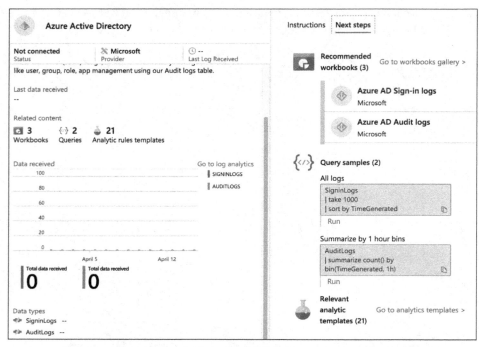

FIGURE 4-16 Next Steps to configure the Azure Active Directory connector in Sentinel

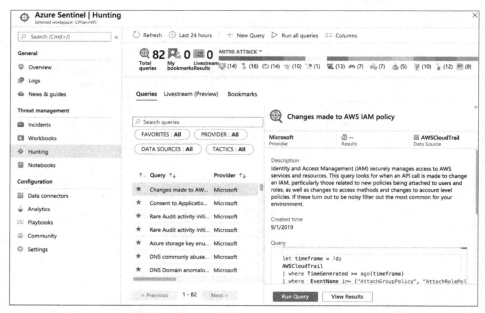

FIGURE 4-17 Hunting for threats in Azure Sentinel

When Sentinel finds a problem, you can have it respond using a *Playbook*. A Playbook is a workflow that runs in response to an alert in Sentinel. To create a Playbook, click **Playbooks** and then click **Add Playbook**, as shown in Figure 4-18.

FIGURE 4-18 Adding a Playbook in Sentinel

When you add a new Playbook, Sentinel will ask you to create a new Logic App. That's because Playbooks use Logic Apps for their workflows. As of this writing, the user experience is a little disconnected. After the Logic App is created, you'll need to click **Blank Logic App**, as shown in Figure 4-19.

FIGURE 4-19 Creating a new Logic App for a Sentinel Playbook

Enter **sentinel** in the search box and click **When A Response To An Azure Sentinel Alert Is Triggered**, as shown in Figure 4-20. After that, you can continue to build your workflow and add the actions you want to perform when the alert is triggered.

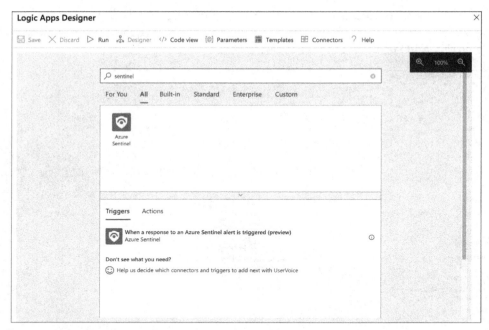

FIGURE 4-20 Adding a trigger for Azure Sentinel in a Logic App

Azure Dedicated Host

When you create a virtual machine—whether in Azure or anywhere else—that VM runs on a host computer. The host computer is a physical computer with a host operating system of its own, and the VM is created on that host computer. VMs that you create in Azure are dedicated to you, but the host computer usually has VMs running on it that are dedicated to other customers.

A dedicated VM on a shared host computer works well for many people, but if you work in an industry or for a company that has compliancy requirements that can't be met with a shared host computer, you might have some applications that you haven't been able to move to the cloud. Fortunately, Azure Dedicated Host provides a solution to compliance for those who need a more secure environment.

When you host your VMs in an Azure Dedicated Host, the physical host computer that runs your VMs is dedicated for your use. No other customer VMs will run on that host computer. Naturally, this means that Azure Dedicated Host isn't the least expensive way to host VMs, but if your compliance requirements mandate strict isolation of your VMs, the cost of using a dedicated host computer are worth it.

Azure Dedicated Hosts run inside of a *host group* that you create inside of an Azure region. Host groups contain one or more Azure Dedicated Hosts and VMs are then deployed to those hosts in the host group. Dedicated hosts support the use of availability zones and fault domains for fault tolerance, and support of Virtual Machine Scale Sets is currently in preview.

Skill 4.2: Describe Azure network security

Another component of security relates to the network. Securing the network requires a completely different set of tools and skills. Just as they do when planning security of data and resources, businesses often pay specialists to help with network security. In Azure, however, a large part of network security is taken care of for you. Even so, you will need to take some actions to keep yourself secure.

This section covers:
- Defense in depth
- Network Security Groups (NSGs)
- Azure Firewall
- Azure DDoS Protection

Defense in depth

Just for a moment, transport yourself back to medieval times and think about what it was like living in a castle. These weren't friendly times in many ways, and there was always a hostile force trying to gain entry into the fortress. To prevent invasion, moats were built around castles. The purpose of the moat was to prevent an opposing force from tunneling under the wall and gaining entry.

Even before an enemy reached the moat, archers along the high wall of the castle would pose a formidable risk to attackers approaching the castle. Assuming an opposing force made it past the archers and traversed the moat, they were met with a high wall and a sturdy gate. If they were able to make it past the gate, they were met with an army of men with swords and other nasty weapons.

Medieval folks had a pretty good idea when it came to security. They realized that a single opposing force wouldn't be enough to keep them secure. They needed layered opposition so that anyone defeating one method of security would be met with several more down the line.

This is a perfect example of defense in depth, and it's why defense in depth is often referred to as the "castle approach." When it comes to network security, this multi-layered approach is also the best way to keep your network safe. Azure Firewall can help prevent a malicious user from making it into your network, Network Security Groups can help you control network traffic inside your network, and Azure DDoS Protection can help to identify and mitigate malicious traffic that might otherwise seem normal.

Network Security Groups (NSGs)

A Network Security Group (NSG) allows you to filter traffic on your network and apply rules on that traffic. An NSG contains several built-in rules provided by Azure that are designed to allow your resources in the virtual network to communicate with each other. You can then add your own rules to the NSG to control traffic into and out of the network, and also between resources in the network.

Figure 4-21 shows a multi-tier application.

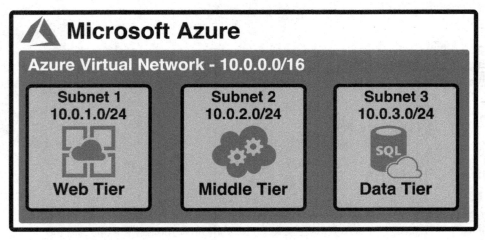

FIGURE 4-21 A multi-tier application

Here's the traffic flow of this application.

- Subnet 1 receives data from another virtual network running Azure Firewall.
- Subnet 1 communicates with Subnet 2 to process requests.
- Subnet 2 communicates with a database server in Subnet 3 in order to access data.

If you want to ensure a secure environment, Subnet 1 should not be able to directly communicate with resources in Subnet 3. Likewise, Subnet 3 should not be able to directly communicate with resources in Subnet 1. Finally, only Subnet 1 should be able to communicate with the other virtual network running Azure Firewall. You can use NSGs to implement rules that will enforce these policies.

NSGs can be associated with a subnet or to a network interface attached to a VM. Each network interface or subnet can only have one NSG associated with it, but you can create up to 1,000 rules in a single NSG, so you should be able to easily apply all the rule logic necessary for any task. If you associate an NSG to both a subnet and to one or more network interfaces inside that subnet, the rules for the NSG associated with the network interfaces are applied first, followed by the subnet's NSG's rules.

EXAM TIP

An NSG that's associated with a subnet affects all VMs inside that subnet, as well as traffic to and from the subnet. For example, let's say you configure an NSG to prevent all traffic except traffic from the Internet and you then associate that NSG with a subnet containing two VMs. In that event, those two VMs will no longer be able to communicate with each other because only traffic from the Internet is allowed by the NSG.

To prevent rules from interfering with each other, each rule you create in an NSG has a priority between 100 and 4,096. Rules with a lower priority take precedence over rules with a higher priority. Network traffic is applied against the rule with the lowest-priority number first. If the traffic matches that rule, the rule is applied, and processing of the rule stops. If the traffic doesn't match the rule, it is evaluated against the next-lowest priority rule. This continues until the traffic has either matched a rule, or there are no additional rules.

MORE INFO   PRIORITY OF DEFAULT RULES

The default rules that Azure applies to all NSGs have a priority in the 65,000 range. This prevents the default rules from ever overriding an explicit rule that you create, and it makes it easier for you to override the default rules if needed.

To create an NSG, search for **Network Security Group** in the Azure Marketplace. When you create an NSG, give it a name, enter a name in the **Name** field or click **Create New** to create a resource group, and choose a location for the NSG from the **Region** drop-down menu, as shown in Figure 4-22.

Create network security group

Basics   Tags   Review + create

Project details

Subscription *

Jim's MSDN Subscription

Resource group *

AZ900

Create new

Instance details

Name *

Subnet-1-NSG

Region *

(US) East US

Review + create   < Previous   Next : Tags >   Download a template for automation

FIGURE 4-22 Creating an NSG

After you create an NSG, you can then add inbound and outbound rules for the NSG. Once you open the NSG in the Azure portal, click **Inbound Security Rules** to add new inbound rules, and click **Outbound Security Rules** to add outbound rules.

In Figure 4-23, **Inbound Security Rules** has been clicked to add a new rule that allows traffic from the virtual network running Azure Firewall. After that, the NSG will be associated with Subnet-1. Note that you can associate the NSG with a subnet or network interface before adding rules.

Subnet-1-NSG | Inbound security rules
Network security group

Search (Cmd+/)   + Add   Default rules   Refresh

	Priority	Name	Port	Protocol	Source
Overview	65000	AllowVnetInBound	Any	Any	VirtualNetwc
Activity log	65001	AllowAzureLoadBala...	Any	Any	AzureLoadBa
Access control (IAM)	65500	DenyAllInBound	Any	Any	Any
Tags					
Diagnose and solve problems					

Settings

Inbound security rules

Outbound security rules

Network interfaces

Subnets

FIGURE 4-23 Inbound Security Rules for an NSG

Click **Add** to add a new NSG rule. Figure 4-24 shows a new rule being added that allows traffic into this subnet from the address space of another virtual network that's running Azure Firewall.

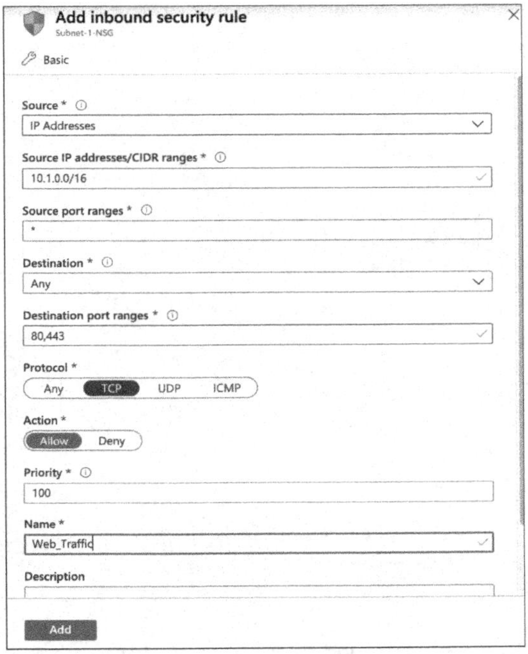

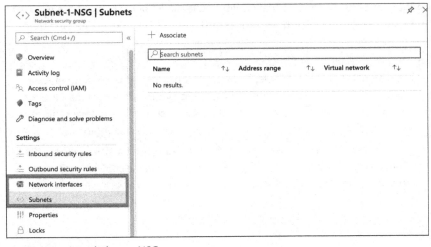

FIGURE 4-24 Creating an NSG inbound rule

The rule being configured in Figure 4-24 uses CIDR notation for the source IP addresses, but you can also enter a specific IP address or change the **Source** drop-down menu to **Any** if you want the rule to apply to all IP addresses. Click Add to create the rule.

Once you've created a rule, click **Subnets** to associate an NSG with a subnet, or click **Network Interfaces** to associate it with a network interface used by a VM. Lastly, click **Associate**, as shown in Figure 4-25.

FIGURE 4-25 Associating an NSG

Figure 4-26 shows the blade where an NSG is associated with a subnet.

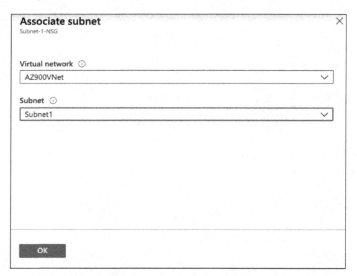

FIGURE 4-26 Associating an NSG with a subnet

Outbound security rules are created in the same way inbound rules are created. You aren't required, however, to create a corresponding outbound rule for every inbound rule. NSGs maintain what's called a *flow record* that stores the state of a connection, and the NSG will allow traffic that corresponds to that flow record without an explicit rule. If a security rule allows inbound traffic to port 80 from IP addresses in the range of 10.1.0.0/16, such as the rule configured in Figure 4-24, the NSG will also allow outbound traffic on port 80 to addresses in that same range using the flow record. The flow record is no longer in effect once traffic stops flowing for a few minutes.

There are some cases where you won't know the specific IP address range. For example, if you want to configure an NSG rule on a virtual network that allows all traffic from the Internet, you wouldn't specify an exact address range. To deal with that, NSGs allow you to use *service tags* when configuring rules.

A service tag is a special identifier created by Microsoft that applies to the Internet or to a specific service type within Azure. For example, if you have some web apps running in Azure App Service, and you want to allow them to communicate with your subnet, you can use the AppService service tag in your inbound rule to allow that. Azure services also have region-specific service tags so that you can allow or deny traffic only from specific regions.

To use a service tag, set the **Source** of your rule to **Service Tag**. You can then select a service tag from the **Source** drop-down menu. In Figure 4-27, the AppService.CentralUS service tag is being used to allow traffic from Azure App Service resources in the Central US region.

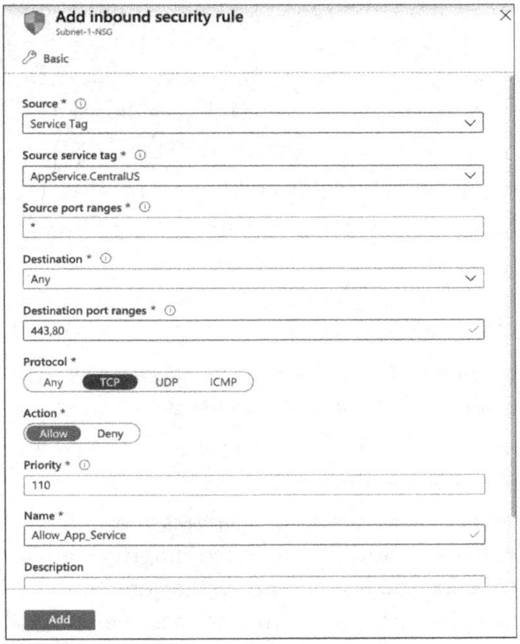

FIGURE 4-27 Using a service tag in an NSG rule

Azure Firewall

In computing parlance, a firewall is an appliance through which network traffic travels into and out of a particular network. The purpose of a firewall is to allow only desired traffic on the network and to reject any traffic that might be malicious or that comes from an unknown origin. A firewall imposes control on the network using rules that specify a source and destination IP address range and port combination.

In a typical firewall configuration, all traffic is denied by default. In order for the firewall to allow traffic to pass through it, a rule must match that traffic. For example, if you want to allow someone on the public Internet to access a web application you have running on a particular server, create a firewall rule that allows communication to ports 80 and 443 (the ports for HTTP and HTTPS traffic). You then configure the rule to send that traffic to your web server.

There are several firewalls available from third parties in the Azure Marketplace, but Microsoft also offers its own firewall called Azure Firewall. Azure Firewall is a PaaS offering in Azure, and it's easily managed and offers a 99.95 percent uptime guarantee. Azure Firewall scales according to your networking needs, so you don't have to worry about traffic spikes causing latency or downtime for your applications.

A typical setup for Azure Firewall consists of the following:

- A centralized hub network that contains the Azure Firewall and a VM that operates as a *jumpbox*. The firewall exposes a public IP address, but the jumpbox VM does not.

- One or more additional networks (called *spoke* networks) that don't expose a public IP address. These networks contain your various Azure resources.

The jumpbox is a VM that you can remote into in order to manage other VMs in your networks. All other VMs are configured to only allow remote access from the jumpbox VM's IP address. If you want to access a VM in a spoke network, you first remote into the jumpbox VM, and then you remote into the spoke network VM from the jumpbox. This set up is referred to as a *hub-and-spoke* configuration, and it provides additional security for your network resources.

Figure 4-28 is an illustration of a typical hub-and-spoke configuration that also includes Azure Firewall. Traffic that comes from the Internet over port 443 (HTTPS traffic) is directed by the firewall to a web server running in Spoke VNet 1. Traffic that comes in over the remote desktop port is directed to the jumpbox VM, and users can then use Remote Desktop Protocol (RDP) from the jumpbox VM to a VM in Spoke VNet 2.

Before you can configure a firewall to handle network traffic, you'll need to create an instance of Azure Firewall. You can choose to include Azure Firewall when you create your virtual network in Azure, or you can create a firewall and add it to an existing virtual network. Figure 4-29 shows Azure Firewall being created during the creation of a new virtual network.

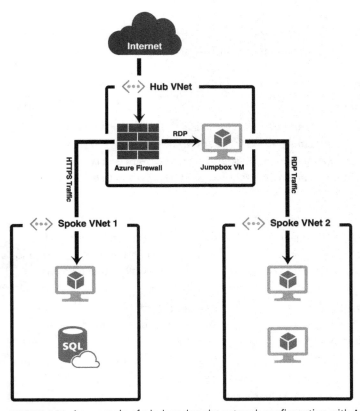

FIGURE 4-28 An example of a hub and spoke network configuration with Azure Firewall

FIGURE 4-29 Creating Azure Firewall

When you create a firewall during the creation of a virtual network, Azure creates a subnet in the virtual network called *AzureFirewallSubnet*, and it uses the address space you specify for that subnet. A public IP address is also created for the firewall so that it can be accessed from the Internet.

> **MORE INFO** **AZURE BASTION**
>
> In this example, we're using a jumpbox and JIT access to explain the benefit of Azure Firewall, but a much better approach to remote access for your VMs is to use Azure Bastion because it doesn't require you to expose a public IP address. Azure Bastion isn't currently covered in the AZ-900 exam, but you can find out more about it by browsing to *https://bit.ly/az900-azurebastion*.

While the PaaS nature of Azure Firewall does remove much of the complexity, using a firewall isn't as simple as enabling it in your virtual network. You will also need to tell Azure to send traffic to the firewall, and then you'll need to configure rules in the firewall so that it knows what to do with that traffic.

To send traffic to your firewall, you need to create a route table. A route table is an Azure resource that is associated with a subnet, and it contains rules (called *routes*) that define how network traffic in the subnet is handled.

A route table is created using the Route Table item in the Azure Marketplace. Once you create a new route table, you must associate it with one or more subnets. To do that, click **Subnets** and then click **Associate**, as shown in Figure 4-30.

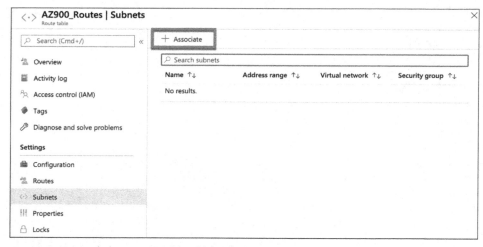

FIGURE 4-30 Associating a route table with a subnet

After you click **Associate**, select the **Virtual Network** and the **Subnet**, as shown in Figure 4-31.

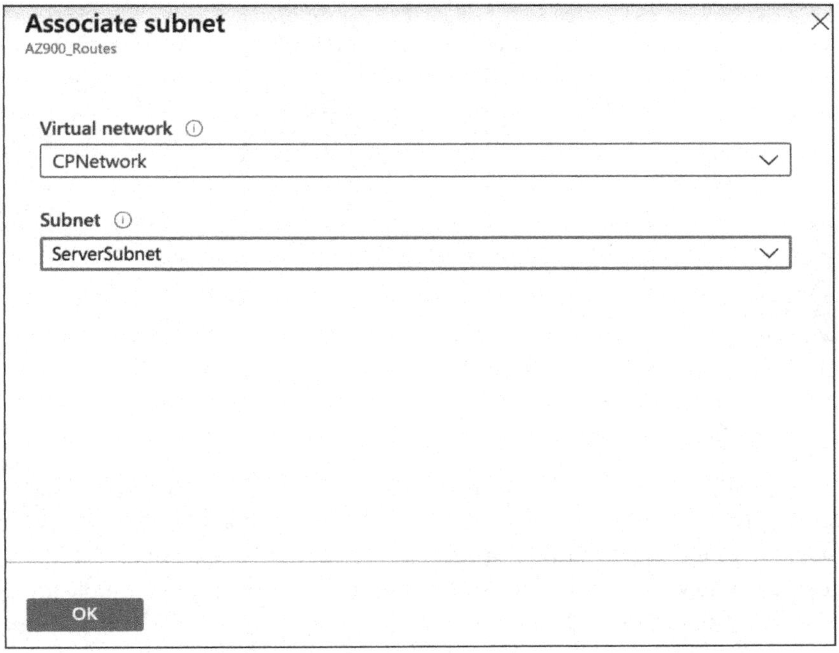

Associate subnet   ✕
AZ900_Routes

Virtual network ⓘ

| CPNetwork | ⌄ |

Subnet ⓘ

| ServerSubnet | ⌄ |

OK

FIGURE 4-31 Choosing a subnet to associate

NOTE   **ROUTE TABLE REGION**

Your route table must be in the same region as your virtual network. Otherwise, you won't be able to associate the subnet with the route table.

In our particular setup, we want to associate both the *JumpboxSubnet* and the *ServerSubnet* with the route table. This will ensure that the firewall will handle all network traffic to the jumpbox VM and all traffic from the *ServerSubnet*.

EXAM TIP

It's important to understand that a firewall can (and should) be used to filter traffic flowing into and out of a network. For example, you want the firewall to handle traffic into your jumpbox, but you also want to ensure that traffic flowing from the subnet where other servers are located is secure and not inappropriately sending data out of your network.

Once we've associated the route table with the subnets, we create a user-defined route so that traffic is directed through Azure Firewall. To do that, click **Routes** and then click **Add**, as shown in Figure 4-32.

FIGURE 4-32 Adding a new user-defined route to the route table

Figure 4-33 shows the configuration of a new user-defined route named `ToFirewall`. This route is configured for 0.0.0.0/0, which is the notation for all traffic. It's then sending that traffic to a virtual appliance (Azure Firewall, in this case) located at IP address 10.1.1.4, which is the internal IP address of this firewall. Once this route is configured, it will immediately apply to all devices on the subnets associated with the route table.

Add route
AZ900_Routes

Route name *
ToFirewall

Address prefix * ⓘ
0.0.0.0/0

Next hop type ⓘ
Virtual appliance

Next hop address * ⓘ
10.1.1.4

ⓘ Ensure you have IP forwarding enabled on your virtual appliance. You can enable this by navigating to the respective network interface's IP address settings.

OK

FIGURE 4-33 Adding a user-defined route

Remember, Azure Firewall blocks all traffic by default, so at this point, there's no way to reach the jumpbox VM that's in the `JumpboxSubnet`. In order to access that VM, you must configure a firewall rule in Azure Firewall that will forward the appropriate traffic to the jump-box VM.

To add a firewall rule, open Azure Firewall in the Azure portal and click **Rules**, select the type of rule, and click the **Add** button to add a new rule collection, as shown in Figure 4-34.

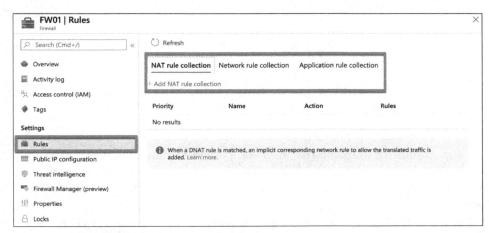

FIGURE 4-34 Azure Firewall rule collections in the Azure portal

There are three types of rule collections available in Azure Firewall.

- **NAT Rule Collection**   Network address translation (NAT) rules are used to forward traffic from the firewall to another device on the network.
- **Network Rule Collection**   These are rules that allow traffic on specific IP address ranges and ports that you specify.
- **Application Rules Collection**   Application rules are used to allow applications, such as Windows Update, to communicate across your network. Also, they can be used to allow particular domain names such as *azure.com* and *microsoft.com*.

Azure Firewall combines all the rules of a specific type and priority into a rule collection. The priority is a number between 100 and 65,000. Lower numbers represent a higher rule priority and are processed first. In other words, if you want to ensure that a rule is always applied before all other rules, include that rule in a rule collection with a priority of 100.

When network traffic enters the firewall, NAT rules are applied first. If the traffic matches a NAT rule, Azure Firewall applies an implicit network rule so the traffic can be routed appropriately, and all further rule processing stops.

If there isn't a NAT rule that matches the traffic, network rules are applied. If a network rule matches the traffic, all further rule processing is stopped. If there isn't a network rule that applies to the traffic, the application rules are applied. If none of the application rules match the traffic, the traffic is rejected by the firewall.

To allow access to remote into the jumpbox VM, you might configure a NAT rule that forwards any traffic on port 55000 to port 3389 (the port for remote desktop) on the internal IP of the jumpbox VM, as shown in Figure 4-35. Because port 55000 is a general port that wouldn't normally be used for remote desktop, someone with malicious intent would likely never discover that it's being used for that purpose.

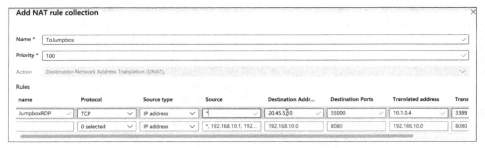

FIGURE 4-35 Adding a NAT rule

In addition to rules that you configure, the threat intelligence feature in Azure Firewall can protect you from known-malicious IP addresses and domain names. Microsoft constantly updates its list of known-bad actors, and the data collected is provided in the Microsoft Threat Intelligence feed.

When you enable threat intelligence, you can choose to have Azure alert you if traffic from a known-malicious IP address or domain name attempts to enter your network. Also, you can choose to have the traffic denied by the firewall automatically, as shown in Figure 4-36.

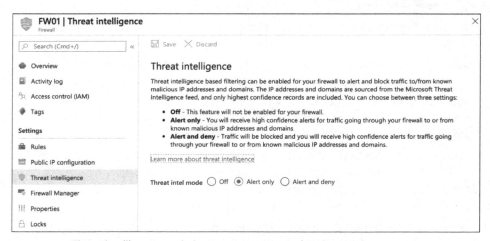

FIGURE 4-36 Threat intelligence can help protect your Azure virtual network

Azure DDoS Protection

Cloud applications that are accessible from the Internet over a public IP address are susceptible to *distributed denial of service* (DDoS) attacks. DDoS attacks can overwhelm an application's resources and can often make the application completely unavailable until the attack is mitigated. DDoS attacks can also be used to exploit security flaws in an application and attack systems to which an application connects.

Azure uses DDoS Protection to help protect against DDoS attacks. DDoS Protection is a feature of Azure Virtual Networks. There are two tiers of DDoS Protection: Basic and Standard.

- **Basic** Basic protects you from volume-based DDoS attacks by distributing large amounts of volume across Azure's entire network infrastructure. Basic protection is provided for you automatically in Azure. Basic DDoS Protection applies to both IPv4 and IPv6 public IP addresses. With the Basic tier, you have no logging or reporting of any DDoS mitigation, and there's no way to configure alerts so that you're notified if a problem is detected. However, the Basic tier is free and provides basic protection.

- **Standard** The DDoS Standard tier offers protection from volume-based DDoS attacks, and when it's used in combination with Azure Application Gateway, it also provides protection from attacks designed to target the security of your applications. It offers logging and alerting of DDoS events and mitigations, and if you need help during a DDoS attack, Microsoft provides access to experts who can help you. The DDoS Standard tier applies only to IPv6 public IP addresses. The Standard tier is targeted at enterprise customers and is billed at $2,994 per month, plus a small fee per gigabyte for data that is processed. The fixed monthly price covers up to 100 resources. If you need to cover additional resources, you pay an additional $30 per resource, per month.

To enable the DDoS Standard tier, click **DDoS Protection** in your virtual network in the Azure portal and select **Standard**, as shown in Figure 4-37.

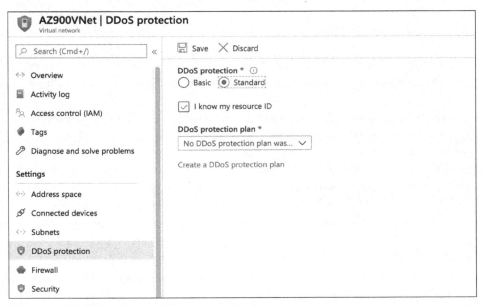

FIGURE 4-37 DDoS Protection in the Azure portal

To enable Standard tier, you'll need a DDoS Protection plan. If you don't currently have one, click **Create A DDoS Protection Plan** to create one in the Azure portal. You can then apply that DDoS Protection plan to your virtual network and to other virtual networks that you have access to in Azure. Virtual networks that use the DDoS Protection plan aren't required to be in the same subscription, so in most cases, an organization will only need a single DDoS Protection plan to protect all its virtual networks.

EXAM TIP

The fact that you can add virtual networks from multiple Azure subscriptions to the same DDoS Protection plan is an important concept. You are billed a large monthly charge for the DDoS Protection plan, and if you create two DDoS Protection plans, you have just doubled your costs.

DDoS Protection Standard tier monitors your network traffic 24/7, and it uses machine learning to profile your traffic over time and adjust itself to accommodate your network's traffic profile. During a DDoS event, Standard tier allows you to stream logs to an SIEM system. SIEM systems are designed to allow for the aggregation of data from a large number of sources for the purpose of analysis and to comply with data retention policies and standards.

Once you've configured any alerts and monitoring for DDoS Protection, you can simulate a DDoS event using a BreakingPoint Cloud account available at: *https://www.ixiacom.com/products/breakingpoint-cloud*. This allows you to ensure that your DDoS Protection is protecting you from DDoS attacks.

Thought experiment

You're now much more informed about security matters in the cloud. Let's put that knowledge to the test with a thought experiment. The answers to this thought experiment are in the section that follows.

ContosoPharm has discovered that you are a now a security guru and they've got some problems they'd like for you to solve for them. First of all, they've got a large number of Azure resources they've just deployed with a new application. Like most of their applications, this new application deals with sensitive data. They want to make sure they're complying with best practices for security. They also have some servers the application uses that are on-premises, so it's important that they find out if they're as secure as they should be.

Another concern ContosoPharm has is access to Azure VMs the app uses. The IT director wants to ensure that only computers on the ContosoPharm corporate network can remote desktop to these VMs, and only during certain time periods during the day.

One portion of the ContosoPharm app uses certificates for authentication, and they want to make sure these certificates are stored in a secure manner. They also need the ability to store encrypted keys so that they comply with FIPS 140-2.

The IT director for ContosoPharm has told her staff they need to implement SOAR and SIEM in their environment. They need this to work for both their Azure resources and resources they have in Amazon Web Services. They don't want to spend a lot of money on consulting, so they need an easy way to accomplish this.

One of the executives at ContosoPharm has pointed out that an upcoming component of the application will have strict compliance requirements, and she's concerned that the VMs hosting the application will be running on a host computer that is also running other customer VMs in Azure. She recommends that they host these VMs on-premises, but the IT director is concerned that doing so would cause a performance bottleneck. You should propose a way for ContosoPharm to deal with these concerns.

The app that they've deployed to the cloud is a multi-tier application. The CTO is concerned that the network engineers didn't secure the app well enough. He wants to ensure that traffic rules are implemented across the various tiers of the application. He also wants to make sure traffic from the outside that shouldn't make it to the network is rejected.

Finally, because this application is critical to ContosoPharm's operation, they are willing to invest the money they can save from your consulting on any solution that can help them prevent a distributed denial of service attack from causing availability problems.

What are your recommendations to ContosoPharm?

Thought experiment answers

This section covers answers to the thought experiment.

To ensure ContosoPharm is complying with best practices, they should use Azure Security Center. Not only can it report on their Azure services, but they can also get details on their on-premises resources. By using the just-in-time VM access features of Security Center, they can ensure that VMs can't be remoted into unless the source computer is on their corporate network. They can also restrict the times of day that VMs are accessible.

To store their certificates securely, they should use Azure Key Vault. They can also store their encrypted keys in Azure Key Vault, but because they need FIPS 140-2 compliance, they'll need to use the Premium tier.

To easily implement SOAR and SIEM in its environment, ContosoPharm should use Azure Sentinel. It can then configure connectors for its Azure and AWS services.

To address the compliance concern with VMs being hosted on the same host computer with other Azure customers, you can recommend the use of Azure Dedicated Host. This would allow ContosoPharm to create a host group and a dedicated host computer for hosting the VMs in an isolated environment, and it would prevent the bottleneck of hosting the VMs on-premises.

To impose rules on network traffic in their virtual networks, they should configure NSGs. To make sure traffic from the outside that shouldn't make it to the network gets blocked, they should use Azure Firewall and configure rules to allow only the inbound traffic that's appropriate. The NSGs they create should also impose rules on which tier of the application can accept traffic from the Internet.

To prevent DDoS attacks, they can purchase DDoS Standard. While the cost for this is relatively high, it does provide a high level of protection against DDoS attacks.

Chapter summary

This chapter introduced you to the security tools you can use to protect Azure resources, on-premises resources, and virtual networks. You also learned some security concepts that can help you to make better sense of how to configure these tools in Azure.

Here's a summary of what this chapter covered.

- Azure Security Center is a best practice analyzer for Azure resources and on-premises resources.
- Security Center covers three primary areas: policy and compliance, resource security hygiene, and threat protection.
- Just-in-time VM access can restrict VM remote desktop access to certain networks and certain times of day.
- Azure Key Vault provides a secure way to store secrets, keys, and certificates.
- Azure Key Vault Premium tier stores keys in hardware security modules (HSMs), making it FIPS 140-2–compliant.
- Azure Sentinel is a solution for implementing SOAR and SIEM in an environment.
- Sentinel can help watch for security threats in Azure, other clouds, and on-premises.
- Sentinel can take an action on a security alert using Playbooks, and Playbooks are built on top of Azure Logic Apps.
- Azure Dedicated Host allows you to host your VMs on a dedicated host computer.
- Azure Dedicated Host uses a host group to contain the dedicated host computers running your VMs.
- Defense in depth is also often called the "castle approach" because it represents multi-layered security strategies.
- Network Security Groups (NSGs) are rules that allow you to filter traffic on a network and control that traffic.
- NSG rules have a priority between 100 and 4,096, and rules with a lower priority number take precedence.
- Azure Firewall denies all traffic into specific subnets unless a rule is configured to allow that traffic.
- Azure Firewall is a stateful firewall that "remembers" the state of connections. This allows it to recognize malicious traffic that might otherwise seem normal.
- Azure DDoS Protection comes in two tiers: Basic and Standard.
- Basic is free and refers to the DDoS protection that Microsoft has in place to prevent Azure from being impacted by DDoS attacks.
- Standard can be used alongside Azure Application Gateway.

CHAPTER 5

Describe identity, governance, privacy, and compliance features

We've talked a lot about security, but when it comes to moving to the cloud, security isn't the only major concern companies have. They also want to have control over how resources are used, and they want to ensure that data is kept private after it's in the cloud provider's ecosystem. Also, many businesses are required to comply with regulations and standards, and by moving to the cloud, they're offloading some of that responsibility to the cloud provider. Therefore, they want to ensure a high level of confidence that the cloud provider is keeping them compliant.

Microsoft takes all these concerns seriously, and they provide powerful tools in Azure to meet their customers' needs. In this chapter, we'll talk about those tools and how to use them.

Skills covered in this chapter:

- Describe core Azure identity services
- Describe Azure governance features
- Describe privacy and compliance resources

Skill 5.1: Describe core Azure identity services

Security isn't only about controlling network traffic. In order to provide a secure environment, you must have some means of identifying who's accessing your application.

> **This section covers:**
> - Authentication and authorization
> - Azure Active Directory
> - Conditional Access, multifactor authentication (MFA), and single sign-on (SSO)

Authentication and authorization

In most business applications, not all users have the same privileges. For example, a website might allow a small number of users to add and revise content. Another smaller group of users might have the ability to decide who can add content. The vast majority of users, however, are just consumers of the content. They can't modify the content in any way, and they also can't grant other people the ability to access the content.

In order to implement this kind of control, you need to know who is using the application so you can determine what their level of privileges should be. To determine who is using the application, you would require that users log in, often with a username and password. Assuming the user provides the right credentials, that user is *authenticated* to the application.

Once a user is authenticated and begins interacting with an application, additional checks might take place to confirm which actions the user is and isn't allowed to perform. That process is called *authorization*, and authorization checks are performed against a user who is already authenticated.

This kind of authentication and authorization scenario isn't limited to a website scenario. When you log into the Azure portal, you are being authenticated. As you interact with Azure resources, you are also being authorized to perform the actions you're taking. Based on your level of privilege, you are only allowed to do certain things. For example, you might be authorized to create Azure resources but not authorized to give other people access to the Azure subscription you're using.

Azure uses a service called Azure Active Directory to enforce authentication and authorization in Azure, but it has many capabilities beyond simply authentication and authorization.

Azure Active Directory

If you have any experience with on-premises Windows Active Directory, you might find understanding Azure Active Directory (Azure AD) to be a challenge. That's because Azure AD isn't the cloud equivalent of Windows Active Directory. It's entirely different.

Azure AD is a cloud-based identity service in Azure that can help you authenticate and authorize users. You can use Azure AD to give users access to Azure resources. You can also give users access to third party resources used by your company and on-premises resources, all using the same username and password.

> **MORE INFO   GRANTING ACCESS TO AZURE RESOURCES**
>
> You'll learn about how you can authorize users to access your Azure resources when we cover role-based access control later in this skill.

The core of Azure AD is a directory of users. Each user has an *identity* that's comprised of a user ID, a password, and other properties. Users also have one or more *directory roles* assigned to them. The user ID and password are used to authenticate the user, and the roles are used for authorization to perform certain activities in Azure AD.

When you sign up for an Azure subscription, an Azure AD resource is automatically created for you, and it's used to control access to Azure resources you create under your subscription. Figure 5-1 shows Azure AD in the Azure portal.

FIGURE 5-1 Azure AD in the Azure portal

To view or manage users in Azure AD, click **Users** in the menu on the left side of the page. This opens the **All Users** blade shown in Figure 5-2.

FIGURE 5-2 The All Users blade in the Azure portal

The Azure AD shown in Figure 5-2 contains two users. The first user's source is Azure Active Directory, and this user was manually added to the directory. The other user is using a Microsoft Account to log in to the directory.

To add a new user from your company to your Azure AD, click **New User** to display the blade shown in Figure 5-3.

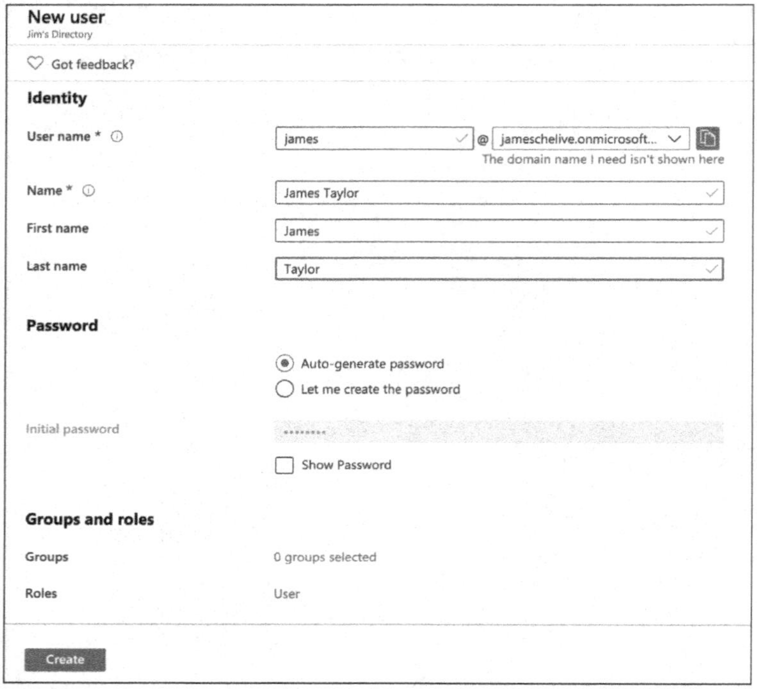

FIGURE 5-3 Adding a new Azure AD user

The specified username is used to log in to Azure AD. The domain name you use must be one that you own and that is associated with your Azure AD. You can also assign the new user to a group or a role. Groups make it easier to manage a larger number of similar users.

Azure AD offers a feature called Azure AD B2B (business-to-business) collaboration that allows you to add users who don't belong to your company. So, you can invite other users from outside of your company to be members of your Azure AD. Those users can then be given access to your resources. Users who are not part of your company are called *guest users*. To add a guest user, click **New Guest User**, as shown in Figure 5-2. This will open the New Guest User blade, as shown in Figure 5-4.

When you invite a guest user, an invitation to join your Azure AD is sent to the email address you specify. In order to accept the invite, the user's email address must be associated with a Microsoft Account. If the user doesn't have a Microsoft Account, the user will be given the option to create one in order to join your Azure AD.

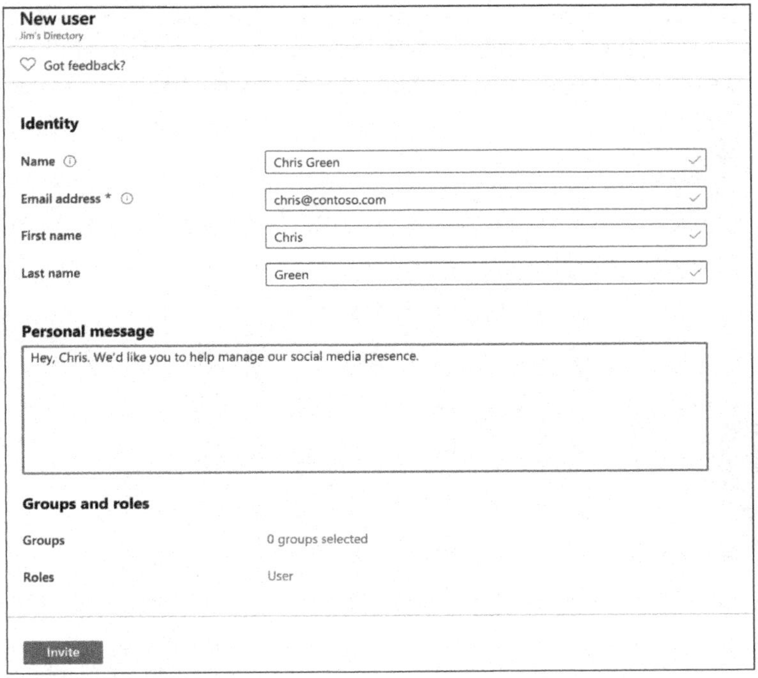

New user
Jim's Directory

♡ Got feedback?

Identity

Name ⓘ	Chris Green	✓
Email address * ⓘ	chris@contoso.com	✓
First name	Chris	✓
Last name	Green	✓

Personal message

Hey, Chris. We'd like you to help manage our social media presence.

Groups and roles

Groups   0 groups selected

Roles   User

Invite

FIGURE 5-4 Adding a new guest user

The user in Figure 5-4 can be given access to the corporate social media accounts by adding those applications to Azure AD. Thousands of applications can be added, including social media apps such as Facebook and Twitter. To add an application, open Azure AD in the Azure portal, click **Enterprise Applications** (shown previously in Figure 5-1) and click **New Application**, as shown in Figure 5-5.

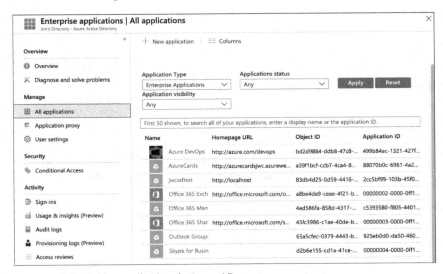

FIGURE 5-5 Enterprise applications in Azure AD

After you click **New Application**, you can choose from popular cloud providers, as shown in Figure 5-6. You can search for an application from here by entering an application name in the search box. You can also filter the view using the filtering buttons to the right of the search box.

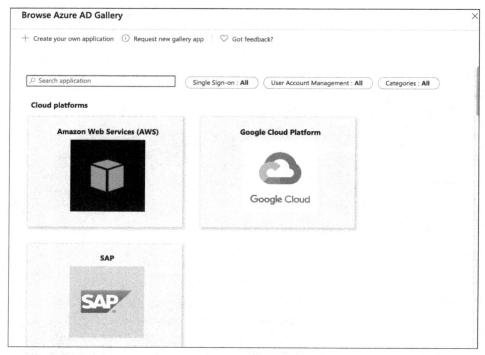

FIGURE 5-6 Cloud providers in the enterprise application gallery

If you scroll down, you'll see a list of many other applications you can add, as shown in Figure 5-7.

You can also add your own application, add an application that exists in your on-premises environment, or integrate any other application. The application that you add needs to expose a log in page to which you can point Azure AD in order to integrate it.

EXAM TIP

You can configure which resources an application can access using a *service principal*. The service principal is created when you give an application access to Azure resources using role-based access control, which is a concept you'll learn about in the next section.

After you add an application, you can configure Azure AD so that users with access to that application can authenticate to it using the same credentials they use to log in to Azure AD. This kind of authentication is known as *single sign-on* (or SSO), and it's one of the key benefits to using Azure AD.

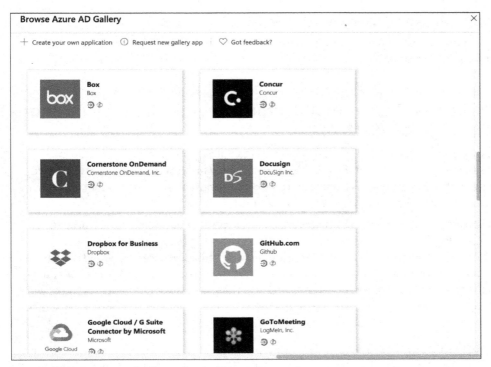

FIGURE 5-7 Enterprise application gallery apps

EXAM TIP

Azure AD B2B allows you to invite guest users to your Azure AD from other businesses. Another AD feature called Azure AD B2C allows you to give users access to Azure AD applications by signing in with existing accounts, such as a Facebook or Google account.

Another important benefit to using Azure AD for managing user access to other applications is that you can easily revoke that access from a single interface. For example, if you give a user the username and password of your social media account so he or she can post to your account, you'd have to change the username and password on your social media account when you no longer want that user to have access. If you grant access using Azure AD with SSO configured, you can remove that access easily within the Azure portal. The user never has to know the username and password you use for the social media account.

All the Azure AD features we've covered so far are included in the free version of Azure AD that everyone with an Azure subscription gets. Azure AD has three other pricing tiers that aren't free: Office 365 apps, Premium P1, and Premium P2. If you upgrade to one of the Premium plans, you can enable multifactor authentication for your users.

Conditional Access, multifactor authentication (MFA), and single sign-on (SSO)

In the simplest sense, administrators of Azure AD can decide if a user has access to a particular resource by requiring that the user be authenticated with a username and password and has the authorization to access that resource. However, most administrators want much more control than that in order to keep resources secure.

Suppose you have given a user named Christine access to your Microsoft 365 account using Azure AD. Because all your sensitive documents are stored in Microsoft 365, you need to be confident that someone can't hack Christine's password and gain access to your data. Azure Conditional Access and multifactor authentication (MFA) can help make Christine's account much more secure, and single sign-on can help Christine access her corporate resources without having to enter her username and password. Let's start by looking at Conditional Access.

Conditional Access

Azure Conditional Access allows you to create policies that are applied against users. These policies use *assignments* and *access controls* to configure access to your resources.

Assignments define who a policy applies to. It can apply to users, groups of users, roles in your Azure AD, or to guest users. You can also specify that a policy only applies to specific applications, such as Microsoft 365 in our example above.

Assignments can also define conditions that must be met (such as requiring a certain platform such as iOS, Android, Windows, and so on), specific locations by IP address, and more.

Access controls determine how a Conditional Access policy is enforced. The most restrictive access control is block access, but you can also use access controls to require that a user use a device that meets certain conditions, that they're using an approved application to access your resources, that they are using MFA, and so on.

To create a Conditional Access policy, search for **Azure AD Conditional Access** in the Azure portal. You can then click the **New Policy** button to create a new policy, as shown in Figure 5-8.

EXAM TIP

Conditional Access is only available in the Premium tiers of Azure AD. Because the free version of Azure AD is being used in these examples, the New Policy button is disabled in Figure 5-8.

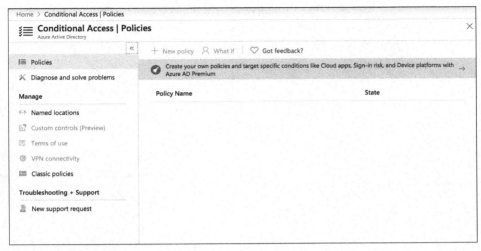

FIGURE 5-8 The Conditional Access policies blade in the Azure portal

Multifactor authentication (MFA)

By default, users can log in to your Azure AD using only a username and password. Even if you require your users to use strong passwords, allowing access to your resources with only a username and password is risky. If a hacker obtains the password by using software that guesses passwords or by stealing if through phishing or some other means, your resources are no longer secure.

Multifactor authentication solves this problem. The concept behind multifactor authentication is that you must authenticate using a combination of:

- Something you know, such as a username and password
- Something you have, such as a phone or mobile device
- Something you are, such as facial recognition or a fingerprint

If multifactor authentication requires all three of these, it's referred to as three-factor authentication, or sometimes 3FA. If only the first two are required, it's referred to as two-factor authentication, or sometimes 2FA. (Microsoft actually calls this *two-step verification*.) Azure multifactor authentication is two-factor authentication.

> **NOTE BIOMETRICS IN MOBILE DEVICES**
>
> Even though Azure multifactor authentication is two-factor, if you are using a mobile device that includes biometric features, you might be authenticating using three-factor authentication. However, the third factor is enforced by your mobile device and not by Azure. Azure multifactor authentication doesn't require three-factor authentication.

To enable multifactor authentication for one or more users of your Azure AD, open the **All Users** blade, click the three dots at the top of the page, and click **Multi-Factor Authentication**, as shown in Figure 5-9. (If you have a large monitor, the **Multi-Factor Authentication** button might be visible by default.)

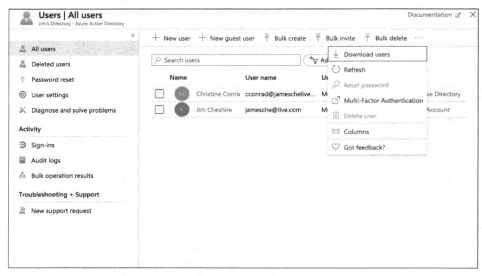

FIGURE 5-9 Enabling multifactor authentication

MORE INFO   COMBINED SECURITY INFORMATION REGISTRATION

For a better user experience, Microsoft recommends you use combined registration to allow users to register for MFA along with self-service password reset in one operation. You can read more about this at *https://bit.ly/az900-combinedregistration.*

When you click **Multi-Factor Authentication**, a new browser window opens and displays the Azure AD user management site. Select one or more users for whom you want to enable multifactor authentication and click **Enable**, as shown in Figure 5-10.

EXAM TIP

It's easier to configure MFA using a Conditional Access policy. Besides ease of use, configuring MFA with Conditional Access also allows you to configure MFA for guest users, something that's not possible using the site shown in Figure 5-10.

Once a user is required to use MFA, he or she needs to take a second step when logging in to the Azure portal. This can be a prompt from the Microsoft Authenticator app (available for iOS and Android), an SMS message with an access number, a phone call requiring you to enter an access code, or an OAUTH hardware token.

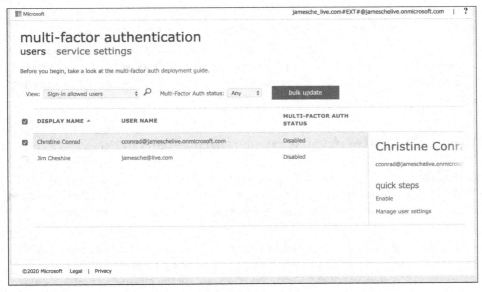

FIGURE 5-10 Enabling Multi-Factor Authentication

Single sign-on (SSO)

Single sign-on (SSO) is a simple concept with a huge impact for users. When using SSO, users can access corporate resources at their companies without having to enter a username and password. Instead, they are authenticated using the log-in credentials they supplied when logging into the computer they're using. SSO not only provides convenience, but it also provides a more secure environment because passwords aren't being entered for every resource.

For a device to work with SSO, it must be joined to Azure AD. Once the device has been added to AD, the user can access Azure resources and other company resources such as SharePoint and Microsoft 365 resources using SSO. Users can also access on-premises resources using SSO.

SSO to on-premises resources is implemented using a component called Azure AD Connect. Azure AD Connect connects your on-premises resources to Azure AD, and you'll need to install and configure Azure AD Connect before you can use SSO with on-premises resources.

> **MORE INFO**   **AZURE AD CONNECT**
>
> For more information on getting started with Azure AD Connect, see *http://bit.ly/ az900-adconnect.*

SSO supports two sign-in methods: password hash synchronization and pass-through authentication. Password hash synchronization copies a user's password in a hashed format to Azure AD. Because the password is hashed, the actual password can't be retrieved. When the user enters the password, an algorithm is used to generate a hash, and that hash is compared against the hash stored in Azure AD. If the two are the same, the user is authenticated.

Pass-through authentication passes a user's login on Azure AD into an on-premises pass-through authentication agent, and that agent sends the authentication to the on-premises Windows Active Directory instance. Once authenticated, Azure AD Connect is used to pass that authentication through to Azure AD and the user's resources.

Skill 5.2: Describe Azure governance features

As your cloud presence grows, you'll likely end up with a large number of Azure resources that span many different Azure services, and it's likely you'lll want to allow access to those resources by multiple users. Role-based access control is a great way to give users a specific level of access to your resources.

Unless you have some control over how those resources are created and managed, costs can spiral out of control. In addition to cost control, you might have other restrictions you'd like in place as well, such as which regions certain resources should be created in, how certain resources are tagged, and so on.

The traditional way of handling such governance issues would be to send out a memo to everyone explaining what the requirements are, and then crossing your fingers that people adhere to them. Fortunately, Azure Policy can ensure your requirements and policies are adhered to.

Ensuring that you can re-create environments is another important aspect of governance, and Azure Blueprints is the perfect way to make sure you can re-create an environment with precision. As you build your cloud environments, you'll want to make sure you're following best practices, and the Cloud Adoption Framework for Azure can help you learn from experts how to do just that.

> **This section covers:**
> - Role-based access control (RBAC)
> - Resource locks
> - Tags
> - Azure Policy
> - Azure Blueprints
> - Cloud Adoption Framework for Azure

> **MORE INFO**   **OAUTH HARDWARE TOKEN**
> An OAUTH hardware token is a small device that displays an access number. When prompted in your browser, enter that access number within a short timeframe in order to complete the authentication.

Role-based access control (RBAC)

Role-based access control (RBAC) is a generic term that refers to the concept of authorizing users to a system that is based on defined roles to which the user belongs. Azure implements RBAC across all Azure resources, so you can control how users and applications can interact with your Azure resources.

You might want to allow users who administer your databases to have access to databases in a particular resource group, but you don't want to allow those people to create new databases or delete existing databases. You might also want some web developers to be able to deploy new code to your web applications, but you don't want them to be able to scale the app to a higher-priced plan. These are just two examples of what you can do with RBAC in Azure.

There are four elements to RBAC:

- **Security principal** The security principal represents an identity. It can be a user, a group, an application (which is called a service principal), or a special AAD entity called a *managed identity*. A managed identity is how you authorize another Azure service to access your Azure resource.

- **Role** A role (sometimes called a role definition) is what defines how the security principal can interact with an Azure resource. For example, a role might define that a security principal can read the properties of a resource but cannot create new resources or delete existing resources.

- **Scope** The scope defines the level at which the role is applied, and it specifies how much control the security principal has. For example, if the scope is a resource group, the role defines activities that can be performed on all resources in the resource group.

- **Role assignments** Roles are assigned to a security principal at a particular scope, and that's what ultimately defines the level of access for the security principal.

RBAC includes many built-in roles. Three of these built-in roles apply to all Azure resources.

- **Owner** Members of this role have full access to the resources.

- **Contributor** Members of this role can create resources and manage resources, but they cannot delegate that right to anyone else.

- **Reader** Members of this role can see Azure resources, but they cannot create, delete, or manage those resources.

All the other built-in roles are specific to certain types of Azure resources.

To give someone access to a resource using RBAC, open the resource to which you you want to give access in the Azure portal. Click **Access Control (IAM)** in the portal to configure RBAC. In Figure 5-11, RBAC is being configured for a web app hosted in Azure App Service. Clicking **Add** in the Add A Role Assignment box allows you to add a role.

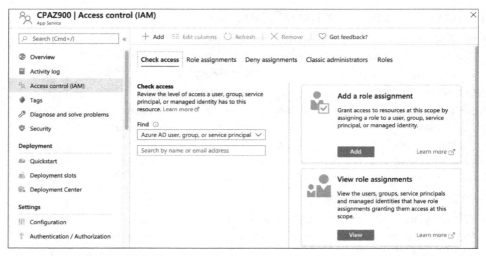

FIGURE 5-11 Configuring RBAC for a web app

EXAM TIP

The scope of RBAC is defined by where the RBAC role is assigned. For example, if you open a resource group in the portal and assign an RBAC role to a user, the scope is at the resource group level. On the other hand, if you open a web app within that resource group and assign the role, the scope is to that web app only.

RBAC roles can be scoped to the management group, subscription, resource group, or resource level.

After clicking **Add**, choose the role you want to assign. The list of roles will differ depending on what type of resource this is. Choose who or what you want to assign the role to, and then click **Save**, as shown in Figure 5-12.

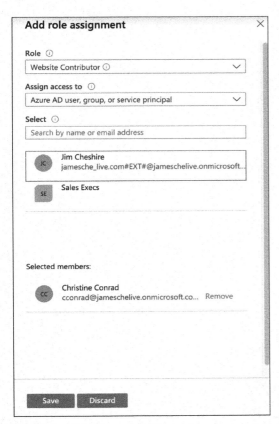

FIGURE 5-12 Adding a role assignment

Figure 5-12 shows a list of users in the AAD because the Assign Access To drop-down menu is set to AAD objects. You can see a list of other types of objects by selecting a different type. For example, in Figure 5-13, we are selecting a built-in managed identity type called Virtual Machine, and this will allow us to select from a list of VMs to assign to the role.

FIGURE 5-13 Using a managed identity to assign a role

 EXAM TIP

It's important to understand that role assignments are additive. Your RBAC abilities at any particular scope are the result of all role assignments up to that level. In other words, if I have the Owner role on a resource group and you assign me the Website Contributor role on a web app within that resource group, the Website Contributor assignment will have no effect because I already have the Owner role on the entire resource group.

RBAC is enforced by Azure Resource Manager (ARM). When you attempt to interact with an Azure resource, whether in the Azure portal or by using a command line tool, you are authenticated by ARM and a token is generated for you. That token is a representation of your identity and all your role assignments, and it's included with all operations you perform on the resource. ARM can determine if the action you are performing is allowed by the roles to which you are assigned. If it is, the call succeeds; if not, you are denied access.

You can ensure that someone has the rights you desire by checking access in the Azure portal. After opening the resource and clicking **Access Control (IAM)**, use the drop-down menu and search box shown in Figure 5-11 to search for a user or object and then click the user or object to see the access level, as shown in Figure 5-14.

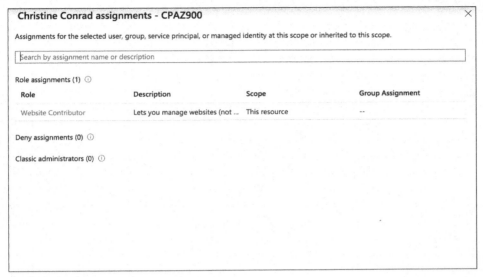

FIGURE 5-14 Showing RBAC assignments for a user

For a greater level of detail on what exact operations are and aren't allowed, click the role that's displayed. This will allow you to see a detailed list of operations and the combination of read, write, delete, and other actions that a security principal can perform.

EXAM TIP

We talked briefly about service principals earlier as they relate to Azure AD applications. Service principals are security principals that specifically represent applications. A security principal that represents a user is called a *user principal*. The important thing to remember is that both user principals and service principals are forms of a security principal.

Resource locks

RBAC is a great way to control access to an Azure resource, but in cases where you just want to prevent changes to a resource, or prevent that resource from being deleted, resource locks (or locks) are a simpler solution. Unlike RBAC, locks apply to everyone with access to the resource.

EXAM TIP

In order to create a lock, you must either be in the Owner or the User Access Administrator role in RBAC. Alternatively, an administrator can create a custom role that grants the right to create a lock.

Locks can be applied at the resource level, the resource group level, or at the subscription level. To apply a lock to a resource, open the resource in the Azure portal and click **Locks** in the **Settings** section of the menu on the left, as shown in Figure 5-15.

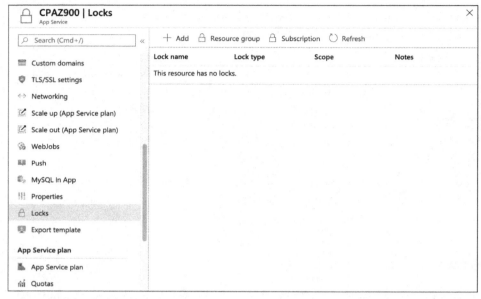

FIGURE 5-15 Locking a resource

To add a lock to the resource, click **Add**. (You can also review and add locks to the resource group by clicking **Resource Group**, or to the subscription by clicking **Subscription**.) In the **Lock Name** box, provide a name for the lock; set the **Lock Type**, and add an optional note, as shown in Figure 5-16.

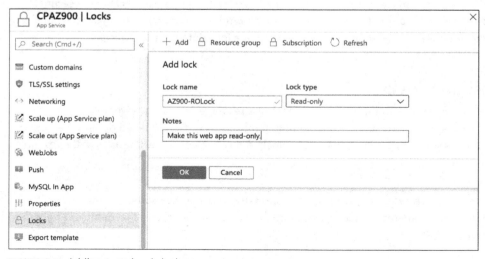

FIGURE 5-16 Adding a read-only lock

A read-only lock is the most restrictive lock. It prevents changing properties of the resource or deleting the resource. A delete lock prevents the resource from being deleted, but properties can still be changed. The result of a read-only lock is often unpredictable because of the way locks are handled by Azure.

Locks only apply to operations that are handled by ARM, and some operations specific to a resource are handled internally by the resource instead of being handled by ARM. For example, if you set a read-only lock on an instance of Azure Key Vault, it will prevent a user from changing access policies on the vault, but users can still add and delete keys, secrets, and certificates because those operations are handled internally by Key Vault.

There are other situations where a read-only lock can prevent operations that occur unexpectedly. For example, if you place a read-only lock on a storage account, it will prevent all users from listing the access keys for the storage account because the operation to list keys makes the keys available for write access.

If a lock is applied to a resource group, all resources in that resource group inherit the lock. Similarly, if a lock is applied at the subscription level, all resources in the subscription inherit the lock. It is possible to nest locks, and in such situations, the most restrictive lock is the effective lock. For example, if you have a read-only lock on a resource group and a delete lock on a resource in that resource group, the resource will actually have a read-only lock applied to it because a read-only lock is more restrictive. The explicit delete lock will be ineffective.

EXAM TIP

Locks are also inherited by newly created resources. If you apply a delete lock to a resource group and add a new resource to the resource group later, the new resource will automatically inherit the delete lock.

When an operation is attempted in the portal and denied because of a lock, an error will display, as shown in Figure 5-17.

EXAM TIP

Not all resource types will tell you that a lock prevented an operation that was attempted in the portal. There are times when you will see only a generic error message. If you try the same operation in the Azure CLI or using the Az module in PowerShell, you should see details on the lock.

You can edit or delete a lock by clicking **Locks** and clicking either **Edit** or **Delete** in the portal, as shown in Figure 5-18. In most cases, you will need to scroll to the right to see the **Edit** and **Delete** buttons.

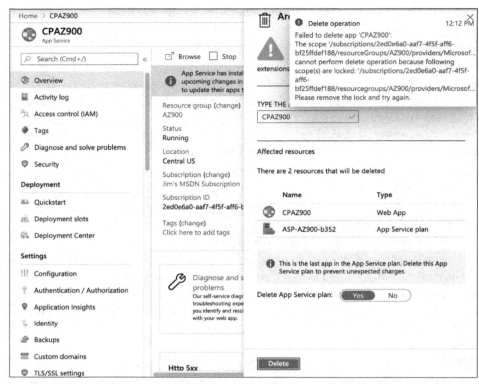

FIGURE 5-17 Denied by a lock

FIGURE 5-18 Editing or deleting a lock

Tags

Another feature in Azure that makes it easy to organize resources is tags. A tag consists of a name and a value. For example, suppose a company is participating in two trade events: one in Texas and one in New York. You have also created a lot of Azure resources to support those events. You want to view all the Azure resources for a specific event, but they're spread out across multiple resource groups. By adding a tag to each resource group that identifies the event it's associated with, you can solve this problem.

In Figure 5-19, you can see the tags associated with a WebStorefront resource group. This resource group has been assigned a tag named EventName, and the value of that tag is Contoso-Texas. By clicking the cube icon to the right of the tag, you can view all resources that have that tag.

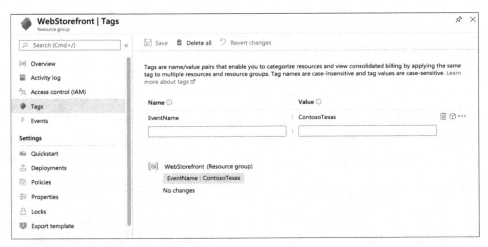

FIGURE 5-19 Tagging a resource group

> **NOTES   SHOWING ALL TAGS**
>
> To view all your tags, choose All Services from the main menu in the portal and then search for *Tags* in the list of services.

You can apply a tag to most Azure resources, not just resource groups. It's also important to understand that by adding a tag to a resource group, you are not adding that tag to the resources within the resource group. If you have a web app in the WebStorefront resource group, that web app does not inherit the tag that is applied to the resource group. This means tags add an additional layer of flexibility and power when viewing your Azure resources.

EXAM TIP

Tags can also help you organize your Azure billing expenses. When you download your Azure invoice, resource tags will appear in one of the columns. Because Azure invoices can be downloaded as comma-separated values, you can use tools like Microsoft Excel to filter based on tags.

Azure Policy

Azure Policy allows you to define rules that are applied when Azure resources are created and managed. For example, you can create a policy that specifies that only a certain size VM can be created and that the VMs must be created in the South-Central US region. Azure will take care of enforcing this policy so that you remain in accordance with your corporate policies.

To access Azure Policy, type **policy** in the search box in the Azure portal and click **Policy**. Alternatively, you can click **All Services** and search for **policy** in the list. This will display the Policy blade, as shown in Figure 5-20.

FIGURE 5-20 Azure Policy in the Azure portal

By default, Azure Policy shows your compliance with policies defined on an Azure subscription. If you want to, you can scope this view to a different subscription or to a resource group by clicking the ellipsis (**...**) button next to Scope and selecting the new scope. See Figure 5-21.

The non-compliance shown in Figure 5-20 is based on policies implemented by Azure Security Center. By clicking the non-compliant item, you can see the full details of what is and isn't within policy, as shown in Figure 5-22.

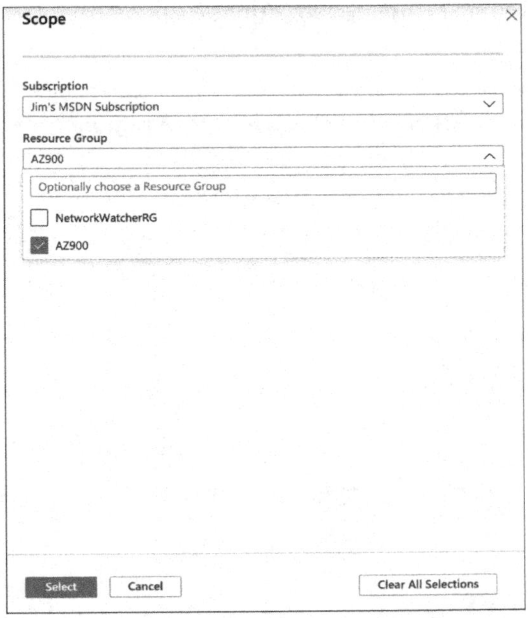

FIGURE 5-21 Changing the scope of the Policy blade in the portal

FIGURE 5-22 Details on compliance

Notice that the title of this item is *ASC Default* followed by a subscription ID. ASC Default is actually a collection of multiple policies that are defined by Azure Security Center. Azure Policy makes it easy to impose a full suite of policies by combining them into a group called an *initiative*. By defining an initiative, you can easily define complex rules that ensure governance of your company's policies.

You can assign a new policy either by selecting a policy from a list of included policies or by creating your own policy. To assign a policy from the list of included policies, click **Assignments > Assign Policy**, as shown in Figure 5-23.

FIGURE 5-23 Assigning a policy

To select a policy, click the ellipses (**...**) next to Policy Definition, as shown in Figure 5-24.

FIGURE 5-24 Selecting a policy definition

In this case, you apply a policy that will flag any App Service app that is not configured to use a virtual network service endpoint. You can do that by entering **app service** in the Search box and selecting the built-in policy that applies to that policy, as shown in Figure 5-25.

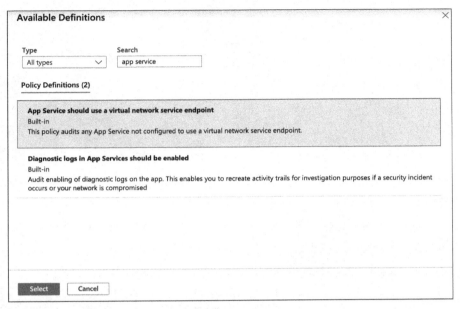

FIGURE 5-25 Adding a built-in policy definition

After clicking **Select** (shown in Figure 5-25), the details of this particular policy are shown. If you click the **Parameters** tab, you can see the effect of the policy. As you can see in Figure 5-26, the effect of this policy is **AuditIfNotExists**.

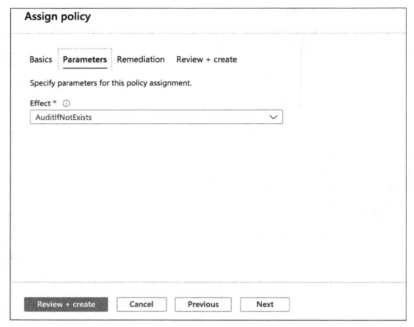

FIGURE 5-26 Completing the assignment

Six effects are supported in Azure Policy. However, not all effects are available for built-in policies. The effects are:

- **Append** Adds additional properties to a resource. It can be used to add a tag with a specific value to resources.
- **Audit** Logs a warning if the policy is not complied with.
- **AuditIfNotExists** Allows you to specify an additional resource type that must exist along with the resource being created or updated. If that resource type does not exist, a warning is logged.
- **Deny** Denies the create or update operation.
- **DeployIfNotExists** Allows you to specify an additional resource type you want deployed with the resource being created or updated. If that resource type is not included, it is automatically deployed.
- **Disabled** The policy is not in effect.

> **MORE INFO** **MORE ON POLICY EFFECTS**
>
> For more information on policy effects, including examples of each, see *https://bit.ly/ az900-policyeffects*.

In addition to using the built-in policies, you can also define your own policies by creating a custom policy definition. Custom policy definitions are ARM templates that define the policy. For more information on creating a custom policy definition, see: *https://bit.ly/az900-custompolicy.*

Azure Blueprints

When a company decides to create a cloud application, it doesn't start by creating a resource in the portal. Instead, a lot of planning happens before a single Azure resource is created. This planning includes a plan for making sure the entire architecture of the cloud app complies with the necessary standards. It also involves concepts like detailed planning of virtual network topologies and rights assignments for users of the app. Also, best practices are likely a part of this planning.

There's a lot of risk involved if a company fails to plan carefully, and for that reason, many companies will hire someone with deep technical knowledge of the cloud to help in that planning. Hiring that kind of resource can add a lot of additional expense, and it can also add a lot of time to a project.

Azure Blueprints is a service that can make the process of deploying to the cloud easier. Blueprints allows you configure an environment just as you need it to be, along with all the policies and other governance aspects in place. That configuration can then be saved so it can be duplicated at any time in other deployments.

Items that you add to a blueprint are called *artifacts*. An artifact can be a resource group, an ARM template, a policy assignment, or a role assignment. Once you've created a blueprint, you can either save it in a subscription or in a management group. A blueprint that's saved in a management group can then be used by any subscription within that management group's hierarchy.

EXAM TIP

You might be wondering how blueprints differ from ARM templates. After all, we did say that ARM templates are used to facilitate predictable and reproducible deployments. Blueprints offer numerous benefits over ARM templates.

Because blueprints are actual Azure resources and not simply files designed to define a deployment, Azure maintains a connection between the blueprint and the resources that use the blueprint. That allows companies to iterate on blueprints and improve them. It also makes it much easier for a blueprint to evolve with a company's needs. Also, blueprints are versioned and can be stored in a source-control system, so tracking of blueprints is easy and effective.

With that said, it's important to understand that blueprints aren't a replacement for ARM templates. In fact, most blueprints make extensive use of ARM templates as artifacts.

To create a blueprint, search for **blueprints** in the Azure portal to open the Blueprints | Getting Started page, as shown in Figure 5-27.

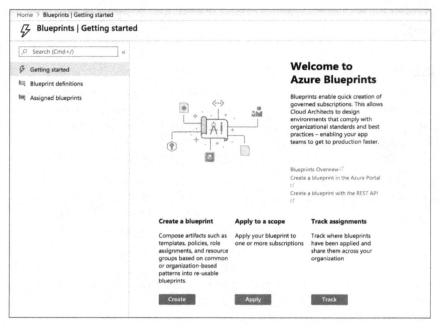

FIGURE 5-27 Azure Blueprints Getting Started page

From the **Getting Started** page, click **Create** to start the process of creating a blueprint. As shown in Figure 5-28, Microsoft provides many sample templates that you can use as a foundation for your blueprint, but you can also start with a blank blueprint.

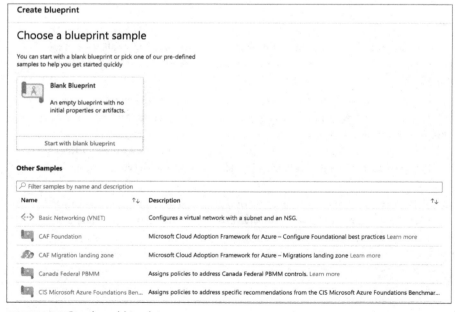

FIGURE 5-28 Creating a blueprint

Click the link to start with a blank blueprint. Enter a name for your blueprint, a description, and set the place where your blueprint definition will be saved. This is either a subscription or a management group. In Figure 5-29, a blueprint is being created that will be saved to a subscription.

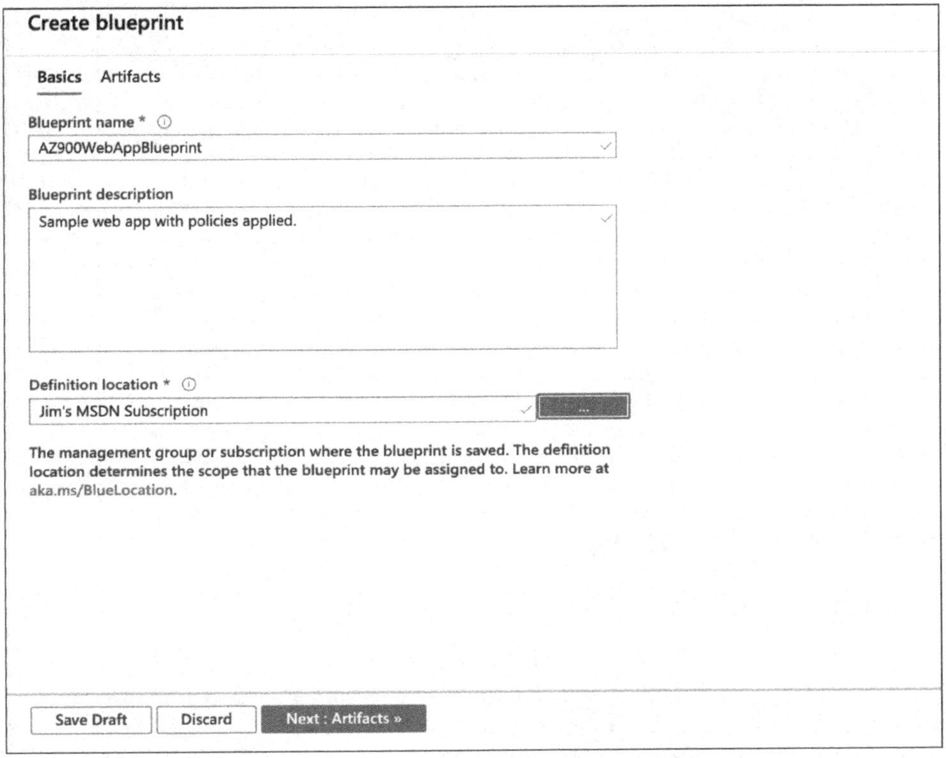

Create blueprint

Basics   Artifacts

Blueprint name * ⓘ

| AZ900WebAppBlueprint | ⌄ |

Blueprint description

| Sample web app with policies applied. | ⌄ |

Definition location * ⓘ

| Jim's MSDN Subscription | ⌄ | ... |

The management group or subscription where the blueprint is saved. The definition location determines the scope that the blueprint may be assigned to. Learn more at aka.ms/BlueLocation.

| Save Draft | Discard | Next : Artifacts » |

FIGURE 5-29 Specifying a blueprint's basic settings

EXAM TIP

You cannot change the name or the definition location of a blueprint after it's created.

To add artifacts to your blueprint, click **Next: Artifacts**, as shown in Figure 5-29. Click **Add Artifact** to add your first artifact. Select the **Artifact Type** and enter the necessary information to add the artifact. In Figure 5-30, a resource group artifact is being added.

In order for this blueprint to remain more generic at this point, you can specify that the resource group name and the location are supplied when the blueprint is assigned by clicking the **This Value Should Be Specified When The Blueprint Is Assigned** checkbox next to the **Resource Group Name** and/or **Location**. (We'll cover blueprint assignment later in this section.) Clicking **Add** will add this artifact to the blueprint.

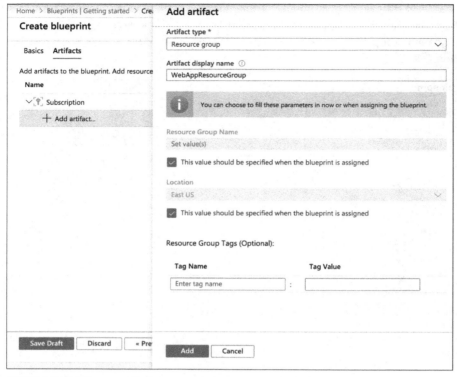

FIGURE 5-30 Adding an artifact

When you're finished adding artifacts, click **Save Draft** (shown in Figure 5-30) to save a draft of the blueprint. While in draft mode, the blueprint can be edited and updated. When you're ready to make the blueprint available, you can publish it.

To publish a blueprint, click **Blueprint Definitions** and click the blueprint, as shown in Figure 5-31.

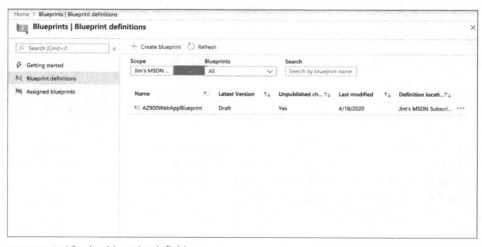

FIGURE 5-31 Viewing blueprint definitions

Click the **Publish Blueprint** button, as shown in Figure 5-32, to publish the blueprint.

AZ900WebAppBlueprint
Blueprints   ×

⬆ Publish blueprint   ✎ Edit blueprint   🗑 Delete blueprint

Name   State
AZ900WebAppBlueprint   ⬚   Draft

Definition location   Description
Jim's MSDN Subscription   Web app with policies

Definition location ID
2ed0e6a0-aaf7-4f5f-aff6-bf25ffdef188

Version
Draft

                                         ⌃

Latest artifacts

Artifact name	Resource type	Parameters
⌄ 🔧 Assigned subscription	Subscription	
🔲 WebAppResourceGroup	Resource group	0 out of 2 parameters popula...

FIGURE 5-32 A blueprint ready to be published

When you publish a blueprint, you need to provide the version number. It's advisable to also add change notes. In Figure 5-33, our new blueprint is being published as Version 1.0. Clicking the **Publish** button completes the process.

Publish blueprint

Version * ⓘ
| 1.0 | ⌄ |
No previous versions

Change notes ⓘ
| Original version | ✓ |

| Publish | Cancel |

FIGURE 5-33 Publishing a blueprint

Once a blueprint has been published, it's available to assign to a subscription. Click the blueprint and click **Assign Blueprint** to assign it, as shown in Figure 5-34.

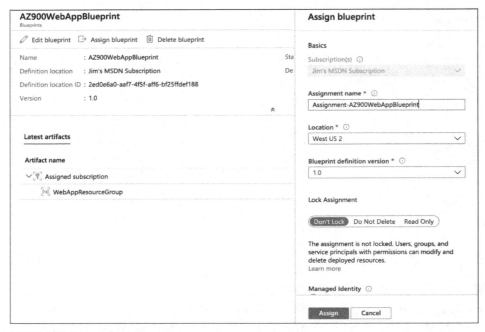

FIGURE 5-34 Assigning a blueprint

To assign the blueprint, enter an assignment name, select a location, and select the blueprint definition version. (You can also accept the defaults for all these settings.) You can also specify a lock assignment for the resources the blueprint creates by clicking the desired lock assignment setting.

Clicking **Assign** completes the blueprint assignment.

> **NOTE BLUEPRINT PARAMETERS**
>
> When this blueprint was created, it was specified that the resource group name and location should be chosen when the blueprint is assigned. Therefore, you will need to enter those values in the spaces provided when you assign the blueprint.

 When the blueprint is assigned to a subscription, resources defined by the blueprint are created in that subscription.

Cloud Adoption Framework for Azure

As you've learned, moving to the cloud isn't as simple as clicking a few buttons in the Azure portal. There's considerable planning that must take place, but before any of that planning even starts, it's important to become educated on how to move to the cloud successfully. You need to learn about things such as best practices, how your cloud apps should be architected, the proper way to migrate resources, setting up governance and policies, and so forth.

As you might expect, Microsoft has this kind of knowledge spread out across its Azure teams. Not only has Microsoft learned from the many customers they've worked with, but Microsoft itself is a huge consumer of Azure, and they're skilled in how to plan, organize, deploy, and govern Azure resources.

In an effort to share their vast knowledge with customers, Microsoft created the Cloud Adoption Framework for Azure. The Cloud Adoption Framework brings together all the best practices from Microsoft employees, Microsoft partners, and lessons learned from Microsoft customers. All this information is made available in a comprehensive website. All the information from the framework is neatly organized, and you can even download assets such as an infographic to help you visualize the Cloud Adoption Framework.

 You can access the Cloud Adoption Framework by browsing to *https://aka.ms/cloudadoptionframework*.

Skill 5.3: Describe privacy and compliance resources

As we've already discussed, companies moving to the cloud are often concerned about keeping information private and compliant with regulations. Microsoft addresses these concerns using many methods, and in this section, we'll talk about Microsoft's approach to security, privacy, and compliance.

This section covers:
- Security, privacy, and compliance
- Microsoft privacy statement
- Online Service Terms (OST) and Data Protection Addendum (DPA)
- Trust Center
- Azure compliance documentation
- Azure sovereign regions

Security, privacy, and compliance

Security, privacy, and compliance are three pillars of trust between you and your cloud provider. Microsoft takes all three seriously and provides information and tools related to each.

Microsoft wants you to be confident that they are doing what's necessary to keep your information and your resources secure, and they offer details on the efforts they take to ensure the security of your data from outside actors who might want to obtain your data for their own use.

At the same time, you want to be assured that Microsoft doesn't use your data in any way that isn't approved by you, and when you store private data in the cloud, you want assurance that Microsoft can't and won't access that data. Microsoft is committed to your privacy, and they provide full disclosure of how your data is handled and kept private.

As you move to the cloud, you offload some of the responsibility for your services and data to your cloud provider. This includes some of the responsibility for compliance with data protection standards. Even though the cloud provider takes care of some of that burden for you, it's still vital that you have confidence in the cloud provider and that you trust them to maintain compliance.

> *NOTE* **SHARED RESPONSIBILITY MODEL**
>
> **Remember when we talked about the shared responsibility model way back in Skill 1.2? The paragraph above is an excellent example of what the shared responsibility model is all about.**

There are many standards with which businesses must comply. For example, in 2016, the European Union passed the General Data Protection Regulation (GDPR). The GDPR regulates the way personal data is handled for individuals within the EU, but it also controls any personal data that is exported from the EU. Companies doing business in EU countries are legally required to abide by the GDPR.

One way that organizations can ensure they are abiding by the GDPR and other regulations that regulate data, is to maintain compliance with industry-wide standards focused on helping organizations keep information secure. One of those standards is the International Organization of Standards (ISO) 27001 standard. Companies that comply with the ISO 27001 standard can be confident that they are maintaining the best practices necessary to keep information secure. In fact, many companies won't do business with a cloud provider unless they can prove ISO 27001 compliance.

Systems that deal with governmental data must maintain compliance with standards that are maintained by the National Institute of Standards and Technology, or NIST. The NIST SP 800-53 is a publication by NIST that outlines all the requirements for information systems dealing with government data. In order for any government agency to use a service, it must first prove compliance with NIST SP 800-53.

Microsoft privacy statement

The Microsoft privacy statement is a comprehensive statement from Microsoft that outlines the following as it relates to handling data and your personal information.

- Personal data Microsoft collects
- How Microsoft uses personal data
- Reasons Microsoft shares personal data

- How to access and control your personal data collected by Microsoft
- How Microsoft uses cookies and similar technologies
- What organizations providing Microsoft software to you can do with your data
- What data is shared when you use a Microsoft Account with a third party
- Specifics about how Microsoft secures data, where it's processed, and retention policies

Microsoft links to the privacy statement in all official communications, and you can access the privacy statement online at *https://aka.ms/privacystatement*.

Online Service Terms (OST) and Data Protection Addendum (DPA)

Your use of Microsoft products and services (including Azure) is governed by the terms that Microsoft documents in the Online Service Terms (OST) for their services and products. The OST outline what you can and cannot use a service for, and they are focused on ensuring that no one uses Microsoft services to cause harm to someone else.

As an addendum to the OST, Microsoft publishes the Data Protection Addendum (DPA) that outlines the data processing and security terms when using Microsoft services.

You can access both the OST and the DPA on the Licensing Terms page located at *http://bit.ly/az900-licensingterms*.

Trust Center

The Trust Center is a web portal where you can learn all about Microsoft's approach to security, privacy, and compliance. You can access Trust Center by browsing to *https://aka.ms/microsofttrustcenter*.

The Trust Center provides information on security solutions, security products, how Microsoft handles privacy and data management, and so on. It also provide white papers and checklists as tools for you to ensure you are secure and compliant.

As the cloud environment evolves and threats change, Microsoft updates the Trust Center with relevant information, so make sure you visit often.

Azure compliance documentation

As we've already discussed, ensuring you are compliant with the proper regulations is a key consideration when moving to the cloud. To make doing so easier, Microsoft provides comprehensive documentation on regulations from around the globe. This documentation contains information on each regulation and information on Microsoft's approach to compliance with the regulation.

You can find the Azure compliance documentation at *http://bit.ly/az900-azurecompliance*.

Azure sovereign regions

Some compliance requirements can't be met by simply applying policies in Azure. For example, some US government compliance scenarios require that data stays within the United States of America and that only citizens of the United States have any access to systems used to store that data. You can't meet this requirement with policies. In fact, you can't meet that requirement at all in the public cloud. To address this type of issue, Microsoft developed completely isolated Azure data centers that make up the Azure Government cloud.

Azure Government data centers are separate from public data centers. All employees working in Azure Government are screened and are citizens of the US. Even Microsoft employees who provide technical support to Azure Government customers are required to be US citizens.

Because Microsoft also wanted to allow for compliant communication between the Azure Government cloud and on-premises government systems, they also developed dedicated Microsoft ExpressRoute locations that are completely isolated from other Azure networks and that use their own dedicated fiber-optic components.

Azure Government isn't only for federal government agencies. Cities and municipalities also take advantage of Azure Government for compliance. When a customer signs up for Azure Government, Microsoft vets that user to ensure they are representative of a government agency. Only then are they given a subscription to Azure Government.

The Azure Government cloud has all the same features and services as the public cloud, but there are small differences. For example, the portal for Azure Government is located at *https://portal.azure.us* instead of *https://portal.azure.com*. URLs for Azure services also use the *.us* top-level domain, so if you create an App Service web app in Azure Government, your default domain name is *https://webapp.azurewebsites.us*. However, outside of that difference, everything else is the same, so developers who have a skill set in cloud development in Azure will find that their skills transfer directly to Azure Government.

The United States Department of Defense has additional compliance requirements called DoD Impact Level 5 Provisional Authorization. Compliance with this relates to controlled unclassified information that requires additional levels of protection. These additional DoD requirements are met by a subset of data centers within Azure Government that are approved for DoD usage.

Microsoft also understands that the strict requirements in the EU need a unique approach, so they developed another cloud called Azure Germany. Much like Azure Government, Azure Germany is a distinct cloud system that's designed to meet specific compliance needs. Azure Germany is available to customers doing business in the EU, the European Free Trade Association, and the UK.

Azure Germany datacenters are physically located in Germany and are operated under strict security measures by a local company named T-Systems International (a subsidiary of Deutsche Telekom) that operates as a data trustee. The data trustee has full control over all data stored in Azure Germany and all the infrastructure used to house that data. Microsoft is involved in managing only those systems that have no access at all to customer data.

Another region where Azure has specific requirements is China. Microsoft operates another separate cloud in China called Microsoft Azure China. Azure China is operated by Shanghai Blue Cloud Technology Co., Ltd. (frequently referred to as simply BlueCloud). BlueCloud is owned by Beijing 21Vianet Broadband Data Center Co., Ltd. (often called 21Vianet), an Internet and data center service provider in China. Because of this relationship, you may see Azure China referred to as "Microsoft Azure operated by 21Vianet" or simply "Azure 21Vianet."

Azure China doesn't offer the full set of features offered in other Azure clouds, but Microsoft is working hard to add additional features and services. For all the details on what is and isn't offered in Azure China, browse to *https://bit.ly/az900-azurechina*.

Thought experiment

You've learned a lot about identity, governance, privacy, and compliance in this chapter. Let's test that knowledge with another thought experiment.

The answers to this thought experiment are in the section that follows.

Your old buddies over at ContosoPharm have gotten back in touch with you to help them with some more of their cloud work. This time around, they have a few new challenges. First, they are creating a new customer portal that they want to integrate with their social media accounts. They need an outside contractor to help with the social media accounts by posting to their followers and answering any customer questions. The IT director is concerned about providing the usernames and passwords of their social media accounts to a third party. He'd like some way to allow the contractor to access their social media accounts without having their password, and he'd like to be assured that when the contract is over, the contractor can easily be removed from the social media accounts.

They also have a few Azure resources the contractor will need to access, but the IT director is worried about security there as well. To keep things secure, he wants to ensure that no one can access ContosoPharm's systems if someone finds out the contractor's username and password. He also wants to make sure that one specific resource is only accessible if the contractor is logging in from a Windows computer. He doesn't want it accessible from mobile devices.

He also needs to make sure the contractor can view a couple of the Azure resources in the Azure portal in case something goes wrong, but he doesn't want the contractor to be able to change any settings.

As developers work on this solution, they'll be creating some Azure VMs. These VMs need to be in the Central US region so they're geographically close to a caching component that also runs in the Central US region. The IT director has sent out a memo to all developers telling them to only create VMs in Central US, but he's concerned that someone will forget and poor caching performance will impact their testing metrics. Also, if someone deletes the caching component, it will completely break the application, so they need to ensure no one is able to delete it.

Some of the VMs created for this application are being billed out to the IT department for development purposes, but the majority of VMs are billed to the sales department. The CEO wants to be able to see a breakdown of expenses for both departments after she gets the Azure invoice.

ContosoPharm has one other huge problem they need help with. They're planning another deployment to the cloud soon, and it's going to be a complex application. They've spent a long time planning the implementation. They know exactly how the network needs to be configured, and they have a record of all the resources that need to be created, along with the ARM template that will do the work of deploying. The network configuration they've devised for the Azure VNets is specific to their needs and enables them to integrate with on-premises systems, and it's a very complicated setup. They would like a way that they can easily recreate this setup in Azure when they need to deploy other applications that use the same network topology.

Thought experiment answers

This section details the answers to the thought experiment.

To give the contractor access to social media accounts without providing the username and password to the social media accounts, they can add the contractor to their Azure Active Directory as a guest user. They can then add enterprise applications for the desired social media platforms and give the user access to them using Azure AD business-to-business, or B2B. When the contractor's contract ends, they can simply remove him or her from Azure AD and that will revoke all future access to the social media accounts.

To ensure that no one can access the systems if the contractor's username and password are compromised, they can use multifactor authentication. Because the contractor is a guest user in Azure AD, they'll need to use a Conditional Access policy, but that will also solve the problem of not allowing access to a resource unless the contractor is using Windows by defining a condition based on the device.

To ensure the contractor can view some of their Azure resources without being able to change any settings, they can use the Reader role in RBAC for the resources. This will allow the contractor to see the resources, but not delete or change any settings.

To ensure that developers only create VMs in the Central US region, they can use Azure policies. To make sure that no one deletes the caching component, they can place a ReadOnly or a Delete lock on the component.

To ensure that the CEO can see a breakdown of VM usage for the IT department and the sales department separately, they can use tags on the VMs. Tags are displayed in the Azure invoice, and because the invoice can be exported to a format that can be opened in Microsoft Excel, they can easily filter on them.

To translate their hard work in planning and to ensure the complicated network configuration is easy to reproduce in future deployments, they can use Azure Blueprints. By creating a blueprint that adds artifacts for the necessary policies, resource groups, ARM templates, and so forth, they can easily make sure to get everything configured correctly.

Chapter summary

This chapter covered a ton of topics related to identity and governance. We ended with details on privacy and compliance and the tools Microsoft provides to help with those areas.

Here's a summary of what we covered in this chapter.

- Authentication is the act of determining who is accessing a resource.
- Authorization is the act of enforcing what the authenticated user can and cannot do.
- Azure Active Directory is a cloud-based identity service in Azure.
- At the core of Azure AD is a directory of users.
- Other users can be invited to join your Azure AD.
- Guest users are typically outside of your organization and are invited to your Azure AD.
- Enterprise applications allow integration of Azure AD with other services and cloud platforms.
- Conditional Access policies are applied against users using assignments and access controls.
- Multifactor authentication is two-factor authentication that requires you to enter a code in addition to entering your username and password.
- Single sign-on allows a user to access company resources without having to re-enter a username and password.
- Role-based access control (RBAC) allows you to control how users and applications can interact with your Azure resources.
- Azure Policy allows you to define rules that are applied when Azure resources are created and managed.
- Resource locks allow you to prevent changes to a resource and to prevent resources from being deleted.
- Tags allow you to easily organize your resources by assigning a name and value that can be seen in the Azure portal and on your Azure invoice.
- Azure Blueprints allows you to save configurations and resources in a blueprint that can be easily deployed in the future.
- Items added to a blueprint are called artifacts. An artifact can be a resource group, an ARM template, a policy assignment, or a role assignment.
- The Cloud Adoption Framework for Azure brings together best practices and information from Microsoft employees, partners, and customers to help you adopt the cloud more easily.
- The Microsoft privacy statement is a comprehensive statement from Microsoft that outlines how Microsoft uses, handles, and protects your data and personal information.

- The Online Service Terms (OST) and Data Protection Addendum (DPA) provide information on the terms of use of Microsoft services and how data can be used with those services.
- The Trust Center outlines Microsoft's approach to security, privacy, and compliance.
- Azure compliance documentation covers requirements for regulations around the globe and how Microsoft addresses compliance.
- Azure Government is a private cloud for governments that is only accessible by US citizens. It has its own datacenters that are completely separate from the public cloud.
- A subset of Azure Government datacenters is approved for Department of Defense usage because they have additional compliance related to DoD Impact Level 5 Provisional Authorization.
- Azure Germany datacenters are in a private cloud designed to comply with EU regulations.
- Azure China is a separate cloud in China that doesn't currently offer all Azure services.

CHAPTER 6

Describe Azure pricing, SLAs, and lifecycles

We've covered most of the important concepts related to the cloud, but we still have a few important concepts to cover. The final topics we'll cover are pricing in Azure, service level agreements (SLAs), and the lifecycle of Azure services.

Pricing doesn't just involve knowing the price of Azure resources. Companies often want to know how much entire cloud solutions are going to cost before applications are deployed to the cloud, and once the application is deployed, they want to minimize costs as much as possible and have visibility into the ongoing costs of Azure resources.

We've already talked about high availability in the cloud, and Microsoft can help you with ensuring your application experiences high availability by following their guidelines related to SLAs. When something goes wrong in Azure and it affects your services, you need to understand what you can do to engage with Microsoft.

Finally, it's important that you understand service lifecycles, especially because some services are at a point in their lifecycles where there is no guaranteed SLA or support from Microsoft.

Skills covered in this chapter:

- Describe methods for planning and managing costs
- Describe Azure service level agreements (SLAs) and service lifecycles

Skill 6.1: Describe methods for planning and managing costs

As you begin to contemplate moving to the cloud, the first thing you'll likely want to do is determine what your costs will be based on your resource needs. Once you've begun deploying and using Azure resources, managing your costs becomes important in order to stay within your budgets. Azure has tools that help you with planning and the management of your costs in Azure.

Factors affecting costs

As you're planning your Azure deployments, you should keep in mind the factors that can affect your costs, such as the resource type, how you purchase the resource, the Azure regions you use, and the billing zone your resources are in.

Azure services are billed according to *meters* associated with a resource. These meters track how much a specific metric has been used by the resource. For example, there is no charge specifically for an Azure virtual network, and you aren't charged for network traffic within a virtual network; however, you are charged per gigabyte for traffic into and out of the virtual network from peered virtual networks.

EXAM TIP

Each Azure service has a pricing page that outlines estimates on pricing for that resource based on typical usage.

As you determine which resources you need to use in your Azure deployment, consider how those resources are going to use the metrics the resources charges for. For example, if you can plan your virtual networks so that you have fewer peered networks, you can save substantially over the long-term.

You might also find that purchasing Azure resources differently might offer cost savings. If you agree to pay in advance using an Enterprise Agreement, Microsoft will offer you a reduced rate. Longer-term agreements offer even more price breaks. Cloud solution partners (CSPs) might also provide you with complete solutions that are more cost-effective than purchasing all the resources yourself.

Microsoft's costs for operating Azure services differ by region, even when those regions are within the same geographic boundary. Therefore, your pricing will differ based on which Azure region you use. For example, a VM deployed to the Central US region will cost more than the same VM deployed to the East US region. Microsoft doesn't provide a breakdown on their costs, but you can assume that electricity and other resources needed for an Azure data center are more expensive in the Central US region than they are in the Eastern US region.

It's also important to keep in mind that you're not charged for network traffic into an Azure datacenter, but you are charged for network traffic out of a datacenter. However, your first 5GB of outbound data is free. After that point, you are charged a set amount on a tiered model.

It's also important to know that Azure regions are broken out into four separate groups for billing purposes. These groups are called *billing zones*, or more commonly, *zones*. Microsoft's costs for network traffic out of each zone differs, so your costs will differ, too.

Table 6-1 lists the zones in Azure and their corresponding regions.

TABLE 6-1 Zones and regions

Zone Name	Included REGIONS
Zone 1	Australia Central, Australia Central 2, Canada Central, Canada East, North Europe, West Europe, France Central, France South, Germany North (Public), Germany West Central (Public), Norway East, Norway West, Switzerland North, Switzerland West, UK South, UK West, and all US regions
Zone 2	East Asia, Southeast Asia, Australia East, Australia Southeast, Central India, South India, West India, Japan East, Japan West, Korea Central, and Korea South
Zone 3	Brazil South, South Africa North, South Africa West, UAE Central, and UAE North
DE Zone 1	Germany Central (Sovereign) and Germany Northeast (Sovereign)

The cheapest outbound networking costs are in Zone 1. DE Zone 1 is the second cheapest, followed by Zone 2 and Zone 3.

Reducing Azure costs

It's important to understand how your decisions can affect your costs, but it's also important to understand those things you can do to reduce the costs you experience in Azure.

If you regularly find that you use VMs month over month, you can save substantially by using Azure Reservations. By committing to resource usage in advance and taking advantage of reserved instances, you no longer have to pay the fees associated with pay-as-you-go pricing. You can also modify your reserved instance reservation to adjust for your usage as you go, so you don't have to sacrifice flexibility.

Similarly, if you have a need for consistent usage of Azure SQL Database, Azure Cosmos DB, or Azure Synapse Analytics, you can save substantially with reserved capacity pricing on those services. Reserved capacity allows you to save by purchasing a one-year or three-year contract, and you are then billed monthly at a reduced amount.

You can save even more on VMs and Azure SQL Database by taking advantage of hybrid use benefit. When you use hybrid use benefit, you bring your own license for Windows Server or SQL Server to Azure. For example, if you use 10 Windows VMs for a typical period over a month's time, you can save more than 40 percent by using your own license with hybrid use benefit.

Another way to save substantially is by taking advantage of Microsoft's unused server capacity to run workloads that only require the use of a computer for a temporary (usually short) timeframe. By using Azure Spot VMs, you can take advantage of this unused capacity for huge savings.

As you can see, there are many factors that can affect your costs in Azure, and it can be difficult to estimate costs based on all these factors. Fortunately, Microsoft offers a pricing calculator that can help you get a handle on estimating your costs as you move to the cloud.

Pricing calculator

The Azure pricing calculator can help you get an estimate of expenses based on the products you intend on using, as well as where those products will be deployed and so on. You can access the pricing calculator by browsing to: *https://bit.ly/az900-pricingcalculator*.

When calculating an estimate of your Azure expenses, the first step is to select which products you want to use. As shown in Figure 6-1, some of the more common Azure products are displayed by default, and you can add any of those products by clicking its tile.

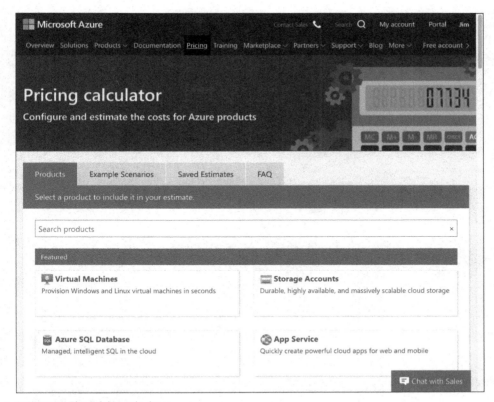

FIGURE 6-1 The pricing calculator

If the product you want is not listed, you can search for your product by entering its name in the Search Products box.

After you add the products you want to use, scroll down to configure the specific details of each service. These details vary based upon how Microsoft charges for the product. Figure 6-2 shows the options for Azure SQL Database.

Clicking the informational icon to the right of the product name displays a menu for quick access to the pricing page for the product, additional product details, and documentation to help you make better decisions about the options you select.

Once you've configured a product based on your needs, you can add another instance of that product to your estimate by clicking the **+** button (**Clone** button) in the upper-right portion of the window. For example, suppose you need two Azure SQL Databases for your app and each of them is going to be using the same service tier, instance size, and so on. The easiest way to add these is to add one Azure SQL Database product to your estimate, configure it with the desired pricing options, and then click the **Clone** button to add the second instance.

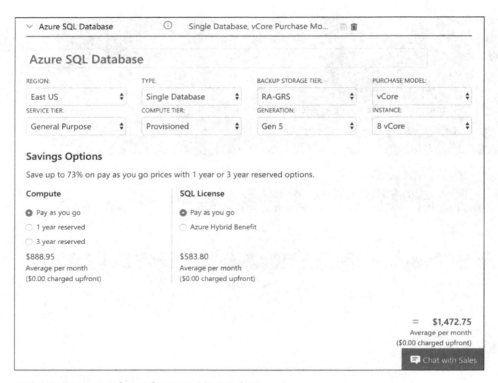

FIGURE 6-2 Estimate of costs for Azure SQL Database

To review your pricing estimate, scroll to the bottom of the page. As shown in Figure 6-3, you can choose a support plan to add to your estimate. If you have a Microsoft Online Services Agreement, an Enterprise Agreement, or a Microsoft Customer Agreement, you can choose it to have that pricing applied to your estimate. You can then click Export to save your estimate as an Excel file and then select **Save** to save your estimate in the pricing calculator to make changes later. You can also click **Share** to create a sharable link to your estimate so others can view it.

> **NOTE** **SAVED ESTIMATES**
>
> If you save an estimate in the pricing calculator, you can access it later by clicking the **Saved Estimates** tab at the top of the page.

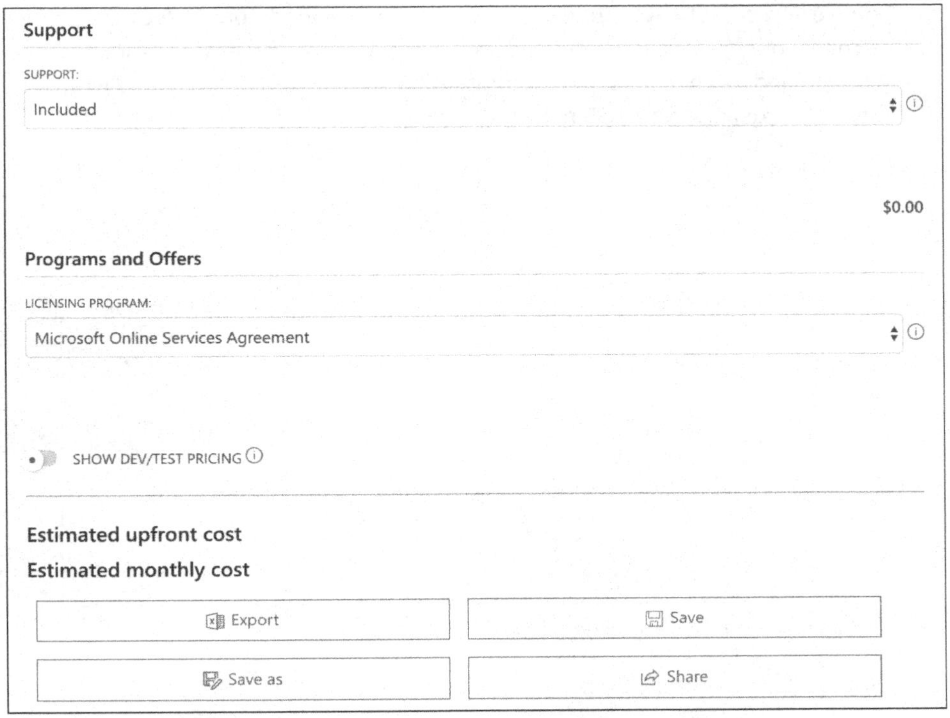

Support

SUPPORT:

Included	⬍ ⓘ

$0.00

Programs and Offers

LICENSING PROGRAM:

Microsoft Online Services Agreement	⬍ ⓘ

● ◗ SHOW DEV/TEST PRICING ⓘ

Estimated upfront cost

Estimated monthly cost

🗷 Export	🖫 Save
🗟 Save as	⮥ Share

FIGURE 6-3 Completing an estimate in the pricing calculator

Total cost of ownership calculator

The pricing calculator is helpful for estimating your expenses for new applications in Azure, but if you have on-premises applications you want to migrate to Azure and you want an estimate of how much you can save in Azure, the TCO calculator is a better choice. You can access the TCO calculator by browsing to *https://bit.ly/az900-tcocalculator*.

When using the TCO calculator, the first step is to add details about your on-premises servers, databases, storage, and network usage. In Figure 6-4, an on-premises server has been configured for a web app. You can configure all the details about the server, including the OS, whether it's a VM or a physical server, and more.

Databases and storage systems that are on-premises should also be added, in addition to any network usage for your application. In Figure 6-5, a storage system has been added, and network usage for the app has been specified.

After entering all your on-premises workloads, you can view the assumptions the TCO calculator uses by clicking **Next**. The TCO calculator uses a comprehensive list of on-premises expense assumptions that Microsoft has put together based on years of experience, and these assumptions are used to provide you with the best estimate possible of your cost savings. As shown in Figure 6-6, assumptions include items such as whether you've purchased a Software Assurance plan for your on-premises servers, details on your current expenses on-premises, your IT labor costs, and much more. For an accurate TCO estimate, it's best to carefully record your expenses before generating a TCO report.

FIGURE 6-4 Configuring an on-premises server in the TCO calculator

Storage

Enter the details of your on-premises storage infrastructure. After adding storage, select the storage type and enter the remaining details.

Image storage					
Storage type ⓘ	Capacity ⓘ	Backup ⓘ	Archive ⓘ		
NAS/File Share	3	3	6		
	TB	TB	TB		
	(1 - 5000)	(0 - 5000)	(0 - 5000)		

(+) Add storage

Networking

Enter the amount of network bandwidth you currently consume in your on-premises environment.

Outboud bandwidth ⓘ

| 2 |
| GB |
| (1 - 2000) |

Next

FIGURE 6-5 Configuring storage and networking

After you adjust your assumptions, scroll to the bottom of the screen, and click **Next** to view your TCO report. Your TCO report shows you how much you can save over the next five years by moving your app to Azure, as shown in Figure 6-7.

Storage costs

Storage procurement cost/GB for local disk/SAN-SSD	3	(USD)
Storage procurement cost/GB for local disk/SAN-HDD	2	(USD)
Storage procurement cost/GB for NAS/file storage	2	(USD)
Storage procurement cost/GB for Blob storage	2	(USD)
Annual enterprise storage software support cost	10	(%)
Cost per tape drive	4500	(USD)

IT labor costs

Number of physical servers that can be managed by a full time administrator	387
Number of virtual machines that can be managed by a full time administrator	516
Hourly rate for IT administrator	50 (USD)

Other assumptions

The following assumptions also affect the TCO model, but typically require less adjustment by customers. You can come back to this section at any time and adjust the assumptions.

⌄ **Hardware costs**

⌄ **Software costs**

FIGURE 6-6 Adjusting assumptions made by the TCO calculator

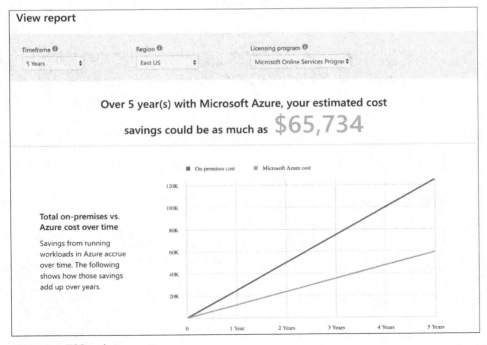

FIGURE 6-7 TCO savings report

A TCO report includes detailed charts of expense savings, and at the bottom of the report, you'll find a breakdown of on-premises costs and Azure costs, so you can easily determine where you'll save money. Just as with the pricing calculator, reports generated by the TCO calculator can be downloaded, saved, and copied by clicking the appropriate button as shown in Figure 6-8.

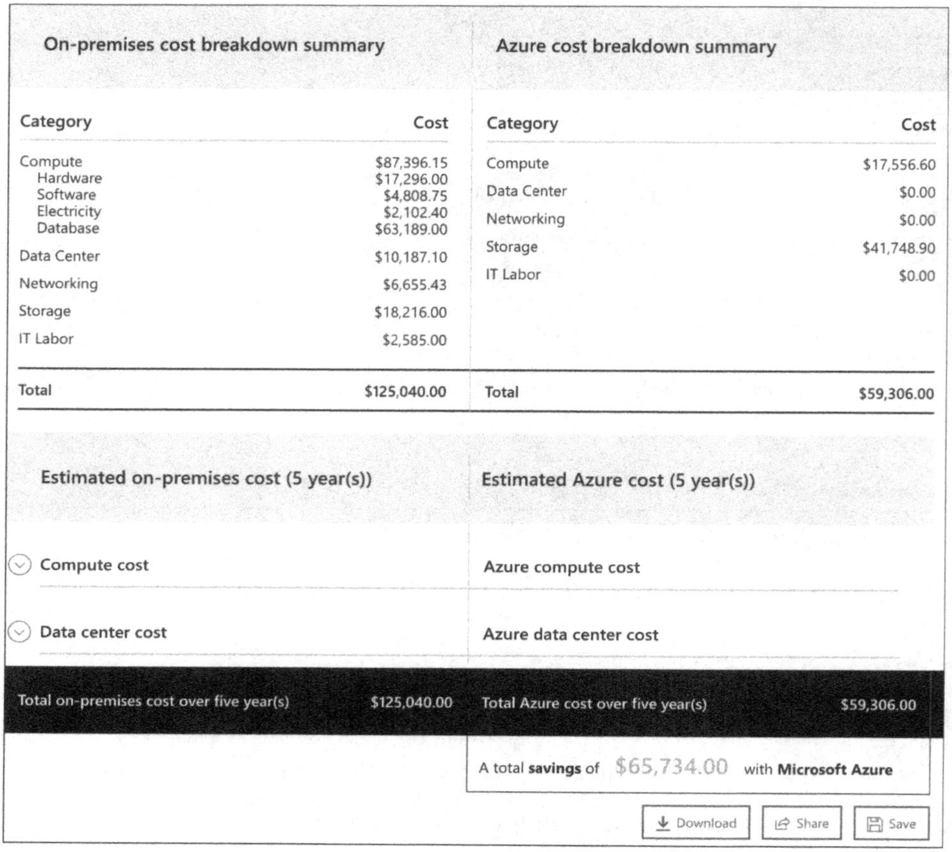

On-premises cost breakdown summary		Azure cost breakdown summary	
Category	**Cost**	**Category**	**Cost**
Compute	$87,396.15	Compute	$17,556.60
Hardware	$17,296.00	Data Center	$0.00
Software	$4,808.75	Networking	$0.00
Electricity	$2,102.40	Storage	$41,748.90
Database	$63,189.00	IT Labor	$0.00
Data Center	$10,187.10		
Networking	$6,655.43		
Storage	$18,216.00		
IT Labor	$2,585.00		
Total	**$125,040.00**	**Total**	**$59,306.00**

Estimated on-premises cost (5 year(s))		Estimated Azure cost (5 year(s))	
⌄ Compute cost		Azure compute cost	
⌄ Data center cost		Azure data center cost	
Total on-premises cost over five year(s)	$125,040.00	Total Azure cost over five year(s)	$59,306.00
		A total **savings** of $65,734.00 with **Microsoft Azure**	

⬇ Download   ↪ Share   💾 Save

FIGURE 6-8 Summary of costs on-premises and on Azure

Azure Cost Management

Azure Cost Management is a tool in Azure that makes it easy to analyze your costs at a granular level. Cost Management allows you to create a budget for your Azure expenses, set configurable alerts so you'll know if you are approaching a budgeted limit, and analyze your costs in detail.

To get started with Cost Management, open the Azure portal, search for **Cost Management**, and click **Cost Management + Billing**.

Once Cost Management + Billing loads in the portal, click **Cost Management** in the menu on the left (shown in Figure 6-9) to access Cost Management.

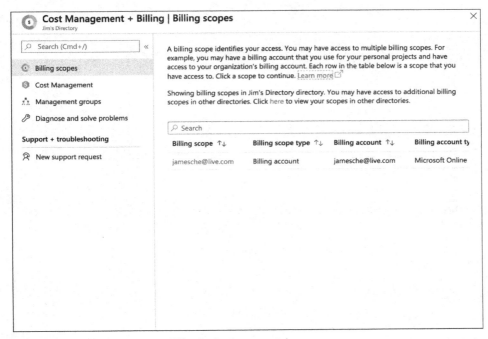

FIGURE 6-9 Cost Management + Billing in the Azure portal

To effectively monitor your costs, you should create a budget in Cost Management. Creating a budget isn't required, but it will allow you to visualize your spending compared to your planned expenses.

1. Click **Budgets** in the left menu, and click **Add**, as shown in Figure 6-10.
2. Enter a name for your budget.
3. Enter a spending amount and the period at which your spending resets.
4. Enter a start date for your budget.
5. Enter an expiration date as shown in Figure 6-11.
6. Click **Next** to complete your budget.

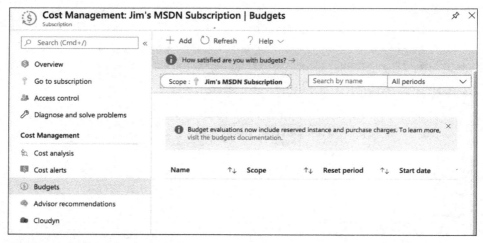

FIGURE 6-10 Adding a new budget

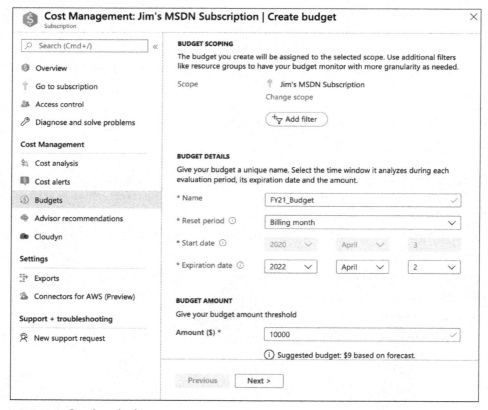

FIGURE 6-11 Creating a budget

7. Configure your alert conditions.

8. Add an email address for someone who should receive the alerts, as shown in Figure 6-12.

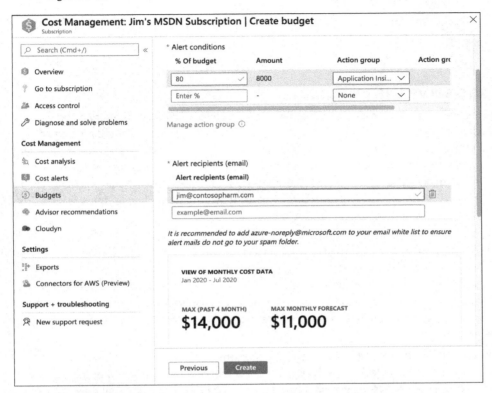

FIGURE 6-12 Configuring alerts for a budget

9. Click **Create** to create your budget.

After you create a budget, click **Cost Analysis** to see how your spending compares to your budget.

Skill 6.2: Describe Azure service level agreements (SLAs) and service lifecycles

Many of the services you use today include a *service level agreement* (SLA) that serves as a contract between you and the service provider for a certain level of service. Microsoft provides SLAs in Azure, and they also provide comprehensive documentation on how the SLA is computed for a service. However, not all services come with an SLA. Microsoft will often make services available in preview prior to releasing them for production use. These preview services often don't come with an SLA.

Azure service level agreement (SLA)

SLAs establish specific targets for availability, and they also define what the service provider will do when those targets aren't met. SLAs are expressed as a percentage and are almost always 99 percent or higher. The highest level of availability expressed in an SLA is 99.999 percent, commonly referred to as *5 nines*. To provide you with some context as we discuss SLAs, a service with an SLA of 5 nines guarantees that downtime over an entire year will not exceed 5.56 minutes. A more reasonable SLA of 99.9 percent guarantees that downtime over the period of a month will not exceed 43.2 minutes.

An important concept in cloud service SLAs is that the cloud provider considers an application to be outside of SLA only when the availability percentage is not met because of an issue that the cloud provider can control. In other words, if you deploy new code to your application, and it causes your application to crash, the cloud provider is not going to consider that a breach of SLA. If you install a component onto your virtual machine and it causes the machine to go down, that's not within the cloud provider's control and isn't classified as not meeting SLA.

Because SLAs only refer to problems within the control of the cloud provider, when an application suffers from lack of availability, it's important to determine whether the problem is a platform issue or an issue with your code or configuration. Answering that question can be more difficult than you might think.

Azure is a highly complex environment involving a large number of services operating together. For example, Azure App Service (one of Azure's most popular services) uses Azure virtual machines, Azure DNS systems, Azure Storage, Azure SQL Database, and other Azure services under the hood. Performance degradation of any of those services can affect the availability of an application running in App Service. If you report that your App Service application is unavailable, Microsoft needs to determine whether it's because of a problem on their end or a problem with your application.

Microsoft maintains an enormous amount of diagnostic data on all Azure operations across all Azure services. When you open a support case with Microsoft to report that your application is unavailable, Microsoft can perform data analytics against this data to determine if there was a problem with the Azure platform itself.

If you believe that your application's availability has fallen below the SLA, it's your responsibility to submit a claim to Microsoft. You can do that by opening a support case. If Microsoft determines that the SLA has not been met, you might receive a credit on your Azure invoice. The amount of the credit depends on the duration that SLA was not met and the specific Azure service's SLA policy.

Most Azure services offer an SLA of at least 99.9 percent, and higher SLAs can be achieved with additional configuration by the customer. For example, a single VM using Premium storage for all disks has an SLA of 99.9 percent. If you deploy two or more VMs into the same availability set, that SLA increases to 99.95 percent. If you deploy those two or more instances across two or more availability zones within the same Azure region, then the SLA moves to 99.99 percent.

Interpret the terms of an SLA

Because SLA varies between Azure services, and because specific configurations can affect the SLA of a single Azure service, it's important to be able to determine the specific SLA for the Azure services you are using. Microsoft provides details on the SLA for every Azure service at *https://bit.ly/az900-azuresla*.

As shown in Figure 6-13, once on the SLA web page, you can select a category to see all Azure services in that category. You can also enter your service name in the search box to find the SLA for that service. Once you locate the service you're interested in, click it to read details on the SLA.

When you click a service, you'll see details on the SLA provided by that service. Figure 6-14 shows the SLA page for Azure Virtual Machines. The three bullet points at the top of the page outline the SLA for Azure VMs.

The Introduction section describes Azure SLAs in general. The General Terms section describes SLA terms that refer to all Azure services, such as Management Portal, Service Level, and Downtime. It also explains how you can make a claim and the limitations for Azure SLAs.

The SLA Details section applies to the specific Azure service you're viewing. For example, this section on the VM SLA page defines VM-specific terms that relate to the SLA for VMs. If you scroll down, you'll see additional details, as shown in Figure 6-15, including how to calculate availability and the amount of credit you might receive if an SLA isn't met.

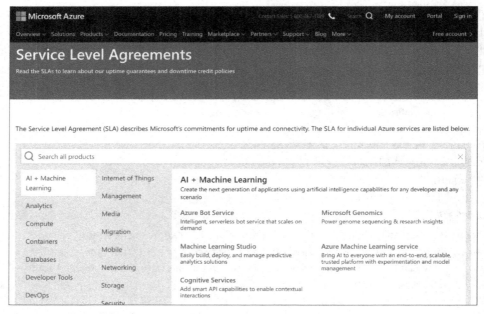

FIGURE 6-13 Azure SLA web page

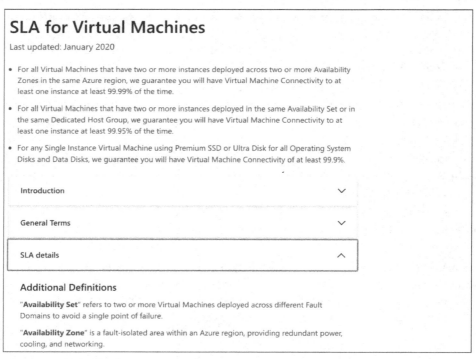

FIGURE 6-14 Azure VMs SLA

Monthly Uptime Calculation and Service Levels for Virtual Machines in Availability Zones

"**Maximum Available Minutes**" is the total accumulated minutes during a billing month that have two or more instances deployed across two or more Availability Zones in the same region. Maximum Available Minutes is measured from when at least two Virtual Machines across two Availability Zones in the same region have both been started resultant from action initiated by Customer to the time Customer has initiated an action that would result in stopping or deleting the Virtual Machines.

"**Downtime**" is the total accumulated minutes that are part of Maximum Available Minutes that have no Virtual Machine Connectivity in the region.

"**Monthly Uptime Percentage**" for Virtual Machines in Availability Zones is calculated as Maximum Available Minutes less Downtime divided by Maximum Available Minutes in a billing month for a given Microsoft Azure subscription. Monthly Uptime Percentage is represented by the following formula:

Monthly Uptime % = (Maximum Available Minutes – Downtime) / Maximum Available Minutes X 100

The following Service Levels and Service Credits are applicable to Customer's use of Virtual Machines, deployed across two or more Availability Zones in the same region:

MONTHLY UPTIME PERCENTAGE	SERVICE CREDIT
< 99.99%	10%
< 99%	25%
< 95%	100%

FIGURE 6-15 Details on Azure VM SLA

If your application uses multiple Azure services, multiple SLAs will apply to you. If you experience downtime, you must submit a claim for all Azure services that fell below SLA if you want to be considered for a credit. However, monetary credit isn't your only concern related to the availability of your application. Downtime in your application affects your business negatively, so you want to always ensure that you have the highest SLA possible. When you're dealing with multiple Azure services with different SLAs, it's important to understand how that affects your overall SLA.

When calculating the SLA for an application using multiple Azure services, you must calculate a composite SLA based on the services you're using. For example, if you have an App Service web app that also uses a single Azure VM using Premium storage, you must combine the SLA for both services to determine your application's overall SLA.

> **NOTE   COMPOSITE SLAs**
>
> It's important to understand that individual service SLAs still apply to you when you're using multiple Azure services. However, understanding composite SLAs is important because it allows you to determine when a specific configuration is increasing the likelihood that you will experience downtime.

The SLA for App Service is 99.95 percent, and the SLA for a single VM running Premium storage is 99.9 percent. Therefore, your overall SLA for your application is 99.95 percent x 99.9 percent, or 99.85 percent. By deploying two VMs into two availability zones in the same region, you can obtain a 99.99 percent SLA for your VMs, and that increases your overall SLA to 99.94 percent.

> **MORE INFO   COMPUTING COMPOSITE SLAS**
>
> For more information on computing composite SLAs, see *https://bit.ly/az900-compositesla.*

Service lifecycle in Azure

As Azure product teams develop new services and features, it's important for them to get feedback from customers using those services and features in a real-world environment. For that reason, Microsoft will often offer new services and features to customers as *preview offerings*. While the Microsoft official term is *preview*, you will often see people refer to these services and features as being a *beta* offering.

Once a feature has reached a certain level of completeness and reliability, it moves to a stage called *general availability*. This is the point where a service is fully supported and has an SLA associated with it.

EXAM TIP

Services and features that are in preview do not offer an SLA, and they are not meant to be used in production applications. Preview features are also usually not offered in all Azure regions. Microsoft will provide documentation on which regions are available for a specific preview.

Preview services and features

Preview services and features are sometimes first offered as a private preview. In private preview, the service or feature is made available to a small set of customers for testing. Access to a private preview is sometimes by invitation from the engineering team that is developing the service or feature. In other cases, Microsoft may provide a way for any customer to sign up for access to the private preview. If registration is open to everyone, Microsoft will close registration after a target number of customers has signed up.

> **NOTE   SERVICES VERSUS FEATURES**
>
> Many previews are for features of an existing service. For example, App Service might add a new feature for the existing service, and before that feature is fully released, it will go through some period in the preview phase.

Private preview services and features commonly expose only a subset of the functionality that will eventually make it into the service or feature. Microsoft will often ask customers using a private preview to test specific scenarios and provide feedback. This helps engineering teams to uncover bugs and usability issues in the complex, real-world environments that customers are using.

Once a service or feature meets a specific bar set by the engineering team, it will transition to public preview. This usually occurs once the service or feature is fully functional or very close to it. However, if there are bugs in a specific part of the functionality that the engineering team feels is critical, they may delay public preview until those bugs are fixed.

Features and services that are in public preview are provided at a discounted rate, but like private preview features and services, they typically don't offer an SLA and are provided as-is.

Customers participating in a private preview are sometimes given a secret link to the Azure portal that enables the service or feature. When the customer uses that link, Microsoft can use their Azure subscription ID to determine if they have registered and are approved for the private preview. If they aren't, the feature or service won't be available, even if they use the secret link.

In other situations, the Azure portal experience hasn't been developed for a private preview feature or service. In those cases, customers are given command-line instructions for using the service or feature. It's more common for the portal user interface to be developed during the private preview phase, so early adopters are usually given command-line access only.

Once a service or feature reaches public preview, it is made available to all customers in the regions where it's available, and no registration is required to use the service or feature. A preview badge will be displayed in the Azure portal so that users will know that the service or feature is a preview offering. Figure 6-16 shows the App Service Editor feature in App Service. Note that this feature has the Preview label.

Services and features that are in public preview are usually supported by Microsoft just as though they were fully released. However, SLAs don't apply to previews, and there are some situations where a service or feature won't be supported by Microsoft support engineers while in preview. In those cases, you might be referred to forums for support.

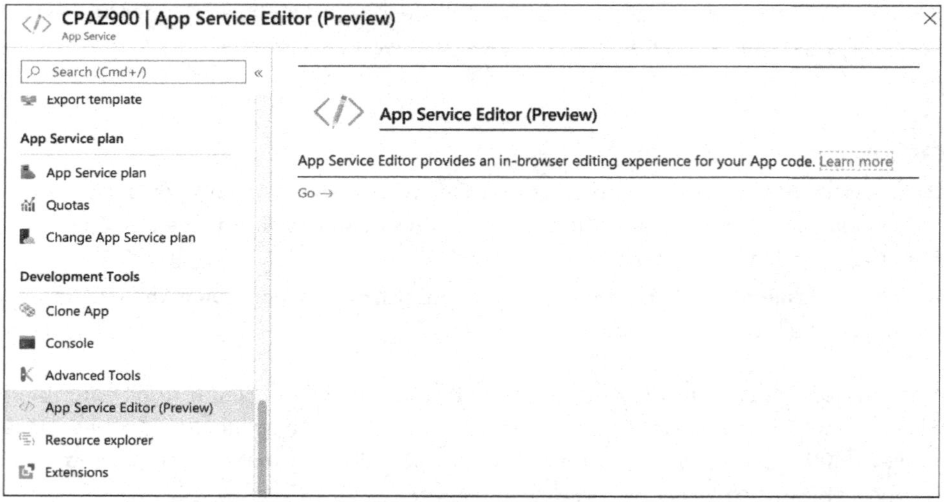

FIGURE 6-16 Preview feature in App Service

General availability

Once a preview service or feature reaches a quality and availability bar suitable to the engineering team, they will declare *general availability* or GA. At this point, the service or feature is fully supported.

Once a service or feature reaches GA, it falls under the SLA Microsoft provides. If it's a new service, a new SLA will be published on the SLA web page. For new features of existing services, once GA is reached, the feature will inherit the SLA of the service it's a feature of.

If you were using a feature or service during public preview, you will usually not have to do anything to be officially supported under GA. However, in some situations, Microsoft will ask that you delete any resources created during preview and recreate them. This usually happens when remnants left over from preview code might cause a problem with a service or feature running in GA.

When a service or feature reaches GA, it may not be GA in all Azure geographies. In those cases, other geographies will usually GA later in the lifecycle of the service or feature. Preview pricing might also remain in effect for some period after GA. Details like this are published on the official GA announcement on the Azure website.

Thought experiment

We've covered a lot of ground, and it's time to put your new knowledge to the test with a thought experiment. Answers to this thought experiment are in the section that follows it.

ContosoPharm has been planning a large deployment to the cloud for the past few months, and it is ready to pull the trigger and get things going. The one person at ContosoPharm who is the most nervous about this deployment is the IT director. She has a fixed budget, so she needs to have a good idea of costs. She also needs to provide a detailed financial forecast to the CFO, and she wants that report to be as accurate as possible. Once again, ContosoPharm has turned to you for advice.

ContosoPharm is going to have a complex network deployment with this new cloud service. They will have numerous VMs connected to the network as well. They want to keep costs as low as possible. What recommendation can you give them related to their network that can help them keep costs lower? What about their VMs?

The IT director has a comprehensive spreadsheet that includes all the resources Contoso-Pharm will need to use in the cloud. She needs to add estimated pricing to that spreadsheet, but she's not sure what to record for pricing. What guidance can you provide to help?

ContosoPharm is currently hosting this service on-premises. They're moving to the cloud with hopes of saving money. The CFO would like a forecast of how much money they can save by moving to the cloud, as opposed to their on-premises costs. What's the best way for the IT director to put that information together?

Once ContosoPharm deploys this service to the cloud, the IT director wants to carefully monitor costs to ensure she doesn't go over budget. If she does go over budget, she'll need to provide a detailed analysis to the CFO that explains where the cost overages came from. How can she accomplish this easily?

The CEO has asked the IT director about reliability of the cloud. She's assured the CEO that the cloud is reliable, but she'd like to be able to back up that claim with some real data. It would be even better if she can offer details on how they've configured some of their services in order to improve reliability. What should you suggest?

Thought experiment answers

This section details the answers to the thought experiment.

To keep costs low on their networks and VMs, there are a few things they can do. First, careful planning on which regions they create services in will help. Costs differ by region, so choosing regions with lower costs can help. However, they'll need to keep in mind that Azure virtual networks are billed for traffic that flows out of a datacenter, so careful planning to avoid that when possible is necessary. They should also take zones into account because network traffic out of each zone will differ.

To get an estimated price on how much their resources will cost, ContosoPharm can use the pricing calculator. The pricing calculator allows them to add and configure all the products they will use in Azure. It will then provide a cost estimate per month that the IT director can plug into her spreadsheet.

To determine how much money ContosoPharm can save by moving to the cloud, the IT director can use the total cost of ownership (TCO) calculator. Using the TCO calculator, the IT director can enter in all the specifics about ContosoPharm's on-premises systems, personnel, and so on. It can then provide a view of how much money can be saved by moving to the cloud.

To monitor costs in an ongoing way and report on what might be causing them to go over budget, ConsotoPharm can use Azure Cost Management. They can create a budget based on their expected usage, and Cost Management will allow them to monitor and report on expenses.

To find information related to the reliability of services in the cloud, the IT director can check the SLA page for each service. This will provide clear information on Microsoft's guarantee for availability. It will also outline what configuration ContosoPharm needs to take to maintain the highest SLA, and that can be helpful for her as she puts together information on how they've configured services for maximum reliability.

Chapter summary

From pricing to costs and from service levels to service lifecycles, we've covered a lot in this chapter. Here's a summary of everything we covered.

- Primary factors that affect costs are the resource type, how you purchase resources, the Azure regions you use, and the billing zone your resources are in.
- Azure services are billed according to meters associated with the resource.
- Purchasing an Enterprise Agreement or purchasing from a cloud solution partner (CSP) can save you money on Azure services.
- Microsoft's costs vary by region, and yours will, too.
- Azure regions are broken out into billing zones, and you're charged differently based upon the zone.
- The pricing calculator helps you to figure out expenses in Azure by providing a cost estimate based on the resources you need.
- The total cost of ownership calculator allows you to enter details on your on-premises resources. It then provides an estimate of how much you can save by moving to the cloud.
- Azure Cost Management allows you to analyze your costs at a granular level.
- Cost Management allows you to create a budget and configure alerts based on that budget.
- An SLA is a guarantee from Microsoft for uptime of a service.
- SLAs often have configuration requirements that must be met. These are documented on the service's SLA web page.
- A service is only considered outside SLA if an availability problem happens because of something that is within Microsoft's control.
- Preview services are offered in advance of production release and often have no SLA. They're also usually offered at a discount.
- When a service is ready for production use, it's declared to be generally available and carries an SLA.

Index

A

access control
>with Azure Conditional Access, 232-233
>RBAC (role-based access control), 237-241
>resource locks, 241-244
>SSO (single sign-on), 235-236

ACI (Azure Container Instances), 56-58

action groups, 181-182

actions, 131, 150-151, 181-182

Active Directory. *See* Azure Active Directory

agility of cloud services, 4-6

AI (artificial intelligence), 115-118

AKS (Azure Kubernetes Service), 58-59

alerts in Azure Monitor, 178-182

analytics. *See* data analytics

Apache Spark, 105

API types, 73-74

App Service. *See* Azure App Service

append blobs, 70

application failures, 3

Application Insights, 3, 12

architectural components, 26-41
>ARM (Azure Resource Manager), 38-41
>availability zones, 28-31
>management groups, 37-38
>regions, 26-28
>resource groups, 31-33
>subscriptions, 33-37

ARM (Azure Resource Manager), 38-41, 240
>Azure portal and, 152
>benefits of, 41

ARM API, 39

ARM templates, 31, 33, 40-41, 80, 173-174, 251

artifacts, 141, 143, 251

Artificial General Intelligence (strong AI), 115

artificial intelligence (AI), 115-118

Artificial Narrow Intelligence (weak AI), 115

assignments with Azure Conditional Access, 232

authentication, 226
>Azure Active Directory, 226-232
>MFA (multifactor authentication), 233-235
>for site-to-site connections, 66
>SSO (single sign-on), 235-236

authorization, 226
>Azure Active Directory, 226-232
>Azure Conditional Access, 232-233
>SSO (single sign-on), 235-236

Auto-Scale, 6

availability
>of cloud services, 2-4. *See also* fault tolerance
>with ExpressRoute, 70

availability sets, 30, 48-51

availability zones, 28-31

Azure
>architectural components, 26-41
>>ARM (Azure Resource Manager), 38-41
>>availability zones, 28-31
>>management groups, 37-38
>>regions, 26-28
>>resource groups, 31-33
>>subscriptions, 33-37
>core resources, 41-81
>>ACI (Azure Container Instances), 56-58
>>AKS (Azure Kubernetes Service), 58-59

C

I

J

K

L

M

Q–R

S

T

U

V

Plug into learning at

MicrosoftPressStore.com

The Microsoft Press Store by Pearson offers:

- Free U.S. shipping

- Buy an eBook, get three formats – Includes PDF, EPUB, and MOBI to use with your computer, tablet, and mobile devices

- Print & eBook Best Value Packs

- eBook Deal of the Week – Save up to 50% on featured title

- Newsletter – Be the first to hear about new releases, announcements, special offers, and more

- Register your book – Find companion files, errata, and product updates, plus receive a special coupon* to save on your next purchase